Joseph V. Ato...
7320 Oakdale
Hammond. Ind.

A PRACTICAL CATHOLIC DICTIONARY

A PRACTICAL CATHOLIC DICTIONARY

Jessie Corrigan Pegis, M.A.

HANOVER HOUSE

GARDEN CITY, NEW YORK

Nihil Obstat: JOHN A. GOODWINE, J.C.D.
          Censor Librorum

Imprimatur: ✠ FRANCIS CARDINAL SPELLMAN
          Archbishop of New York
          January 21, 1957

CONTENTS

Introduction

If I could have avoided the use of the word *dictionary* in this work, I would have done so. Dictionaries often define without explaining their definitions, so that one is sometimes as much in the dark after reading a definition as before doing so. I have attempted in this work to define simply and to add explanations where they seemed necessary. Since I could not avoid the word *dictionary,* I have called the present work a *practical* Catholic dictionary. I hope that *A Practical Catholic Dictionary* will be of more practical or working use to the general reader than more technical dictionaries often are.

While working on this dictionary I have had in mind those Catholic and non-Catholic readers who want a dictionary of Catholic words that is neither too technical nor too specialized for ordinary needs. I have also had in mind the convert who, even after he has received instruction in the Catholic faith, realizes only too well how much he has still to learn about his religion. More than once I have thought back to what I would have liked to know and did not know about my faith when I entered the Catholic Church thirty years ago. Finally, I have hoped that this dictionary might be of some help to students in junior and senior high schools. For this reason I have tried to keep close to the catechism in many of my explanations.

In line with these aims, I have left out long historical accounts and involved or detailed theological explanations. I have included the titles of the books of the Bible as well as the better-known Biblical names, but I have not attempted to go into Biblical history or tell Biblical stories in any complete fashion. Originally, I had planned to include a number of short biographies of the saints in the body of the dictionary; but since this would have given a disproportionate amount of space to the entry, *Saints,* I have left these biographies for the Appendix (which also includes a list of the popes and their pontificates and a list of the more famous

9

encyclicals of the last hundred years). St. Joseph and St. John the Baptist are the only two saints who have separate entries in the dictionary, while the saints who were apostles are considered under the entry, *Apostles.*

The famous lexicographer, Dr. Samuel Johnson, defined a lexicographer, not without deep reflection, I am sure, as "a harmless drudge." I would here like to make an acknowledgment to the person who invited me to undertake this harmless drudgery. Miss Lucy Murphy of the Buffalo Public Library suggested this work some five years ago and helped me in my first selection of words for it. I would also like to acknowledge the generous help and guidance of the Rev. Vincent L. Kennedy, C.S.B., of the Pontifical Institute of Mediaeval Studies, Toronto, Canada, who went through the manuscript twice and gave me the benefit of his wide knowledge and serious scholarship. To Mrs. Isabella Beach Dougherty, who typed the manuscript several times, from its first to its final form, and who never complained at the many and hardly readable changes I wrote into the copy, I want to express my sincerest thanks.

20 August, 1956   J.C.P.
Yonkers, New York

A PRACTICAL CATHOLIC DICTIONARY

A

abbess The superior of a community of nuns belonging to religious orders whose male communities are governed by abbots.

abbey A monastery or convent under an abbot or abbess. Sometimes the name abbey is given to a church. Westminster Abbey in London, England, is a large church in which many of England's famous men are buried. It was once a Roman Catholic monastic church, but since the time of Henry VIII it has belonged to the Church of England.

abbot The superior of a community of monks in an abbey. The abbot is elected for life and has considerable authority.

Abdias A book of the Old Testament of the Bible. *Abdias* is the smallest book in the Old Testament, consisting of only one chapter. It is the prophecy of Abdias, a minor prophet, concerning the destruction of the land of Edom.

Abel The second son of Adam. Abel kept the flocks for his father while his elder brother, Cain, tilled the soil. Cain and Abel both offered sacrifices to God. Abel was a good man, and his offering of a lamb from his flock was pleasing to God, while Cain's offering of the fruit of the ground was not. Cain was jealous of the favor which his brother had found with God, and he killed Abel out of jealousy.

abjuration (1) Denial, under solemn oath, of apostasy, heresy, or schism by one who has been excommunicated. Such a denial is necessary before the heretic can be received back into the Church. (2) A similar denial of heresy, apostasy, or schism required of adult converts (those over fourteen) before their confession of faith and baptism.

ablution (1) The washing of the chalice and of the priest's fingers after the Communion of the Mass. After the people have received Communion, the priest puts the ciborium containing the Sacred Hosts back in the tabernacle. He takes the chalice and holds it out to the server who pours wine into it from a cruet. The priest washes the chalice with this new wine so that the Blood of Christ

will not remain in it. He drinks the wine and takes the chalice to
the Epistle side of the altar. Here the server pours wine and water
over the priest's thumbs and index fingers which are held over
the chalice. This is done so that no particle of the Blessed Sacrament which might be clinging to his fingers will be lost. Returning
to the center of the altar, the priest drinks the wine and water
from the chalice. (2) The water and wine with which the priest
washes his fingers after the Communion of the Mass and which
he drinks from the chalice.

Abram (Abraham)   One of the great patriarchs and the only one
to be referred to as *our patriarch* in the Canon of the Mass. God
chose Abram, who lived in the city of Ur in Chaldea, to be the
Father of His chosen people. *See* **chosen people.** God led Abram
into the land of Chanaan and promised him that He would give
this land to his descendents. He established His covenant with
Abram and changed his name from Abram to Abraham, which
means Father of Many. God tested the faith of Abraham by asking him to offer his son Isaac as a sacrifice. However, God did
not require this sacrifice but accepted a ram in Isaac's place.

absolution (from sin)   The freeing of a sinner from his sins by God
Himself through the priest who hears his confession. In the Sacrament of Penance sins are forgiven providing the penitent is truly
sorry for them. The actual words of absolution which the priest
says in Latin while making the Sign of the Cross over the penitent
are: "I absolve thee from thy sins in the name of the Father and
of the Son and of the Holy Ghost." The priest does not give
absolution until he has listened carefully to the confession and
imposed a penance. If he thinks that the sinner is not sorry for his
sins, he may refuse absolution.

When the priest received the sacrament of Holy Orders he
received this power to give absolution. The power to forgive sins
comes from God Himself. The first Apostles received this power
to forgive sins from Jesus Christ. When Jesus Christ came to His
Apostles after His Resurrection He breathed upon them and said
to them: "Receive the Holy Spirit; whose sins you shall forgive,
they are forgiven them; and whose sins you shall retain, they are
retained." *John XX 22-23.* These same words are used by the
bishop at the ordination of a priest.

absolution (of the dead) The prayers said over the coffin (or catafalque if the body is not present) after a Requiem Mass. *See* **catafalque.**

abstinence, day of A day on which the use of meat is not allowed. Anyone seven years of age or over must keep the days of abstinence. Complete abstinence means that meat and soup or gravy made from meat may not be taken. Friday, Ash Wednesday, the Vigils of Christmas and the Assumption, and Holy Saturday are days of complete abstinence. Partial abstinence means that meat and soup or gravy made from meat may be taken at the principal meal only. Ember Wednesdays and Saturdays and the Vigil of Pentecost are days of partial abstinence. *See* **Ember days.** The priest announces at the Sunday Masses which days, besides Friday, are days of abstinence for the coming week. Days of abstinence are noted on a Catholic calendar.

accident *See* substance.

acolyte (1) A member of the clergy in the highest of the four minor orders. (2) An altar boy who performs some of the duties of an acolyte, such as lighting the altar candles.

Acta Apostolicae Sedis Latin name for the *Acts of the Apostolic See*, the official publication containing decrees, decisions, encyclical letters, etc., of the Holy See. *See* **Holy See.**

Acts of the Apostles The book of the New Testament written by St. Luke and giving an account of the early growth of the church established by Jesus Christ.

actual grace *See* grace.

A.D. *Anno Domini*, Latin words meaning *in the year of the Lord*. Time is measured on the calendar before and after the year Jesus Christ was born. A date followed by the abbreviation A.D. means so many years after the birth of Jesus Christ.

Adam The name of the first man created by God. God created man in His sixth and last period of creation before He rested on the seventh day. "God said, 'Let us make mankind in our image and likeness; and let them have dominion over the fish of the sea, the birds of the air, the cattle, over all the wild animals and every creature that crawls on the earth.'" *Genesis I 26*. God gave Adam, the first man, many gifts and privileges, the greatest of which was sanctifying grace, but He did expect perfect obedience in return. This obedience was the one thing that Adam did not give to God, and through his disobedience he lost God's friendship. Because of Adam's sin all men are born with original sin on their souls. *See* original sin.

adoration Worship which is given to God alone. The veneration given to the saints is different from divine worship. *See* veneration.

Adoration of the Cross One of the ceremonies of Good Friday. The word *adoration* here means the solemn veneration given to the Cross on Good Friday. The ceremony comes from Jerusalem where on Good Friday a relic of the True Cross was venerated. While holding the Cross for all to see, the priest sings three times: "Behold, the wood of the Cross, Upon which hung the Savior of the world." After each time, all kneel to adore the Cross and answer, *"Venite, Adoremus"* (*Come, let us worship*). The priest, his assistants, and his servers solemnly adore and kiss the Cross. The Cross is then brought to the altar rail to be adored by the people.

Advent The season or time of year leading up to Christmas. The word *advent* means coming, and during Advent we are waiting for the coming of Jesus Christ. Advent begins on the Sunday nearest St. Andrew's Day, November 30, and ends at midnight, December 24. The first Sunday of Advent is the first day of the ecclesiastical year. *See* year, ecclesiastical. Advent is the first liturgical season of the Church calendar. During Advent the Church, through its prayers, Gospels, etc., shows the Jewish world waiting for the Messias, the Redeemer who was to save man from his sins. Advent is a period of penance, though not so much a period of penance as Lent. The Redeemer has not yet come, and only by penance can the way be prepared for Him.

advocate, devil's Popular name for the Promoter General of the Faith, an official of the Sacred Congregation of Rites. He is called the devil's advocate because it is his duty to raise possible objections to the beatification or canonization of a saint.

affinity Relationship acquired through a valid Christian marriage. A man is related by affinity to the blood relations of his wife, and a woman is related by affinity to the blood relations of her husband. In Canon Law affinity can be an impediment to marriage.

age of reason The age at which a child knows the difference between right and wrong and must answer for what he does. Seven years of age is usually considered the age of reason.

Aggeus A book of the Old Testament of the Bible consisting of four short prophecies of the minor prophet, Aggeus.

agnosticism The philosophy of the Agnostics who taught that one can know only things that appear to the senses, and that, therefore, one cannot know God.

Agnus Dei (1) A prayer said by the priest during the Mass just before the Communion. *Agnus Dei* is Latin for *Lamb of God*. The prayer is said three times: "Lamb of God, who takest away the sins of the world, have mercy on us. Lamb of God, who takest away the sins of the world, have mercy on us. Lamb of God, who takest away the sins of the world, grant us peace." At Masses for the dead, "Grant them rest" is said twice instead of "Have mercy on us," and "Grant them rest eternal" is said instead of the last "Grant us peace." In the Old Testament the Messias, He who was to save the world, was sometimes spoken of as a lamb. The Jewish people often offered a lamb in their sacrifices to God. Jesus Christ was the Lamb of God because He sacrificed Himself on the Cross. John the Baptist said of Jesus, "Behold, the lamb of God, who takes away the sin of the world!" *John I* 29. (2) A small disc of wax with the figure of a lamb representing Our Lord stamped on it. These are solemnly blessed by the Pope at certain set times. *See* **Appendix, Saints, St. Agnes, January 21.**

Agony in the Garden, the The first Sorrowful Mystery of the Rosary. The night before He was crucified, Jesus Christ went with His disciples into the garden of Gethsemani near the Mount of Olives. He went a little apart from His disciples and began to pray to His Father, "saying, 'Father, if thou art willing, remove this cup from me; yet not my will but thine be done.'" *Luke XXII* 42. He knew the suffering that He would have to endure the following day, but He accepted it willingly. Burdened with the sins of all the world, He shed drops of blood like sweat through His skin. *See* **bloody sweat, the.**

alb A white linen garment reaching almost to the ground. It covers the cassock and has tight-fitting sleeves. The Romans used to wear a garment similar to the alb as an undertunic. The word *alb* comes from the Latin word *alba,* meaning *white.* The alb signifies purity of heart. *See* vestments.

All Hallows'   Another name for All Saints' Day. *See* **Halloween.**

All Saints' Day   One of the important feast days of the Church and a holyday of obligation. This feast, on November 1, is in honor of all God's saints, even those who have not been declared saints by the Church.

All Souls' Day   A day in memory of the souls still in Purgatory. All Souls' Day is November 2, the day after the feast of All Saints. If November 2 should fall on a Sunday, All Souls' Day is November 3. On this day the Church remembers the souls in Purgatory by praying that they will soon enjoy the happiness of Heaven. Each priest is allowed to say three Requiem Masses (Masses for the Dead) on All Souls' Day. It is not a holyday of obligation, but everywhere Catholics go to Mass and pay visits to the church in order to pray for the dead. "It is therefore a holy and wholesome thought to pray for the dead, that they may be loosed from sins." *II Machabees XII 46.*

Alleluia   Praise to the Lord. A song of joy in praise of God. The word *Alleluia* is Hebrew and is found in the Psalms of the Old Testament. The Alleluia in the Mass, between the Epistle and Gospel, is like a chant, sung and repeated. During the Easter season it appears more frequently in the Mass, sometimes taking the place of the Gradual. The great Easter Alleluia is sung after the Epistle at the Mass of the Easter Vigil. The celebrant of the Mass sings it three times, each time in a little higher voice, and all in the church answer after each singing. During Lent, at Masses for the Dead, and at other times of mourning or penance, the Alleluia is not used.

almsgiving   Giving to the poor the things they need—food, clothing or money. Alms must be given in the spirit of charity, that is, because of love of God and one's neighbor. In the Bible almsgiving is mentioned as one means of penance. John the Baptist, who was teaching repentance while he was making ready the way of the Lord, said, "Let him who has two tunics share with him who has none; and let him who has food do likewise." *Luke III 11.* Almsgiving is a corporal work of mercy. *See* mercy, the works of.

Alpha and Omega   The first and last letter of the Greek alphabet.

These letters are used to refer to Jesus Christ as the beginning and the end. During the Easter Vigil, the priest, after cutting a cross on the Easter candle which is to be blessed, cuts the first letter, Alpha, above the cross, and the last letter, Omega, below the cross.

altar   The place or table at which Mass is offered by the priest. Jesus Christ said the first Mass at a table at the Last Supper the night before He died. So today the priest offers the Sacrifice of the Mass at a table.

Every altar must have a consecrated stone slab which contains the relics of at least two saints who were martyrs. This is in remembrance of the days when Mass was said upon the tombs of martyrs. If the altar stone is the whole top of the altar, the altar is called a fixed altar. If the altar stone is only a small part of the altar, then it is called a movable altar. Five crosses are cut in the top of the stone slab or the altar stone. These represent the five wounds of Our Lord.

There may be more than one altar in a church. The high altar is in the center of the sanctuary end of the church. Other smaller altars may be on either side or down the aisle of the church.

altar boy   *See* server.

altar bread   *See* Host.

altar cards   Three cards on which are printed some of the prayers the priest says during Mass. One is at the middle of the altar, one on the left, and one on the right side. On the middle card are prayers said at the center of the altar. On the left is the Last Gospel and, on the right, prayers said over the water and wine and at the washing of the fingers. When Mass is not being said, these cards are laid flat down or taken away.

altar cloths   Three cloths, made of white linen, which cover the altar at Mass. In case any of the wine is spilled, these cloths, which are blessed before they are used, will absorb the wine. Beneath these three cloths is a cerecloth. *See* cerecloth.

altar draperies   Coverings or hangings which are used to protect or decorate the altar. Three *altar cloths* cover the altar at Mass. *See* **altar cloths**. The *tabernacle veil,* which is hung over the tabernacle, is either white or the color of the vestments of the day, but never black. At Masses for the Dead violet is used. The *frontal,* sometimes called an *antependium,* hangs in front of the altar. This, like the tabernacle veil, is either white or the color of the vestments of the day, but never black. A *baldachin* or *tester* is a canopy hung over the main altar and covering the platform on which the priest stands, as well as the altar. If this is made of wood or metal rather than cloth, it cannot properly be called an altar drapery. Decorative screens, called *reredos,* stand behind the altar while decorative curtains, called *riddels,* hang at the sides of the altar. The decorative curtain hung behind the altar is called a *dossal.*

altar piece   A painting at the back of the main altar, sometimes part of the reredos. *See* **altar draperies.**

altar stone   A square flat stone with an opening to contain the relics of martyrs. *See* **altar.** This stone is either the whole top of the altar or it is a smaller slab fitting in the altar top. The early Christians said Mass over the tomb of a martyr on his feast day, and so the priests of today continue to say Mass on the stone which contains relics of martyrs.

ambry   A small boxlike recess which is set into the wall of the sanctuary and in which the sacred oils are kept.

amen   *So be it.* The word *amen* is a Hebrew word meaning *so be it. Amen* is used as an expression of belief or agreement at the end of prayers.

amendment, purpose of   The firm resolve of the penitent not to sin again and to avoid as far as possible the near occasions of sin. The penitent must have this firm purpose of amendment in order to receive the Sacrament of Penance worthily. If he has only venial sins to confess, he must have the firm purpose of avoiding at least one of these sins.

amice   White linen cloth with two long strings to fasten it to the shoulders. It is worn under the alb and is the first vestment the priest puts on over his cassock. The amice is a symbol of the priest's helmet of salvation. *See* **vestments.**

Amos   The book of the Old Testament of the Bible concerning the prophecies of Amos. Amos is one of the minor prophets of the Old Testament.

Angelical Salutation   A name for the *Hail Mary.* The first part of the prayer is the Angel Gabriel's greeting to Mary at the time of the Annunciation: "Hail, full of grace, the Lord is with thee. Blessed art thou among women." *Luke I 28.*

angels Pure spirits created by God. They are the creatures who are most like God and most reflect His eternity. Angels have no bodies and can never die, so they are very different from men who have bodies and will die some day. Yet, like men, they are natural beings, for God is the only supernatural being. They do not, however, have any of the needs or characteristics of the human body.

Angels are independent of time and space and change. One does not associate angels with the idea of number or say that there were so many angels present. The word multitude is often spoken of in connection with angels, but even here multitude does not mean a particular number, but rather a certain perfection.

Angels cannot be seen, though they are sometimes pictured as pretty, winged creatures. The wings given to angels are only symbols of the swiftness of their minds in comparison with human minds. Like men, angels have understanding and free will. However, the intelligence of angels is much higher than human intelligence. The little that man can learn, even after years of study, would seem very small beside what the angels know even at the moment of creation. An angel's knowledge comes from God Himself. He does not have to learn it in this world.

Angels have free will and can choose to be good or to be bad. Unlike man, an angel chooses only once. He never has a second chance. Some of the angels chose to love and obey God, and these are the good angels. Heaven is their home, and they see God in the Beatific Vision. Among these angels are those appointed to help those here on earth. *See* **guardian angels.** Some of the angels chose to disobey God and these, who are known as bad angels or devils, were cast into Hell. The angels who were cast into Hell did not lose their great power and knowledge, and that is why their power to tempt those who are in the world is so great.

Angels are mentioned frequently in the Bible. In the Old Testament an angel spoke to Abraham, telling him not to harm his son Isaac whom he was willing to sacrifice to God. In his sleep Jacob, Isaac's second son, saw angels ascending and descending a ladder which reached from earth to Heaven. The Angel Raphael protected the young Tobias on his long journey to a distant city. In the New Testament, it was the Angel Gabriel who made known to Our Lady that she was to become the mother of God. An angelic host announced the birth of Jesus Christ. An angel told St. Joseph to take Our Lady and her Divine Son and flee into Egypt with them. Angels came to minister to Our Lord when He was tempted in the desert and during His Agony in the Garden. At His Resurrection an angel rolled the stone away from His grave.

At Mass the priest and the people confess their sins to Michael the Archangel. They sing *Holy, Holy, Holy* with the angels at the Sanctus. After the consecration at Mass the priest asks God to accept the sacrifice and to carry it by the hands of His holy angel to Heaven.

There are nine choirs of angels. *See* choirs of angels.

Angelus, the A prayer in honor of the Incarnation, Our Lord becoming man. It is said three times a day: in the morning, at noon, and at night. In convents the Angelus is always said at the sound of a bell. The name of the prayer comes from the Latin word *angelus* meaning *angel*.

THE ANGELUS

V. The angel of the Lord declared unto Mary

R. And she conceived of the Holy Ghost. Hail Mary, etc.

V. Behold the handmaid of the Lord.

R. Be it done unto me according to thy word. Hail Mary, etc.

V. And the Word was made flesh

R. And dwelt among us. Hail Mary, etc.

V. Pray for us, O Holy Mother of God,

R. That we may be made worthy of the promises of Christ.

Let us pray. Pour forth, we beseech Thee, O Lord, Thy grace into our hearts, that we to whom the Incarnation of Christ, Thy Son, was made known by the message of an angel, may by His passion and Cross be brought to the glory of His Resurrection, through the same Christ Our Lord. Amen.

At Eastertime the Angelus is replaced by the Regina Coeli, which see.

anger *See* capital sins.

Anniversary Mass A Requiem Mass offered for the repose of the soul of one who is dead on the third, seventh, and thirtieth day after his death, or a year after his death.

Annunciation, the The announcement of the Angel Gabriel to the Blessed Virgin Mary that she was to be the mother of Jesus Christ. The angel greeted Mary with the words, "Hail, full of grace, the Lord is with thee. Blessed art thou among women." Mary did not understand this strange greeting. The angel said, "Do not be afraid, Mary, for thou hast found grace with God." He told her that she was to have a son whom she was to name Jesus. "He shall be great and shall be called the Son of the Most High; and the Lord God will give Him the throne of David His father, and He shall be king over the house of Jacob forever, and of His kingdom there shall be no end." Mary knew that one of the prophecies concerning the Messias was that he was to come from the race of David. Still troubled at the angel's words, she asked him how these things would be possible. The Angel Gabriel answered, "The Holy Spirit shall come upon thee, and the power of the Most High shall overshadow thee; and therefore the Holy One to be born shall be called the Son of God." Mary freely accepted God's will when she said, "Behold the handmaid of the Lord; be it done to me according to thy word." *Luke I 28–38.*

The Feast of the Annunciation is celebrated March 25 and is one of the principal feasts of Our Lady. If March 25 occurs in Holy Week or Easter Week, the celebration is transferred to the Monday after Low Sunday. The first Joyful Mystery of the Rosary is the Annunciation.

anoint To put holy oil on persons or things in a Church ceremony. Anointing is used in many of the sacraments, in Baptism, Holy Orders, Confirmation, and Extreme Unction. Churches and altars are anointed when they are consecrated, and oil and chrism are poured into the holy water font when it is blessed. The Sacrament of Extreme Unction is sometimes called the anointing of the sick.

antichrist Christ's enemy who will spread hatred through the world before Christ's second coming and will cause many to fall away from the Church before he is destroyed by Jesus Christ.

antiphon A short prayer said or sung at the beginning and at the end of the Psalms of the Divine Office.

antiphonal chants At High Mass the Introit, Offertory, and Communion are called antiphonal chants sung by the choir.

antiphons of Our Lady Four prayers in honor of Our Lady sung in Divine Office at different times of the year. They are *Alma Redemptoris Mater, Ave Regina Coelorum, Regina Coeli,* and *Salve Regina.*

Apocalypse The last book of the New Testament written by St. John the Evangelist. In the *Apocalypse,* St. John writes that he was commanded by Jesus Christ to set down the things that he had seen, the things that were happening at that time, and a revelation of things that were to come. The word *apocalypse* means *revelation* and comes from the Greek word *to uncover* or *reveal.* In Protestant versions of the Bible the book is called *The Revelation of St. John the Divine.*

apologetics That branch of theology concerned with defending Christianity.

apologist One who defends Christianity in speech or writing. *The apologists* were early Christian writers who defended the Christian Faith against heresies.

apostasy (from the faith) The giving up of the true Christian faith by a baptized person. One who has been a Catholic and leaves his faith for another faith or becomes an unbeliever is called an apostate from his faith.

apostle (1) One of the twelve Apostles. *See* **Apostles.** The word *apostle* comes from the Greek and means *one sent.* (2) A missionary who brings Christianity to a country for the first time is known as the apostle of that country. For example, St. Augustine of Canterbury is known as the apostle of England.

Apostles The name given, first of all, to the twelve men who were chosen by Jesus Christ to work with Him when He was on earth and to carry on His work preaching the gospel after His return to Heaven. The Gospel according to St. Luke relates how these twelve were chosen from among the disciples: "Now it came to pass in those days, that He went out to the mountain to pray, and continued all night in prayer to God. And when day broke, He summoned His disciples; and from these He chose twelve (whom

He also named apostles): Simon, whom He named Peter, and his brother Andrew; James and John; Philip and Bartholomew; Matthew and Thomas, James the son of Alpheus, and Simon called the Zealot; Jude the brother of James and Judas Iscariot, who turned traitor." *Luke VI 12–16.* James, the son of Alpheus, is sometimes called James the Less because he was younger than James, the son of Zebedee. Jude, whom St. Luke points out as the brother of James the Less, in order to distinguish him from Judas Iscariot, is sometimes referred to as Thaddeus. The apostles were simple men, men of no great learning. Simon Peter and Andrew were fishermen as were James and John. Our Lord told these four that He would make them catchers of men. Matthew, called Levi in the Gospels according to St. Mark and St. Luke, was a tax-collector and a publican. This was a despised profession, and the Pharisees could not understand why Jesus would associate with Matthew and the other publicans.

After Judas Iscariot betrayed Our Lord, the Apostles chose Matthias to take his place. He was not chosen, however, until after the Ascension of Jesus Christ, so at the time of the Resurrection there were only eleven apostles. The first chapter of the *Acts of the Apostles* tells how Matthias was chosen. After praying to God to direct their choice, the Apostles drew lots between Joseph and Matthias.

St. Peter was the chief of the Apostles and became the first head of the Catholic Church on earth. Our Lord said to him, "And I say to thee, thou art Peter and upon this rock I will build my Church, and the gates of hell shall not prevail against it." *Matthew XVI 18.* After the Ascension, St. Peter went to Antioch for a time and from there to Rome, where he was bishop for twenty-five years. He was crucified under Nero and buried on Vatican Hill. All of the Apostles were martyred except St. John, called "the beloved disciple." He escaped martyrdom miraculously and died a natural death about the year 100 A.D.

Later the names of other saints, such as Paul and Barnabas, were added to the list of the Apostles, but these, of course, were not chosen by Jesus Christ when He was on earth. Paul had persecuted the Christians until Our Lord appeared to him and transformed him. Then he upheld the Christian religion as strongly as he had formerly opposed it. St. Paul is often called "the Apostle." Barnabas was a friend of Paul and also a friend and relative of Mark, who wrote the second Gospel.

The Apostles were the first bishops of the Church. Christ's Church on earth was founded on them. They were to lay the foundations of the teaching authority of the Church. When Jesus Christ said to the Apostles, "And behold I am with you all days, even unto the consummation of the world" (*Matthew XXVIII 20*) He meant that the Apostles, to whom He had given authority, would hand down that authority to the bishops who came after them.

Apostles' Creed A profession of faith thought to be handed down by the Apostles and formulated by the Church. It is the oldest creed of the Church and in an early form was in use in the first years of Christianity. The word *creed* comes from the Latin word *credo* which means *I believe,* and a creed is a statement of what is believed. The Apostles' Creed is the creed given in the catechism. It is recited at the Sacraments of Baptism and Ordination and in the Divine Office.

THE APOSTLES' CREED

I believe in God, the Father Almighty, Creator of Heaven and earth; and in Jesus Christ, His only Son, Our Lord; who was conceived by the Holy Ghost, born of the Virgin Mary, suffered under Pontius Pilate, was crucified, died, and was buried. He descended into hell; the third day He arose again from the dead; He ascended into heaven, sitteth at the right hand of God, the Father Almighty; from thence He shall come to judge the living and the dead. I believe in the Holy Ghost, the Holy Catholic Church, the communion of saints, the forgiveness of sins, the resurrection of the body, and life everlasting. Amen.

apostolic succession The unbroken line from the first Apostles to the pope and bishops of today. The duties and powers given to the first Apostles by Jesus Christ have been handed down, without any interruption, to the Pope and the bishops who came after them.

apparition A vision in which a supernatural being takes a bodily form, such as the apparition of Our Lady to Bernadette at Lourdes. *See* **vision.**

appearances (of bread and wine)   The outward aspect of the bread and wine, what can be seen, felt, touched, smelled, or tasted. Only the appearances of bread and wine were left after the substance of the bread and wine had been changed into Our Lord's body and blood at the Last Supper the night before He died. In the Sacrament of the Holy Eucharist, the Host which the priest lays on the tongue of the communicant looks like bread. It tastes like bread to him and feels like bread to the priest, but it is not bread. It has been changed entirely into the body and blood of Our Lord, and only the appearances remain.

apse   The back portion of the sanctuary.

Aramaic   The language of Palestine at the time Our Lord lived on earth and the language which He spoke. The Gospel according to St. Matthew was originally written in Aramaic.

archangel   A spirit just above an angel in rank. *See* **choirs of angels.** Three archangels mentioned in the Bible are Michael, the captain of the heavenly host; Gabriel, who announced to Our Lady that she was to be the mother of Jesus Christ; and Raphael, who accompanied the young Tobias to the city of Rages.

archbishop   The bishop of an archdiocese who has limited authority over the bishops of the several dioceses in his territory. Sometimes the title of archbishop is given to a prelate who has no bishops under him or who does not have the special duties of an archbishop. Such an archbishop is called a titular archbishop. An archbishop is addressed as Your Excellency.

archdiocese   An ecclesiastical territory governed by an archbishop. An archdiocese is the principal diocese within a province.

Arianism   The heresy of Arius. Arius, a priest of Alexandria in the fourth century, denied that the Son was equal to the Father. He claimed that Jesus Christ was a mere creature. St. Athanasius wrote against Arianism, which was condemned at the Council of Nice in 325.

ark, Noe's (Noah's)   The vessel built by Noe (Noah) at the command of God, to keep his family safe during the great flood sent by God. Noe was a just man who loved God. When God saw the wickedness in the world, He planned to destroy man. He did not wish to destroy Noe and his family, so He commanded him to build an ark for their safety. He described to Noe in detail how the ark should be built. God also told Noe to take into the ark with him and his family two of every living creature, male and female.

When the flood came, Noe did as God had commanded. The flood lasted for forty days and then the waters slowly drew back from the earth. When at last Noe and his family came out of the ark, Noe built an altar to God and sacrificed to Him. God was pleased and said to Noe: "I will never again curse the ground on account of man, for the inclination of man's heart is evil from his youth; I will never again destroy every living creature as I have done. As long as the earth shall last, seed-time and harvest, cold and heat, summer and winter, day and night, shall not cease." *Genesis VIII 21–22.*

Ark of the Covenant   A small box of precious wood carried by the people of Israel in their wanderings and placed in the Temple at Jerusalem. This box contained the two Tablets of the law which had been given to Moses by God and on which were written the ten commandments.

art, liturgical   Liturgical or sacred art used in the worship of the Church. On June 30, 1952, the Sacred Congregation of the Holy Office stated that the function and duty of sacred art is "to enhance the beauty of the house of God, and to foster the faith and piety of those who gather in the Church to assist at the divine service." Sacred art includes architecture, painting, sculpture, and whatever pertains to the interior decoration of churches. The best sacred art is truly artistic in form and serves the spirit and mission of the Church.

Ascension   The departure of Jesus Christ, body and soul, into Heaven on Ascension Day, forty days after His Resurrection. Jesus had led His Apostles to the Mount of Olives where He spoke to them for the last time, telling them to go into the whole world and preach the Gospel. The Gospel according to St. Luke describes the Ascension: "Now He led them out towards Bethany and He lifted up His hands and blessed them. And it came to pass as He blessed them, that He parted from them and was carried up into Heaven." *Luke XXIV 50–51.*

The Feast of the Ascension, known as Ascension Thursday, is forty days after Easter Sunday and is a holyday of obligation.

Ash Wednesday The Wednesday on which Lent begins. On this day ashes are blessed and placed on the foreheads of the priests and the people. The ashes are made by burning the palms blessed on Palm Sunday almost a year before. The priest says in Latin, while he places the ashes on the foreheads of the people: "Remember, man, that thou art dust and to dust thou shalt return." Ash Wednesday, which reminds man of his short stay in this world, ushers in Lent in the spirit of penance.

Asperges The ceremony before the principal Mass on Sunday of sprinkling the altar, priests, and people with holy water. During this ceremony an anthem is sung beginning, "Thou shalt sprinkle me with hyssop, O Lord, and I shall be cleansed." In Latin the word *asperges* means *thou shalt sprinkle,* and the ceremony takes its name from the anthem. A hyssop was a leafy branch used to sprinkle the water.

aspiration A short prayer or ejaculation. The word *aspiration* comes from the Latin word *aspirare* (*to breathe*), and an aspiration is the breathing out of a prayer. "My Jesus, mercy," is an aspiration.

assist at Mass To be present at Mass. Since the word *assist* really means to help or join with others in some particular work, to assist at Mass means to join with the priest in offering the Mass.

The first commandment or precept of the Church is *To assist at Mass on all Sundays and holydays of obligation.*

Assumption of the Blessed Virgin Mary The taking into Heaven of the body of the Blessed Virgin Mary soon after her death. The word *assumption* comes from the Latin word *assumere* (*to take up*) and the body of the Blessed Virgin Mary, who was free from original sin and so was not subject to death in the same way that creatures are, was taken into Heaven and united to her soul. The Feast of the Assumption is August 15 and is a holyday of obligation in the United States.

Belief in Our Lady's Assumption goes back to early Christian days. On November 1, 1950, Pope Pius XII defined the Assumption as a dogma of the Church. *See* **dogma.** A new Proper for the Mass for the day shows Mary in her bodily glory. The Introit begins, "A great sign appeared in heaven: a woman clothed with the sun, and the moon was under her feet, and upon her head a crown of twelve stars." *Apocalypse XII 1.*

Athanasian Creed Declaration of Christian belief principally concerning the Trinity and the Incarnation. This creed is found in the Breviary and is recited on the Feast of the Holy Trinity. It is called Athanasian because it was long thought to be composed by St. Athanasius. The Athanasian Creed is one of the principal creeds of the Church.

atheism The denial of the existence of God. Atheists are of two kinds: the speculative atheists who assert that there is no God, and the practical atheists who act as if there were no God.

attention The act of keeping the mind, through the help of the will, on one particular thing. In prayer and in receiving the sacraments one should have at least external attention.

attributes of the Church Characteristics of the Catholic Church. Authority, infallibility and indefectibility are the three chief attributes (characteristics) of the Catholic Church. *See* **authority, infallibility, indefectibility.**

attrition Imperfect contrition for sins. *See* **contrition.**

audience, papal A formal visit to the Pope by a person or a number of persons. Public audiences, in which a number of people visit the Pope in a group, are much more common than private audiences when a single person is allowed to pay his respects to the Pope. A visit to the Pope must be arranged in advance, and certain manners of dress and greeting must be observed. The Pope is addressed as Your Holiness.

Augustinian hermits *See* **religious orders and congregations of men.**

Augustinianism *See* **scholasticism.**

aureole The gold band surrounding the figure in sacred pictures and showing the glory of the persons represented. The Three Divine Persons and the Blessed Virgin are usually shown with an aureole around them. The word *aureole* is used in theology to refer to a reward added to the bliss of Heaven and given to martyrs, virgins, Doctors of the Church, and other heroic persons.

authority of the Church One of the three chief attributes (characteristics) of the Catholic Church. An attribute is a quality which seems to belong to a certain person or thing. Authority belongs to the Catholic Church. It is the power, given by Jesus Christ Himself, to teach, to sanctify, and to govern the faithful in spiritual matters.

The authority of the Catholic Church to teach is called *magisterium*. This authority was given to the Church by Jesus Christ when He said to the Apostles after His Resurrection, "Go, therefore, and make disciples of all nations, baptizing them in the name of the Father, and of the Son, and of the Holy Ghost, teaching them to observe all that I have commanded you; and behold, I am with you all days, even unto the consummation of the world." *Matthew XXVIII 19–20*. The Pope has the highest teaching authority in the Church.

The Catholic Church also has the authority to sanctify, that is, to administer the sacraments. Each one of the seven sacraments was given to the Church by Jesus Christ Himself to give grace.

The power of the government to rule is called jurisdiction. The authority of the Catholic Church to govern is also called jurisdiction. The Catholic Church is a spiritual society founded by Jesus Christ, and it has a government. Jesus Christ is the real Head of the Church which is under the guidance of the Holy Ghost. He is the invisible Head of the Church, while the visible Head of the Church and the deputy of Jesus Christ is the Pope. With the bishops under him, the Pope holds the governing authority of the Church.

Jesus Christ first gave this power to govern to St. Peter and the other Apostles. To Peter He said, "And I say to thee, thou art Peter, and upon this rock I will build my Church, and the gates of hell shall not prevail against it. And I will give thee the keys of the kingdom of heaven; and whatever thou shalt bind on earth shall be bound in heaven; and whatever thou shalt loose on earth shall be loosed in heaven." *Matthew XVI 18–19*. The keys of the kingdom, given to St. Peter, are a symbol of authority. *See* **power of the keys.**

Ave Maria   The Latin words for *Hail Mary*. *See* **Hail Mary.**

Avignon Popes   Seven Popes from Clement V (1305–1314) to Gregory XI (1370–1378) who governed the Church from Avignon instead of from Rome.

B

Babel, the Tower of A tower, built by the descendants of Noe. Noe's descendants all spoke one language. They discovered a valley in the land of Sennaar (Babylonia) and decided to settle there. They planned to build a city in this valley and a tower which would have its top in the heavens. God did not approve of their plans, and He confused their language so that they would not understand each other. God scattered them over the earth, and they stopped building the city. The city and the tower are called Babel "because there the Lord confused the speech of all the earth." *Genesis XI* 9.

Babylonian captivity (1) The taking of the principal men of Jerusalem and some of the sacred vessels of the Temple of Solomon into Babylon by Nabuchodonosor, King of Babylon. The Babylonians took as captives many of the people of Jerusalem, and they seized the treasures of the city. They finally destroyed the city of Jerusalem by setting fire to the houses and breaking down the wall of the city. During their captivity the Jews did penance for their sins. God told them to live in peace in Babylon, to build houses and plant orchards and to marry and give their children in marriage. He promised that after seventy years He would bring them back to Jerusalem. The history of the Babylonian captivity is told in the *Prophecy of Jeremias,* in the Old Testament of the Bible. (2) An expression used for the exile of seven popes (Clement V to Gregory XI) from Rome to Avignon, France. During this period (1309–1377) the popes governed from France instead of Rome and are known as the Avignon Popes.

baldachin *See* **altar draperies.**

balm-balsam Fragrant juice of the balsam tree. It is mixed with olive oil to make chrism, which is blessed by the bishop on Holy Thursday.

banns of marriage A public announcement in the parish church of the promise of marriage between two persons. This announcement must be made at the principal Mass in the parish church of

each party on three successive Sundays or holydays of obligation.
If there are any reasons why these two persons may not marry
each other, anyone hearing the announcement and knowing such
reasons is bound to report them to the parish priest.

Baptism   The sacrament by which a person is cleansed of original
sin, made a child of God and an heir of Heaven. A person must
receive Baptism before he may receive any of the other sacraments. Baptism brings sanctifying grace into the soul and takes
away original sin, which is the sin inherited from Adam and with
which everyone is born. Baptism also takes away any actual sins
and the punishment due to them, if the person baptized is guilty
of any actual sins. In Baptism a person is made alive for the first
time with the life of grace. Since the one who is baptized is in
the state of original sin before receiving this sacrament, Baptism
is called a Sacrament of the Dead. Baptism can be received only
once, because it leaves on the soul an indelible mark called a
character. *See* character.

The ordinary minister of the Sacrament of Baptism is the priest,
because he has the power from God to give the sacrament. However, if there is danger that a person may die without Baptism,
anyone else (including a non-Catholic) may and should baptize.
In case of necessity, the Sacrament of Baptism is given by pouring
ordinary water on the forehead of the person to be baptized.
While pouring it, the minister of the sacrament says: "I baptize
thee in the name of the Father, and of the Son, and of the Holy
Ghost." The minister of the sacrament must say the words at the
same time as he pours the water so that the matter of the sacrament (the water) and the form (the words spoken) are joined.
In solemn baptisms, the priest performs other ceremonies besides
pouring the water, and the water used is baptismal water.

Baptism is necessary for salvation. However, those who have
not received the baptism of water may be saved by the baptism
of blood or the baptism of desire. Baptism of blood is baptism
through suffering death or a wound which leads to death for
Christ or some Christian virtue. Baptism of blood gives grace
and takes away sin and the punishment due to sin, but it does not
imprint a mark on the soul, because it is not a sacrament. A
person who has a mortal sin on his soul cannot receive the

baptism of blood unless he has at least attrition (imperfect sorrow for his sins). Even infants can receive the baptism of blood. The Holy Innocents, those babies killed at King Herod's command in the hope that Jesus might be among them, received the baptism of blood.

Baptism of desire is pure love of God and the desire to do everything necessary to be saved. Many people who have never received the baptism of water may be saved through the baptism of desire. Sometimes this baptism of desire is clearly indicated. If a person who knows the truths of his religion and is being prepared for his Baptism dies before he has actually been baptized with water, he has already received the baptism of desire provided he has perfect contrition and the desire to do what God wants him to do for his salvation. Sometimes, however, this baptism of desire is implied rather than expressly stated. If a person loves God because He is infinitely good in Himself but does not know of the necessity of the Sacrament of Baptism, he has received the baptism of desire through his desire to do what God wants.

Baptism of desire takes away sin and the punishment due to sin, but it does not imprint a spiritual mark (a character) on the soul, because it is not a sacrament.

baptismal font The usual place of Baptism. The font consists of a basin on a stand. The basin which contains the baptismal water has a smaller one in its rim. The water poured over the child's head runs into this smaller basin. Both basins have drains running into the earth. The font is blessed on Holy Saturday, during the Easter Vigil.

baptismal garment The white linen cloth laid by the priest on the head of the child being baptized, with the words "Receive this white garment, etc."

baptismal name The name given in Baptism, preferably a saint's name.

baptismal water Water specially blessed during the Easter Vigil on Holy Saturday for use in solemn Baptism. In case of necessity any ordinary water may be used for Baptism.

baptistery That part of the church which contains the baptismal font and in which baptisms take place. The baptistery is sometimes a separate room or building.

Barabbas   The thief who was released by Pilate at the demand of the people in place of Jesus Christ whom Pilate wanted released. Because it was festival time, the time of the Passover, it was necessary for Pilate to release one prisoner to the people. Pilate could find no guilt in Jesus, and so he wanted to release him. "But the whole mob cried out together, saying 'Away with this man and release to us Barabbas.'" *Luke XXIII 18.* Barabbas, who had been thrown into prison for riot and murder, was released, while Jesus Christ was led away to be crucified.

Baruch   A book of the Old Testament of the Bible. It was written by Baruch who was a close companion of the prophet Jeremias.

basilica   A name given to ancient Roman churches built in the style of Roman public buildings. The name now is a title of honor given to thirteen churches at Rome and other Catholic churches which have certain privileges. St. John Lateran, St. Peter, St. Paul Outside the Walls, and St. Mary Major are major basilicas in Rome.

B.C.   Abbreviation meaning *Before Christ.* A date followed by the abbreviation B.C. means so many years before the birth of Christ.

beads, Rosary   Small beads strung together in a Rosary and used to count prayers. *See* **Rosary.** Beads have been used to count prayers for many ages.

bear false witness, to   To hurt the good name of another person either by telling lies about him or by revealing his hidden faults. *See* **calumny and detraction.**

Beatific Vision   The sight of God and His mysteries which will be the reward of those who attain the happiness of Heaven. With the eyes of the soul they will be able to see God in all His perfections and in the three persons, Father, Son, and Holy Ghost. They will also be able to understand the mysteries of their religion which they could not understand while they were on earth. They will be able to see creatures in God and to be aware of the souls on earth which ask for their prayers. While all persons who attain Heaven will enjoy this vision of God, they will not receive it in the same degree of perfection but according to individual merit.

beatification   The official act of the Pope which gives a person the right to be called blessed. When a person is beatified, it means that he is certainly in Heaven. Sometimes canonization follows beatification very quickly. *See* **canonization.** For example, St.

Thérèse (the Little Flower) was beatified April 29, 1923, and was canonized May 17, 1925.

beatitude   Perfect happiness in Heaven enjoyed by the blessed who see God in the Beatific Vision.

Beatitudes, the eight   Eight blessings given by Jesus Christ at the beginning of the Sermon on the Mount. *See* **Sermon on the Mount.** The eight Beatitudes are:

1. Blessed are the poor in spirit, for theirs is the kingdom of heaven.
2. Blessed are the meek, for they shall possess the earth.
3. Blessed are they who mourn, for they shall be comforted.
4. Blessed are they who hunger and thirst for justice, for they shall be satisfied.
5. Blessed are the merciful, for they shall obtain mercy.
6. Blessed are the pure of heart, for they shall see God.
7. Blessed are the peacemakers, for they shall be called children of God.
8. Blessed are they who suffer persecution for justice' sake, for theirs is the kingdom of heaven.

The eight Beatitudes, along with the fruits of the Holy Ghost, are called effects of the gifts of the Holy Ghost. The word *beatitude* means *perfect happiness*. Beatitude is not possible to a creature until he sees God in the Beatific Vision. However, those who have grace in their souls find happiness through the performance of good acts.

Beelzebub   Another name for Satan used in the New Testament.

belief, divine   Acceptance of a truth because God has said it.

bells   (1) Church bells. Bells which have been blessed by the bishop and which are used to call people to Mass or to sound the Angelus. The ceremony of the Blessing of the Bells is so solemn that it was once known as the Baptism of Bells. (2) Bells at Mass. Small bells rung by the server at the solemn parts of the Mass. *See* **Sanctus bell.**

Benedictine Order   *See* **religious orders and congregations of men.**

Benediction, Apostolic   The word *benediction* means a blessing. An Apostolic Benediction, which comes from the Pope himself, is a solemn blessing carrying a plenary indulgence. *See* **indul-**

gence. Bishops and priests have the power to give this benediction only at special times or to a sick person in danger of death.

Benediction of the Blessed Sacrament A religious service in which the Blessed Sacrament is used to bless the people. At the beginning of Benediction the priest takes the consecrated Host from the tabernacle and places it in a Monstrance. *See* **Monstrance.** He places the Monstrance, with the Blessed Sacrament exposed, on a throne above the tabernacle where the people can see and adore Jesus Christ in the Blessed Sacrament. The priest incenses the Blessed Sacrament while a hymn (usually *O Salutarus Hostia*) is sung. Sometimes the Litany of the Blessed Virgin or other prayers are said. The *Tantum ergo* is sung, and the Blessed Sacrament is again incensed. At the end of the service the priest takes the Monstrance, containing the Host, and makes the Sign of the Cross over the people with it.

For Benediction the priest wears a vestment called a cope. It is a long cloak reaching to the heels and open at the front. Before the priest gives the benediction, the humeral veil is placed over his shoulders by the server.

Benediction of the Blessed Sacrament is not a part of the liturgy of the Church. It is not one of the forms of public worship formally set down by the Church, but it is a very popular devotion because it honors Jesus Christ in the Blessed Sacrament.

Benedictus, the The prayer which Zachary, the father of John the Baptist, spoke in praise of God at the time John received his name.

THE BENEDICTUS

Blessed be the Lord, the God of Israel,
  because he has visited and wrought redemption for
  his people,
And has raised up a horn of salvation for us
  in the house of David his servant,
As he promised through the mouths of his holy ones,
  the prophets from of old:
Salvation from our enemies
  and from the hands of all our foes.
He has fulfilled his kindness to our fathers,
  and been mindful of his holy covenant

In the oath to Abraham our father,
  by which he swore to grant us
That, delivered from the hands of our enemies,
  we should serve him without fear
In holiness and justice before him
  all our days.
And you, O child, shall be called the prophet of the
  Most High;
For you shall go before the Lord to prepare his ways,
To give his people knowledge of salvation
  through forgiveness of their sins,
Because of the compassionate kindness of our God
  with which the Orient from on high will visit us,
To shine on those who sit in darkness and the shadow
  of death,
  to guide our feet into the way of peace. *Luke I* 68–79.

The Benedictus is said in the Divine Office at Lauds. At the Christian burial of an adult person it is said at the grave.

Bethlehem A village in Palestine where Jesus Christ was born. Mary and Joseph lived in Nazareth, but they had gone to Bethlehem to have their names written in the register for the census, a list of names for the purpose of taxation. Bethlehem was their family city, since they were both descendants of David. In Bethlehem Mary and Joseph could find no place to stay because the inns were filled with others who had come to register for the census. A poor stable was offered to them as lodging, and it was here that Jesus was born on Christmas day.

betrothal The promise to marry made in writing and signed by both parties, the parish priest, and two witnesses.

Bible, the Holy The sacred writings composed of the Old Testament of forty-five books written before the birth of Our Lord and the New Testament of twenty-seven books written after His birth. The Bible contains truths which God has revealed to us by inspired writing, that is, by writing which has been guided by divine influence. Since the Church, through the guidance of the Holy Spirit, explains divine revelation, the faithful depend on the Church to interpret the Bible for them. The faithful, however, are encouraged to read the Bible, provided they read an approved text, and certain indulgences are granted for such reading.

bigamy The contracting of a marriage by a person who is already validly married.

biretta A stiff square cap with three upright ridges on top worn by the clergy. A priest's biretta is black while a cardinal's is red and a bishop's purple. The biretta is worn on entering the church for service, and on leaving the church, and at certain other times.

bishop The ruler of a diocese. A bishop, as a successor of the Apostles, is a representative of Christ on earth. His authority is conferred on him by the Pope at his appointment. His authority, however, unlike that of the first Apostles, is limited to his own diocese. He has received the fullness of Holy Orders and has special spiritual powers to confirm, ordain, and consecrate. A bishop is addressed as Your Excellency.

bishop, auxiliary A bishop appointed by the Holy See to assist a ruling bishop. An auxiliary bishop is sometimes called a titular bishop because he is given the title of an ancient diocese which no longer exists or in which there are few Catholics.

bishop, coadjutor A bishop appointed to a diocese when the bishop who holds the office is unable to perform his duties. He usually has the right of succession to the diocese to which he is appointed.

bishopric The diocese or office of a bishop.

Black Mass A name given to a Requiem Mass (Mass for the Dead) because black vestments are worn. *See* **Requiem Mass.**

Blaise, St., blessing of A blessing usually given on February 3, the Feast of St. Blaise. It is often called the blessing of the throats. The people kneel at the communion rail while the priest touches their throats with two crossed candles and says: "May God deliver thee from trouble of the throat and from every other evil through the intercession of St. Blaise, the bishop and martyr. In the name of the Father and of the Son and of the Holy Ghost. Amen." *See* **Appendix, Saints, St. Blaise, February 3.**

blasphemy Use of insulting words about God, the saints, or holy things.

blessed A title given to a person after he has been beatified. In the Mass the saints are often referred to as blessed rather than as saints, as in the Confiteor.

blessed in Heaven The souls of the dead who are enjoying the perfect happiness of Heaven. *See* **Church Triumphant.**

Blessed Sacrament, the The sacrament of the Holy Eucharist, called *blessed* because it is the source of all blessings and graces. It contains Jesus Christ Himself who is the source of all grace. The Blessed Sacrament is the sacrament of the body and blood of Our Lord Jesus Christ, who comes in Holy Communion to be the food of the soul. The consecrated bread itself, the Host, is often referred to as the Blessed Sacrament.

Blessed Trinity, the One and the same God in three divine persons, the Father, the Son, and the Holy Ghost. There are three distinct persons who are one God. Each of these persons is divine because each one is God. They all have one and the same divine nature. The Father is God and the first person of the Blessed Trinity. The Son is God and the second person of the Blessed Trinity. The Holy Ghost is God and the third person of the Blessed Trinity.

Jesus Christ Himself revealed the doctrine of the Blessed Trinity. In the Gospel according to St. John He said to His Apostles, "Dost thou not believe that I am in the Father and the Father in me? The words that I speak to you I speak not on my own authority. But the Father dwelling in me, it is he who does the works." *John XIV 10.* Again He says, "And I will ask the Father and he will give you another Advocate to dwell with you forever, the Spirit of truth whom the world cannot receive, because it neither sees him nor knows him. But you shall know him, because he will dwell with you and be in you." *John XIV 16–17.*

God the Father is the Creator. Father, Son, and Holy Ghost are all uncreated. God the Father sent His Divine Son, Jesus Christ, to redeem man from sin. The Son proceeds from the Father. The Holy Ghost proceeds from both the Father and the Son. The Holy Ghost was sent by God the Father and God the Son, as a comforter to give new strength and grace to the Church.

The Blessed Trinity is honored in the Sign of the Cross and in the *Glory Be to the Father*. The Holy Sacrifice of the Mass is offered to the Holy Trinity. The Feast of the Most Holy Trinity is the Sunday after Pentecost.

Blessed Virgin Mary, the   The virgin mother of God. Mary was
a young Jewish virgin, the daughter of Joachim and Anne and a
descendant of the family of David. Joachim and Anne named
their daughter Miriam, which is Hebrew for Mary. Mary was
immaculate, without any stain of sin, from the moment of her
conception. At the very moment her soul came into being it was
free from original sin, which is the sin of Adam with which
everyone is born. She was also free from actual sin, and she was
never to commit a single sin in her life. From the moment she
was conceived, she had sanctifying grace, and she never lost it.

It is said that at three years of age Mary was taken to the
Temple where she was dedicated to God in a special way. For
a number of years she lived a holy life among other young girls
and no doubt meditated with them over the prophecies concerning the Messias, the Savior for whom the Jews were waiting.

When Mary became of an age to be married, she was espoused
(formally engaged) to a carpenter named Joseph, who was also
of the family of David. It was about this time that the Angel
Gabriel appeared to her and announced to her that she was to
become the mother of God. *See* **Annunciation, the.**

Mary's life was filled with the greatest joy and the greatest
sorrow. She was full of joy to hold the Infant God in her arms,
to show Him to the wondering shepherds and the adoring wise
men, but she was sad to have only a poor cave for His first home
and a manger meant for animals in which to lay Him. Her joy
at presenting Him in the Temple of Jerusalem was turned to
sorrow at the words of Simeon, who prophesied that a sword
would pierce her soul. The flight into Egypt and the loss of
Jesus in the Temple when He was twelve years old were also
sorrows to her. *See* **Sorrows of Our Lady, the Seven.** Mingled
with the happiness of having her Divine Son with her in Nazareth
during the thirty years of His hidden life was the knowledge that
He would have to die a cruel death for the sins of men. At His
Crucifixion her sorrow reached its height, and her soul was indeed
pierced with a sword. Yet joy came to her again three days after
His death when the stone was rolled away from His tomb and He
appeared to the Apostles.

Mary lived on earth many years after the death of her Divine

Son to help the Apostles and to mother the new Church. At her death, God took her pure body into Heaven where it was united to her spotless soul. *See* **Assumption, the.** According to tradition all the Apostles except St. Thomas were present at her death. When St. Thomas came and asked to see her body, the tomb was empty. No relics of Our Lady, as of so many of the other saints, remained on earth. Mary is the greatest of the saints, the Queen of all Saints, and the Queen of Heaven. *See* **Queen of Heaven.**

In the Canon of the Mass, at the Communicantes, Mary's name is mentioned first: "In communion with and venerating the memory in the first place of the glorious ever Virgin Mary, Mother of Our God and Lord Jesus Christ." Mary is a spiritual mother to everyone in the world. Jesus Christ gave her to mankind on the Cross when He said to St. John, the beloved disciple, "Behold thy mother." *John XIX* 27.

blessing   A prayer which asks God to look with favor on the person or thing blessed. A blessing is one kind of sacramental. *See* **Sacramentals.** A blessing given by the priest gives a spiritual value to that which is blessed. It calls down God's help upon a person or thing. There are so many kinds of blessings in the Church that it would be impossible to mention all of them. Some blessings given in the Church are of (1) persons—the bride and bridegroom at their wedding ceremony, children, a dying person, people who ask for a blessing; (2) places—a school, a home; (3) things—bells, rosaries, scapulars, medals. Some unusual blessings are of farm animals, fire engines, airplanes, bridges, railways.

A consecration is a special kind of blessing that dedicates the person or thing blessed to God. The vessels used in the celebration of Mass are consecrated. The form of words used for blessings and consecrations is found in the Roman Ritual. *See* **Ritual, the Roman.**

blessing before meals   Prayer said before eating: "Bless us, O Lord, and these Thy gifts, which we are about to receive from Thy bounty, through Christ Our Lord. Amen." A longer form in Latin is used in convents and religious houses.

Blessing, the Last   (1) A blessing given by the priest to the people at Mass, except at a Mass said with black vestments. The Last Blessing is given just before the Last Gospel. The people kneel to receive it. The words of the Last Blessing are: "May God Almighty bless you: Father, Son, and Holy Ghost." (2) A special blessing given by the priest to a sick person. To it is attached a plenary indulgence at the moment of death.

Blessing, Papal   A solemn blessing from the Pope himself, carrying a plenary indulgence. *See* **Benediction Apostolic.**

bloody sweat, the   One of the chief sufferings of Jesus Christ. In His bloody sweat, the sweat of Jesus became drops of blood falling on the ground. The first Sorrowful Mystery of the Rosary, the Agony of Our Lord in the Garden, commemorates His bloody sweat. *See* **Agony in the Garden, the.**

boat (for incense)   A boat-shaped vessel for holding incense before it is burned.

body, glorified   The body which the soul will take after the resurrection of the body. When the blessed in Heaven take their glorified, or risen, bodies they will recognize them as being the same as bodies they had on earth but spiritual. Being spiritual, they cannot die. *To glorify* means *to change into something more splendid.* A glorified body will be much more splendid than an earthly body.

bread, the breaking of the   At the Last Supper Our Lord took bread, blessed and broke it, and, giving it to His Apostles, said, "Take and eat; this is my body." *Matthew XXVI 26.* In the Mass the breaking of the bread (called the fraction of the Host) takes place between the Lord's Prayer and the Agnus Dei. The priest blesses himself with the paten and slips it under the Host. He uncovers the chalice, genuflects, and holds the Host over the chalice. He breaks the Host, first into two pieces, one of which he puts on the paten. He breaks a third piece from the other half before he puts it on the paten. Taking this small piece in his right hand, he makes the Sign of the Cross three times over the chalice, saying, "May the peace of the Lord be always with you." The server answers, "And with thy spirit."

Breviary   A book containing the Divine Office, that is, the prayers which the clergy must say every day. If the Breviary were in one volume, it would be so big that a priest could not easily carry it around with him. Therefore it is usually printed in four volumes, one for each season of the year. Each part contains the psalms arranged for every day of the week, the Proper of the Season (hymns, lessons, etc., for each day of the Church year), the Proper of the Saints, and the Common of the Saints. The Breviary also contains many litanies, prayers, forms, and blessings.

brief A papal letter stamped with the Pope's ring.

brother A title used for laymen or for members of religious orders whose members do not become priests.

bull Formal papal letter used on solemn occasions.

burial, Christian The act of burying the corpse (the dead body) of a Catholic according to the religious service of the Church, in ground which has been consecrated. Before the burial, the Mass of the Dead is said in the church.

burse A small square case in which the corporal is carried to and from the altar. It is the same color as the vestments.

buskins Silk stockings which a bishop wears over his purple stockings at a High Mass.

B.V.M. Abbreviation for the Blessed Virgin Mary.

Byzantine Rite Form of worship used by the Orthodox Eastern Church and some Eastern Catholic Churches.

C

Cain The first son of Adam. Cain raised the crops while his brother Abel kept the flocks. His sacrifice of the fruits of the ground was not acceptable to God because his heart was not pure. Cain was angry because God did not accept his sacrifice, while He accepted that of Abel. He was so jealous of his brother that he killed him.

Caiphas The high priest of the Jews before whom Jesus Christ was taken after He had been arrested. When Caiphas asked Jesus if He were Christ, the Son of God, He answered, "Thou hast said it." *Matthew XXVI 64.* Caiphas thought that by these words Jesus was guilty of blasphemy and should be condemned to death.

calendar, ecclesiastical A calendar of the days of the year noting feasts, vigils, fasts, and saints' days of the Church. Ecclesiastical calendars change from year to year because the date of Easter changes from year to year. *See* **Easter, date of.** Calendars in different dioceses may differ slightly, just as the calendars of different religious orders may vary.

calumny The sin of slander. Harming another's good name by telling lies about him or by exaggerating the facts so that they are no longer true is the sin of calumny or slander. The eighth commandment forbids calumny.

Calvary The place where Jesus Christ was crucified. Mount Calvary was a hill outside Jerusalem, and it was here that the soldiers dragged Our Lord to be crucified. This was the usual place for the execution of criminals. Golgotha is the Aramaic name for Calvary and means a skull. *See* **Aramaic.**

Cana, marriage at The place of Our Lord's first public miracle. Mary, the mother of Jesus, was present at a marriage in the town of Cana in Galilee. Jesus and His disciples had also been invited to the marriage. During the feast the wine was used up, and there was no wine to serve. This was most embarrassing to the young couple and their relatives, and Mary brought the problem

45

to her Divine Son. "They have no wine," she told Him. *John II* 3. Jesus was not yet ready to begin His miracles but, because His mother asked Him to do it, He worked this first miracle at her request. He told the servants to fill the pitchers with water, which He changed into wine.

Candlemas Day   The feast of the Purification of Our Lady, February 2. It is called Candlemas Day because candles are blessed before the principal Mass, and the Candlemas procession is held. Candlemas Day commemorates the day that Our Lord was presented in the Temple. Simeon, that holy old man who had been waiting for this moment, held the Child Jesus in his arms and called Him "A light of revelation for the Gentiles and the glory of your people Israel." *Luke II 32. See* **Purification of Our Lady, the,** and **Nunc dimittis.**

candles at Mass   Candles were originally carried before an important person as a sign of honor to him. There are always lighted candles on the altar at Mass. The number of candles lighted changes according to the religious service. Two candles are usually lighted for a priest's low Mass, though four may be lighted if the Mass is said for the parish or under certain other conditions. Six are lighted for High Mass, seven for the Mass of a bishop, and at least twelve are lighted for Benediction. Candles must be lighted when Communion is given, whether in church or at home. Lighted candles are also used in several of the sacraments.

Candles used in church should be made principally of beeswax. Their color is white except at a Mass for the Dead, when they may be yellow.

candles, blessed   Candles blessed on February 2, Candlemas Day. These may be obtained at the church on that day. Blessed candles in the home may be lighted in times of trouble, temptation, sickness, or death.

candles, votive   Candles which are burned before the Blessed Sacrament, relics, shrines, or statues.

canon   A measuring stick by which other things are measured, while the measuring stick itself does not change. The word *canon,* which comes from the Greek word meaning *a rule,* has a great number of meanings in the Church. (1) The *Canon of the Mass* is that part of the Mass which does not change except for the

Communicantes and the *Hanc igitur*. It is the most solemn part of the Mass and begins after the Sanctus and continues to the Pater Noster. This part of the Mass contains the real sacrifice of the Mass, the consecration of the bread and of the wine. The priest says the Canon in a voice that cannot be heard except during the first words of the prayer, *Nobis quoque peccatoribus* (*To us also sinners*). The silence of the Canon is not kept at a Mass at which priests are ordained. (2) The *Canon of Holy Scripture* is the list, made by the Church, of the inspired books which make up the Old and New Testament. (3) Ecclesiastical *canons* are the laws, rules, etc., which make up the laws of the the Church. *See* **Law, Canon.** (4) The *Canon of the Saints* is a list of the saints recognized by the Church. (5) The title *canon* is given to certain persons in the Church. In Europe and in French Canada, members of a cathedral chapter or a collegiate are called chapter canons. Members of certain religious orders are also called canons, for example, Augustinian canons.

canonical hours   The eight hours making up the Divine Office: Matins, Lauds, Prime, Terce, Sext, None, Vespers, and Compline. Hours of the Divine Office are distributed throughout the day. In the Roman Breviary Matins and Lauds, the first division, are usually joined. Approximate times for the other hours when sung in choir are: Prime, 6:00 A.M.; Terce, 9:00 A.M.; Sext, about midday; None, between noon and 3:00 P.M.; Vespers, between 3:00 and 6:00 P.M. Compline is the last hour of the Divine Office.

canonization   Public declaration from Rome that a person has been made a saint. His name is then placed in the roll (canon) of the saints. A person cannot be canonized until he has been beatified. After his beatification, two miracles which are the result of his intercession must be proved before he can be canonized. Since before beatification two miracles must be proved, this means that before a person is canonized four miracles must be proved. Canonization is carried out solemnly at St. Peter's by the Pope. A Mass is sung in honor of the new saint, and a day is appointed as his feast.

canopy   A covering of honor. Cardinals, bishops and abbots have canopies over their thrones. A canopy is carried over the Blessed

CANTICLE 48

Sacrament in processions. This canopy is made of rich material and is attached to four poles.

canticle A hymn taken from the Bible. Many of the canticles are sung in the Divine Office.

Canticle of Canticles A book of the Old Testament of the Bible possibly written by Solomon. It is called Solomon's Canticle of Canticles and is the description of the love between God and a human soul. Parts of it are used in the Office of the Blessed Virgin Mary. In Protestant versions of the Bible this book is called the Song of Solomon.

cantor The leader of the choir.

capital sins The seven chief or deadly sins: pride, covetousness, lust, anger, gluttony, envy, and sloth. They are called capital sins because they are the chief reasons men commit sin. (1) Pride, which is too high an opinion of one's self, leads to the sin of presumption. The proud man begins to think he can save his soul without God's help. This does not mean that a person cannot take normal pride in a neat appearance or good work or that he cannot be ambitious for his own future. Pride that goes beyond a normal desire to excel because one wants to do his best in whatever work he attempts can lead to sin. (2) Covetousness is too great a love of the goods of this world. It is normal for a man to want to earn a good salary and to provide well for his family. But greed in gaining money or goods, or carelessness of the rights of others in gaining it, may lead to the sin of injustice. Too great a love of the goods of the world also leads a man to forget spiritual values. (3) Lust, which is too great a desire for bodily pleasure, may lead to the sin of impurity. (4) Anger, which is an immoderate desire to take revenge, is opposed to the spirit of charity and may lead to the sin of murder. (5) Gluttony is eating or drinking too much. It dulls the mind and may lead, through the weakening of will power, to serious sins. (6) Envy is a feeling of discontent because of the success of one's neighbor. Envy leads to the sin of hating one's neighbor and wishing him misfortune. The sin of envy, along with the sin of anger, is opposed to the virtue of charity. (7) Sloth is laziness that makes one neglect his duty. It may lead to serious sins of omission, such as missing Mass on Sunday or holydays of obligation.

cappa magna   A great cloak worn by a bishop or cardinal at special functions in the church. It covers the whole person in front and has a hood lined with silk or fur according to the season. A cardinal's *cappa magna* is scarlet and a bishop's is purple.

capsula   Round metal container in which the Host used for Benediction is kept. A veil covers the *capsula*.

cardinal   A member of the Sacred College of Cardinals who are the advisers of the Holy Father and who upon his death elect a new pope. The name *cardinal* comes from the Latin word *cardo*, meaning *a hinge*, and the cardinals are as necessary to the Church as are hinges to a door. They are the fixed clergy of the Church— appointed by the Pope himself and by the Pope given their red birettas and red hats. The cardinals take an active part in the government of the Church and have many duties and privileges. A cardinal is addressed as Your Eminence. *See* **College of Cardinals, the Sacred.**

Carmel   A Carmelite monastery, usually of nuns.

Carmelite Nuns   *See* **religious orders and congregations of women.**

Carmelite order   *See* **religious orders and congregations of men.**

carol   A hymn sung at a festival. The name *carols* is most often given to Christmas hymns.

Carrying of the Cross, the   The third Sorrowful Mystery of the Rosary. Jesus Christ was made to carry a heavy cross on His shoulders already wounded by the scourging. When He could no longer carry it, the soldiers forced Simon the Cyrene to carry it for Him.

cassock   A long close-fitting garment worn by a priest. It is sometimes called a soutane. It buttons down the front and reaches almost to the heels. Most cassocks are black, but the cassock of the Pope is white, of cardinals red, and of bishops and archbishops purple.

catacombs   Underground tunnels built in the early days of the Church for the burial of the dead. The early Christians met in these catacombs to celebrate the anniversary of a martyr's death, but not for normal religious services.

catafalque   A wooden framework covered with a black cloth and resembling a coffin. It is sometimes used at anniversary Masses for the Dead, to represent the body which is not present.

catechism A summary of Christian doctrine in the form of questions and answers.

catechumen Name for a person who, in the early days of Christianity, was preparing to become a Christian. Catechumens were excluded from the Mass of the Faithful. *See* **Mass of the Catechumens.**

cathedra The bishop's throne or chair which is kept in the cathedral (church of the diocese) usually at the right side of the altar. When the Pope is speaking *ex cathedra* he is speaking as leader of the Church on earth, from his throne of authority, and has the intention of making a statement to be accepted as infallible. *See* **infallibility, papal.**

cathedral The mother church of a diocese in which the bishop has his cathedra (throne or chair).

Catholic (1) The word *catholic* comes from the Greek and means *universal* or *concerning all.* One of the marks of the Church is that it is catholic or universal. The Church is catholic or universal because it is for all people and because it teaches all the truths revealed by God. This means that the Church is open to everyone, that it is not for any one class, nation, or race. It also means that the Church teaches all the doctrines which Christ taught. (2) The name *Catholic* usually refers to any person who is a member of the Roman Catholic Church.

Catholic Action The sharing of the laity in the apostolic work of the bishops and other clergy of the Church. In 1932 Pope Pius XI called upon all Catholics to become interested in Catholic action. In Catholic action the laity coöperate with the clergy for the salvation of souls. A large number of official Catholic action groups are engaged in mission work under the supervision of the Church.

Catholic Church, the The one true Church established by Jesus Christ. It is called the Catholic Church from the word *catholic* which means *universal* or *concerning all. See* **Catholic.** Jesus Christ intended the Catholic Church to be for all men and for all time. Just before His Ascension, He said to His Apostles, "All power in heaven and on earth has been given to me. Go, therefore, and make disciples of all nations, baptizing them in the name of the Father, and of the Son, and of the Holy Spirit, teaching them to observe all that I have commanded you; and behold, I am with you all days, even unto the consummation of the world." *Matthew XXVIII 18–20.* He told the Apostles not to leave Jerusalem after His Ascension but to wait there for the coming of the Holy Ghost. On Pentecost the Holy Ghost came to the Apostles who were gathered together in the Cenacle, and the Holy Spirit began to dwell in the Church. From that time on, St. Peter and the other Apostles began to teach "all nations," as Jesus Christ had commanded them, and to strengthen the Church on earth.

celibacy (of the clergy)   Unmarried state of the clergy. Men in Holy Orders, beginning with the subdeacon, are not allowed to marry.

cell   The small, separate room of a monk, friar, or nun. It usually contains a bed, chair, table, necessary books, and writing equipment.

cemetery   A place for burying the dead. Catholics must be buried in consecrated ground, either in a Catholic cemetery or in a grave consecrated by itself.

Cenacle, the   The upper room in Jerusalem in which the Last Supper took place. Here Our Lord appeared after His Resurrection. Here, too, the Holy Ghost came down upon the Apostles who had assembled there with Mary, the Mother of Jesus Christ, and the followers of Jesus. The word *cenacle* comes from a Latin word which means dining room.

The Cenacle Nuns (the Institute of Our Lady of the Retreat in the Cenacle) are an enclosed active congregation which engages in catechetical instruction and opens its houses to women and children making retreats.

censer   Also called a thurible. A metal bowl in which incense is burned. The censer hangs on a chain and can be swung back and forth to spread the odor of the incense.

censor   One appointed by the bishop to examine books on religious or moral matters before they are printed, in order to see that they contain nothing contrary to faith or morals.

censure   A spiritual penalty imposed by the Church on a baptized person for serious reasons. *See* **excommunication**.

cerecloth   A linen cloth placed beneath the three altar cloths. *See* **altar cloths.** The cerecloth is waxed on the side next to the altar.

chalice   The cup used at Mass to contain the wine which becomes, at the consecration, Christ's blood. It is not unlike the cup used by Our Lord at the Last Supper when He changed wine into His blood. It is usually made of gold or silver, and the inside of the cup, at least, must always be gold. The chalice must be specially consecrated by the bishop with chrism.

chalice veil   A square piece of silk which covers the chalice and paten when they are not being used in the Mass. It is of the same material and color as the vestments.

chancery, diocesan   The business office of a diocese, where official documents are kept and from which documents issued by the bishop in his official capacity go out.

chapel   A place of worship smaller than a church. A chapel may be a separate part of a church with its own altar, or it may be a separate building, usually not of any great size. Often a chapel is a room set aside for worship in a school, a seminary, convent, or even a home. Such chapels are sometimes spoken of as oratories.

chaplain   A priest appointed to care for the souls of particular groups of people, not people in general. A chaplain might be appointed to a convent, an orphanage, or a prison, and his work would be to care for the souls of those who were in these places. A chaplain appointed to a school would care for the souls of the students. A chaplain appointed to the army or navy would care for the souls of the soldiers or sailors.

character (of the sacraments)   A spiritual mark on the soul, lasting forever, which is given in the Sacraments of Baptism, Confirmation, and Holy Orders. It is a spiritual quality which gives to him who receives it a special power to serve God. The mark of Baptism makes the person baptized a follower of Jesus Christ and gives him the power to receive the other sacraments. The mark of Confirmation makes those who are confirmed soldiers in the army of Christ and gives them the strength to defend their religion in the face of enemies. The mark of Holy Orders gives the priest the power to perform certain sacred duties.

charity   Love of God for His own sake and one's neighbor for the love of God. Through charity man can share in the life of God Himself. Charity is one of the three theological virtues. *See* virtues, theological. St. Paul says that it is the greatest of the three virtues:

"If I should speak with the tongues of men and of angels, but do not have charity, I have become as sounding brass or a tinkling cymbal. And if I have prophecy and know all mysteries and all knowledge, and if I have all faith so as to remove mountains, yet do not have charity, I am nothing. And if I distribute all my goods to feed the poor, and if I deliver my body to be burned, yet do not have charity, it profits me nothing.

"Charity is patient, is kind; charity does not envy, is not pretentious, is not puffed up, is not ambitious, is not self-seeking, is not provoked; thinks no evil, does not rejoice over wickedness, but rejoices with the truth; bears with all things, believes all things, hopes all things, endures all things.

"Charity never fails, whereas prophecies will disappear, and tongues will cease, and knowledge will be destroyed. For we know in part and we prophesy in part; but when that which is perfect has come, that which is imperfect will be done away with. When I was a child, I spoke as a child, I felt as a child, I thought as a child. Now that I have become a man, I have put away the things of a child. We see now through a mirror in an obscure manner, but then face to face. Now I know in part, but then I shall know even as I have been known. So there abide faith, hope, and charity, these three; but the greatest of these is charity." *I Corinthians XIII 1-13.*

charity, act of (1) Any act which shows a perfect and supernatural love of God. (2) The form of words expressing perfect love of God and neighbor. "O my God, I love Thee above all things, with my whole heart and soul, because Thou art all-good and worthy of all love. I love my neighbor as myself for the love of Thee. I forgive all who have injured me, and ask pardon of all whom I have injured."

chastity The virtue or habit of purity. Chastity is practiced by keeping the mind free from impure thoughts and the body free from sinful pleasures. The sixth commandment of God, "Thou shalt not commit adultery," and the ninth commandment of God, "Thou shalt not covet thy neighbor's wife," forbid sins against chastity.

chastity, vow of *See* vows, religious.

chasuble A vestment which covers the priest like a little house. The word *chasuble* comes from the Latin word *casula*, meaning *a little house*. The Romans wore such a garment as an overcoat. The chasuble signifies the yoke of Christ. *See* vestments.

Children of Mary Members of the sodalities of the Blessed Virgin Mary. *See* sodality.

choir (1) A group of people who sing certain parts of the Mass. A choir should be made up of men and boys wearing cassocks and surplices, but in many churches both men and women, or boys and girls, sing in the choir, and they wear ordinary clothes. (2) The place where the singers sit, sometimes called a choir loft.

choirs of angels The whole company of angels arranged in hierarchic (graded) order. The nine choirs, from the lowest hierarchy to the highest, are: angels, archangels, principalities, powers, virtues, dominations, thrones, cherubim, and seraphim. These nine choirs are usually divided into three orders. The last three—seraphim, cherubim, and thrones—are spoken of as being closest to God and are sometimes called counselors. The middle three—dominations, virtues, and powers—are sometimes called rulers, because their names seem to indicate a certain governing power. The first three—principalities, archangels, and angels—are spoken of as workers. They are God's messengers, and among them are the guardian angels. *See* guardian angels.

chosen people The Jewish people—the Israelites whom God chose to keep alive the faith in God. *See* Abram (Abraham).

chrism, holy Mixture of olive oil and balm, blessed by the bishop on Holy Thursday morning. It is used in the Sacraments of Baptism, Confirmation, and Holy Orders and in solemn consecrations such as of bishops, churches, chalices, etc.

Chrism, Mass of the The only Mass now permitted on the morning of Holy Thursday. The Mass of Chrism is offered in the cathedral church by the bishop who blesses the holy oils to be used in his diocese during the year. Holy Communion is not given during the bishop's Mass on Holy Thursday morning.

Christ   A title meaning *anointed one*, added to Our Lord's name, Jesus. *See* **Messias.**

Christ the King, the Feast of   A feast, instituted by Pope Pius XI, in honor of Our Lord as the King of all saints. It is celebrated the last Sunday in October, shortly before the Feast of All Saints on November 1.

christening   A name given to the Sacrament of Baptism.

Christian   Name given to a follower of Jesus Christ.

Christian name   Name given to a person when he is christened (baptized). *See* **baptismal name.**

Christmas   Christ's Mass. The name given to the feast of Our Lord's birth, the Nativity. On the first Christmas day, Jesus Christ was born to the Virgin Mary in the town of Bethlehem. Some shepherds living in the district saw a great light while they were keeping watch over the flocks at night. An angel of the Lord stood by them and said to them: "Do not be afraid, for behold, I bring you good news of great joy which shall be to all the people; for today in the town of David a savior has been born to you, who is Christ the Lord. And this shall be a sign to you: you will find an infant wrapped in swaddling clothes and lying in a manger." *Luke II 10-12.*

In almost every corner of the earth the feast of Christmas is celebrated, sometimes with religious ceremony, sometimes without it. Very often the true meaning of Christmas, the birthday of Jesus Christ, is forgotten in the worldly celebration of the year's most important holiday. There has been an attempt, among thoughtful persons and organizations, to "bring Christ back into Christmas." *See* **Nativity, the Feast of the.**

Christmas Masses, the three   By a special privilege, a priest is allowed to say three Masses on Christmas day, each of which has a different Proper. The first is said at midnight, the second at dawn, and the third during the day. The Gospels for the first and second Masses are taken from the Gospel according to St. Luke, and they tell of Our Lord's birth to the Blessed Virgin Mary in Bethlehem. The Gospel for the last Mass is the Last Gospel which begins, "In the beginning was the Word, and the Word was with God, and the Word was God." The three Masses are a symbol of Christ's triple birth, of His Father, of the Blessed Virgin Mary, and in the soul through grace.

Christmastide That part of the cycle of Christmas which begins with the Vigil of Christmas, December 24, and ends on January 13. The season of Christmastide is a time of rejoicing at the birth of the Savior whose coming was awaited during Advent. Three great feasts (Christmas, the Circumcision, and the Epiphany) are celebrated during Christmastide.

Christophers, the (Christ-bearers) A name taken by the members of the Christopher movement which was started in 1945 in the United States by Father James Keller, a Maryknoll missioner, The Christophers believe that every person should go into the world carrying Christ. By doing this he will bring love where there is hate and truth where there is error. The Christophers take their name from St. Christopher, who, according to an old legend, carried the Christ Child across an angry river.

church (buildings) The word *church* comes from the Greek word meaning *the Lord's house*. A church is a place for worshipping God. There is only one papal church, the Basilica of St. John Lateran in Rome. The principal or mother church of a diocese is called a cathedral. *See* **cathedral**. Most churches are parish churches, churches used by the Catholics of the particular district which makes up the parish.

church history The written record or history of the Catholic Church from its founding by Jesus Christ Himself to the present day. Eusebius who was bishop of Caesarea in the first part of the fourth century is said to be the father of church history. He wrote an ecclesiastical history in ten books.

Church Militant, the Members of Christ's Church on earth. *See* **communion of saints.**

Church Suffering, the The souls of the faithful who are suffering in Purgatory. *See* **communion of saints.**

Church Triumphant, the The blessed in Heaven. *See* **communion of saints.**

churching of women A mother's public act of thanksgiving after the birth of a child. She comes to the church to receive a blessing according to ritual. Mothers are not obliged to receive this blessing after childbirth, but many wish to do so.

ciborium   A metal cup, the inside of which must be gold, in which the hosts given at Communion are kept. It is goblet-shaped like a chalice and its cover has a cross on top.

cincture   A cord, with two tassels, tied about the priest's waist at Mass to hold the alb in place. *See* **alb.** The word *cincture* comes from the Latin word *cingulum,* meaning *girdle.* It signifies priestly chastity. *See* **vestments.**

Circumcision, Feast of the   Holyday of obligation on January 1. This feast is in memory of the day on which Jesus received His proper name, Jesus, at His circumcision, eight days after His birth. On this day Our Lord shed His first blood for humanity. The Feast of the Circumcision is the octave day of Christmas.

clapper   A wooden clapper used instead of bells from the consecration at the evening Mass of the Lord's Supper on Holy Thursday until the solemn midnight Mass of the Easter Vigil on Holy Saturday.

clergy   The body of men in the Church who have received the Sacrament of Holy Orders.

cloister   (1) A covered walk around an open court. This covered walk usually connects parts of a monastery or of a convent. (2) Another word for *enclosure.* An enclosure is that part of a monastery or convent where the religious live and which they cannot leave without special permission. With few exceptions, no one can enter the enclosure.

clothing, the   The putting on of the habit (clothes) of religious life. This is an outward sign of accepting the religious life.

coats of arms (of the hierarchy)   Heraldic bearings worn by certain high-ranking members of the clergy. In the middle ages knights wore a garment embroidered with heraldic arms over their armor. The Pope, patriarchs, cardinals, archbishops, and bishops show their coats of arms on their seals and thrones. The coat of arms of the Vatican City is a tiara above two crossed keys, gold on red. A cardinal's coat of arms is a scarlet hat with two cords each of which has fifteen tassels. The coat of arms for the archbishop and the bishop are green hats. The archbishop has ten tassels on each cord and the bishop six.

coif   A hood-shaped cap worn under the veil of most nuns.

Collect   A short prayer (*oratio*) said before the Epistle at Mass.

The Collect directs our attention to the particular feast of the day and changes according to the day and the feast. *Collect* means the collected prayers of the people. Sometimes there is more than one Collect.

collection, church Money for the support of the parish given by those present at Mass. The collection is usually taken up following the Creed. In the early days of the Church, offerings of bread and wine, as well as gold and silver, were made by the people at the Offertory of the Mass. The collection takes the place of these offerings, and it is a symbol that the people offer themselves to God.

College of Cardinals, the Sacred An association of all the cardinals with a dean at its head. When a pope dies, the College of Cardinals takes over his duties until a new pope has been chosen. The cardinals come together and meet in solemn conclave (in private) to elect the new pope. The name *conclave* which comes from the Latin and means *with a key* is the name of the meeting of the cardinals for the election of the pope and also the name of the place where they meet.

Colossians A book of the New Testament of the Bible. It is the Epistle of St. Paul the Apostle to the Colossians.

commandments, the ten The ten commands given by God to Moses and further explained by Jesus Christ. God asked Moses to go up on the mountain (Mt. Sinai) to receive from Him the stone tablets on which He had written the commandments intended for the instruction of the Israelites. On the mountain God gave Moses instructions for making the Ark of the Covenant in which the stone tablets were to be placed. *See* **Ark of the Covenant.** On the first tablet were written the commands dealing with man's relationship to God (the first three commandments); and on the second tablet were written the commands dealing with man's relationship to his neighbor (the last seven commandments). These commandments were the center of the Jewish religion. In the *Sermon on the Mount* Jesus Christ said of the ten commandments: "Whoever does away with one of these least commandments, and so teaches men, shall be called least in the kingdom of Heaven; but whoever carries them out and teaches them, he

shall be called great in the kingdom of Heaven." *Matthew V 19.*
These are the ten commandments:

(1) *I am the Lord thy God; thou shalt not have strange Gods
before me.* The first commandment requires that men give to God
alone the highest worship that is due Him. God must be loved
above everything and everyone else, because He created man
who is dependent on Him. Man offers God public or exterior
worship when he assists at Mass and takes part in public devotions. He gives God private worship when he worships Him
in his heart. A person keeps the first commandment well when
he does everything for the love of God.

The first commandment forbids dependence on any power that
is not God's power, such as that of fortunetellers, magic, charms.
It also forbids taking part in non-Catholic worship, that is, joining
in religious services that are not Catholic. (This does not mean
that a person cannot attend the wedding or the funeral of a non-
Catholic friend or relative.)

The first commandment does not forbid honor paid to the
saints in Heaven. *See* veneration.

(2) *Thou shalt not take the name of the Lord thy God in vain.*
The second commandment requires a deep respect for God, the
saints, and holy things. The name of God and the holy name of
Jesus Christ must be used reverently. When God's name is used
without reverence, to express surprise or anger, the speaker is
taking God's name in vain. This is commonly known as swearing.
Ordinarily swearing is only a venial sin, but it sets a bad example
to others and is not in keeping with the respect and love which
are due God's name. Cursing and blasphemy are forbidden by
the second commandment. *See* **cursing, blasphemy.**

The swearing of an oath or the taking of a vow for a good
reason is not contrary to the second commandment of God. However, a person must be truthful in taking vows and swearing
oaths. When he calls God to witness the truth of what he is
going to say, he must be certain that it is the truth.

(3) *Remember thou keep holy the Lord's day.* The third commandment obliges man to worship God in a special manner on
Sunday, the Lord's day. *See* **Lord's Day, the.** To worship God in
a special manner on Sunday one must assist at the Holy Sacrifice

of the Mass. The third commandment forbids all unnecessary servile work on Sunday, that is, work which requires labor of the body rather than labor of the mind. Servile work is allowed when God's honor, one's own need, or the need of one's neighbor requires it. For example, a sacristan could care for the sacred vessels on Sunday; a housewife could do the necessary work of the day about her home; and a person could go into the home of a sick neighbor and help with necessary work.

(4) *Honor thy father and thy mother.* The fourth commandment tells children to love and respect their parents and other lawful superiors. Among their lawful superiors are their teachers, the spiritual authorities of the Church, and the authorities of the government. Children must obey their parents and lawful superiors in all that is not sinful, that is, in anything that is not contrary to the law of God. Children should also aid their parents if they are in spiritual or bodily need. The fourth commandment forbids disrespect, unkindness, and disobedience to parents and lawful superiors.

The fourth commandment also considers the duties of a superior toward those under his care and the duties of a citizen toward his country. Parents should love their children and take care of their spiritual and bodily welfare. Superiors, according to the responsibility which they have, should care for those under them. A citizen should love his country, be interested in its welfare, and obey its laws. A citizen should use his right to vote, pay just taxes to his government, and help his country in a just war.

Both the fourth and fifth commandments have directly to do with the virtue of charity.

(5) *Thou shalt not kill.* The fifth commandment obliges a man to take proper care of his own body and soul and that of his neighbor. The fifth commandment forbids murder and suicide, fighting, anger, hatred, revenge, drunkenness, and bad example. Murder is the voluntary, unjust taking of the life of another person. Human life can be taken only by one who is protecting his own life or that of his neighbor, by a soldier fighting in a just war, or by a person appointed to execute a criminal. Suicide, which is the taking of one's own life, is forbidden, and a person

who commits suicide deliberately and while in his right mind may not receive Christian burial.

(6) *Thou shalt not commit adultery.* The sixth commandment says that a person must be pure and modest in words, looks, and actions, whether alone or with others. The sixth commandment is concerned with outward behavior, while the ninth commandment is concerned with internal sins of impurity—impure thoughts and desires. Purity is a moral virtue, and purity in relation to the sixth commandment of God is called chastity. Chastity has many enemies. Idleness, sinful curiosity, bad company, drinking to excess, dressing immodestly, reading indecent books, and attendance at offensive shows often lead to sins against chastity. On the other hand, the virtue of chastity is best kept by seeking God's grace in the sacraments and by having a true love and devotion to Our Blessed Mother.

(7) *Thou shalt not steal.* The seventh commandment states that a man must respect the property of others, live up to his business agreements, and pay his just debts. It forbids him to take or damage anything that belongs to another person. It also forbids cheating and the accepting of bribes by public officials. The word *steal* means to take or to keep something which belongs to another against his will. Theft and robbery both come under the heading of stealing. *Theft* means *to take secretly,* while *robbery* means *to take violently.* The gravity of the sin depends on the value of the thing stolen, the violence with which it is taken, and the need of the person from whom it is stolen. One who steals or damages the property of another is obliged to return the stolen property or to repair the damage as far as he is able.

(8) *Thou shalt not bear false witness against thy neighbor.* The eighth commandment obliges man to speak the truth in all things, especially in what concerns the good name of another. The eighth commandment forbids lies, rash judgment, detraction, calumny, and the telling of secrets one is bound to keep. A person lies when he deliberately keeps the truth from someone who has a right to know the truth, or when without any good reason he tells a person something that is plainly untrue. One is not lying when he jokingly says something that is not true, when it is clear to those to whom he says it that it is not true. Rash judg-

ment, detraction, and calumny are particularly serious sins against the truth, because they are also sins against charity. *See* **detraction and calumny.** Lying under oath is perjury and is always a mortal sin.

A man is obliged to keep a secret when he has promised to do so, when his office requires it (the priest in the confessional, the doctor, lawyer, or any other person entrusted with professional secrets), or when the good of another demands it. A person who has sinned by detraction or calumny or has told a secret he was bound to keep should repair the harm he has done as far as he is able.

(9) *Thou shalt not covet thy neighbor's wife.* Like the sixth commandment, the ninth commandment is concerned with the virtue of chastity. To covet means to desire or to want something wrongfully. The ninth commandment forbids all thoughts and desires contrary to chastity.

(10) *Thou shalt not covet thy neighbor's goods.* The tenth commandment is similar to the seventh commandment. It forbids all desire to take or keep unjustly what belongs to others and also forbids envy at their success.

commandments, the two great The two commandments that contain the whole law of God and on which the ten commandments are based: (1) Thou shalt love the Lord thy God with thy whole heart, and with thy whole soul, and with thy whole mind, and with thy whole strength. (2) Thou shalt love thy neighbor as thyself. Jesus Christ spoke these two commandments to the Pharisees who, trying to test Him, asked Him which was the great commandment in the Law. After giving them these two commandments, Jesus said, "On these two commandments depend the whole Law and the Prophets." *Matthew XXII 40.*

commandments of the Church Laws or precepts given to the faithful by the Church and binding under pain of sin to all baptized persons over seven years of age unless specially exempted. These are the chief laws or precepts of the Church:

(1) *To assist at Mass on all Sundays and holydays of obligation.* The second commandment of God obliges man to worship God in a special manner on Sunday, the Lord's Day. The first precept of the Church obliges the Catholic to keep holydays of

obligation in the same manner as Sunday. *See* **holydays of obligation.**

(2) *To fast and to abstain on the days appointed.* The law of fasting binds all Catholics between the ages of 21 and 60 who have not been exempted for some good reason. Fasting limits the amount of food taken. *See* **fast day.** The law of abstinence binds those seven years of age or over. It forbids them to eat meat or meat soup on certain days, including all Fridays. *See* **abstinence, day of.**

(3) *To confess our sins at least once a year.* This third precept of the Church obliges a Catholic to go to Confession at least once a year if he has a mortal sin to confess. The fourth precept of the Church obliges him to receive Holy Communion during the Easter time, and he must go to Confession before he receives Communion, providing he has a mortal sin to confess. A Catholic must go to Confession also when he is in danger of death, if he has a mortal sin on his soul. Even though one has committed no mortal sin, it is customary to go to Confession during the period before Easter, though it is not strictly an obligation for those free from mortal sin.

(4) *To receive Holy Communion during the Easter time. See* **Easter duty.** This fourth precept of the Church indirectly obliges a Catholic to keep the third precept. Since it is a sacrilege to receive Holy Communion in mortal sin, one must keep the third precept in order to keep the fourth, providing one is in the state of mortal sin.

(5) *To contribute to the support of the Church.* This precept obliges each Catholic to bear his fair share of the financial burden of the Holy See, the diocese, and the parish.

(6) *To observe the laws of the Church concerning marriage.* This precept obliges all Catholics to observe the marriage laws of the Church. *See* **marriage, laws concerning.**

Commemoration (1) Remembrance of a saint or a feast on a day which happens to be a feast of higher rank. The greater feast is celebrated while the lower feast is commemorated. (2) Commemoration of the living is the remembrance of the living made at Mass towards the beginning of the Canon. One asks God to be mindful of his friends and relatives who are living and of all those present at Mass. (3) **Commemoration of the dead** is the fourth prayer after the consecration. Remembrance is asked for loved ones who are dead and for all the souls in Purgatory.

Common of the Mass   Another name for the Ordinary of the Mass, especially those parts sung by the choir. *See* **Ordinary of the Mass.**

common of the saints   That part of the Missal or Breviary which contains Masses and Offices of saints who do not have special Masses and who have only certain parts of the Proper.

Communicantes   The third prayer of the Canon of the Mass. In this prayer those present in the church put themselves in communion with the Blessed Virgin Mary, the Apostles, the first popes, the early martyrs, and all the saints. The word *communicantes* with which the prayer begins means *communicating* with someone. In the Communicantes the faithful on earth communicate with the saints in Heaven who are close to them because of Jesus Christ. The Communicantes is one of the few parts of the Canon of the Mass that ever change. For the feasts of Easter, Ascension and Pentecost, some slight variations in the prayer are given.

Communion, Holy   The receiving of Jesus Christ in the Sacrament of the Holy Eucharist. Whoever receives Holy Communion worthily shares in the Sacrament of the Eucharist. Jesus Christ meant that the Holy Eucharist should be the food of the soul. At the Last Supper He gave His own body and blood to be this food.

Even before the Last Supper He explained the meaning of Holy Communion to the Jewish people: "I am the bread of life. Your fathers ate the manna in the desert, and have died. This is the bread that comes down from Heaven, so that if anyone eat of it he will not die. I am the living bread that has come down from Heaven. If anyone eat of this bread he shall live forever; and the bread that I will give is my flesh for the life of the world." *John VI 48–52.*

When the Jews wondered how He could give them His flesh to eat, He went on to explain, "Amen, amen, I say to you, unless you eat the flesh of the Son of Man, and drink His blood, you shall not have life in you. He who eats my flesh and drinks my blood has life everlasting, and I will raise him up on the last day.

For my flesh is food indeed, and my blood is drink indeed. He who eats my flesh, and drinks my blood, abides in me and I in him." *John VI 54–57.*

The priest receives the body and blood of Our Lord under the appearances of both bread and wine. The people receive His body and blood under the appearance of bread alone. In some Eastern churches Holy Communion is received by the faithful under the appearances of both bread and wine. *See* **Eastern churches.** Jesus Christ is entirely present under the appearance of bread alone or wine alone.

Those who wish to receive Holy Communion at Mass go to the altar rail and kneel when the bell is rung before the priest's Communion. Usually a shallow metal dish is held by the server under the chin of each person as he receives Communion. If the Host should be dropped by accident, the dish would save it from falling to the floor. As the priest gives Holy Communion to each person, he says: "May the body of Our Lord Jesus Christ preserve thy soul to life everlasting. Amen."

Certain conditions are necessary for the reception of Holy Communion. A child must have reached the age of reason (about seven years of age) so that he can understand at least the difference between the consecrated Host and ordinary bread before he is allowed to receive Holy Communion. A person must also be in the state of grace (that is, be free from mortal sin) in order to receive Holy Communion. Certain rules of fasting must also be observed. *See* **fast, Eucharistic.**

A Catholic must receive Holy Communion at least once a year, during the Easter time, and when in danger of death. Holy Communion is given every day of the year, including Good Friday.

Communion antiphon A short prayer said by the priest after the Communion. It changes with the Proper of the day.

communion of saints The union of the faithful on earth, the blessed in Heaven, and the souls in Purgatory, with Christ as their Head. All three belong to the great spiritual kingdom of Jesus Christ. Members of Christ's Church on earth are spoken of as the Church Militant. The word *militant* means *to be engaged in warfare,* and those who are on earth are still engaged in the struggle to save their souls. The blessed in Heaven are those who have already attained the happiness of Heaven, and they belong to the Church Triumphant. They have already triumphed over the flesh and the devil, while those who are on earth are still struggling. The souls in Purgatory, who have not yet made up for their sins, are called the Church Suffering. They are still suffering because of the sins they committed while on earth, but they have hope of attaining the happiness of Heaven.

These three—the Church Militant, the Church Triumphant, and the Church Suffering—are joined in the communion of saints to each other with Christ as their head. They are bound together by a supernatural bond, and they can help one another. The faithful on earth (the Church Militant) can venerate the saints in Heaven (the Church Triumphant—Our Lady and all the other saints who are close to God). The saints in Heaven can intercede with God for those still on earth. Both the faithful on earth and the blessed in Heaven can pray for the souls in Purgatory (the Church Suffering).

Communion prayers, the three Three prayers said after the Agnus Dei in preparation for Holy Communion. The first is a prayer for peace, which is omitted at Masses for the Dead; the second is for perseverance to keep God's commandments; and the third is for health and strength of soul and body.

communion with, to be in To be united with in religious matters. All Catholics are in communion with the Pope.

Compline The last hour of the Divine Office. *See* **canonical hours.**

conclave (1) The place where the cardinals come together for the election of a pope. (2) The assembly itself.

Confession, annual The yearly Confession which every Catholic who has reached the age of reason must make at Easter time. If there are no mortal sins to be confessed, this yearly confession is not absolutely necessary, but it is advised. *See* **commandments of the Church.**

confession (of faith) *See* **profession of faith.**

Confession (sacramental) The telling of one's sins to a priest in the Sacrament of Penance. In Confession a person must tell every mortal sin committed since his last confession, the number of times it was committed, and any circumstances which might change its nature. He is not bound to tell his venial sins, but it is good to confess them, especially those most often committed. If he purposely conceals a mortal sin, he is committing another mortal sin by not confessing it, and his sins are not forgiven. If a penitent forgets to confess a mortal sin which he has committed, his sins are forgiven, but he must confess the sin at his next Confession. *See* absolution, penance, Penance, the Sacrament of.

confessional The enclosed place where Confessions are heard. This is usually divided in three parts. The center part has a seat for the priest who hears the Confession. The parts on either side have a place for the person who is making the Confession to kneel. A grating (a frame of crossed bars) separates the priest from the one confessing. The priest closes the grating on the one side before he turns to hear the confession on the other side.

confessor (1) The priest who hears Confession. In the confessional he acts in the name of Christ in forgiving sins and gives the Sacrament of Penance. (2) A name sometimes used for men who are canonized saints but not martyrs.

Confirmation The sacrament through which the Holy Ghost comes to a baptized person in a special way, gives him more grace, and makes him a soldier in the army of Jesus Christ. The word *confirmation* means a strengthening. One who has just been baptized becomes a member of the Church and subject to its laws, but in Confirmation he becomes a citizen of the Church, able to assume the responsibilities of that citizenship and to defend his faith against its enemies. In Baptism, when he received the new life of the soul, a sharing in God's life, he received the Holy Ghost with the Father and the Son. In Confirmation, however, he receives the Holy Ghost more fully, its gifts of wisdom, understanding, counsel, fortitute, knowledge, piety, and fear of the Lord.

The Sacrament of Confirmation is given by the bishop. He stretches out his hands over those who are to be confirmed and prays that they may receive the Holy Ghost. He lays his right hand on the head of each person and anoints the forehead of each with holy chrism in the form of a cross. While anointing the person being confirmed, he says: "I sign thee with the Sign of the Cross, and I confirm thee with the chrism of salvation, in the name of the Father and of the Son and of the Holy Ghost." He then gives the confirmed person a slight blow on the cheek, saying: "Peace be with you." This is to remind the person who is being confirmed that he must be willing to endure many hardships for the love of Christ.

The Sacrament of Confirmation can be received only once, because it leaves on the soul a spiritual mark called a character, which lasts forever. The character of Confirmation makes the Christian a witness to the truth of the Christian faith and gives him the strength to defend the faith more vigorously.

In the days of the early Church Confirmation was given immediately after Baptism. Today it is usually given when a child is about ten years old, some time after his first Holy Communion.

Confiteor The word *confiteor* means *I confess.* The Confiteor is a prayer of sorrow for sin, a general confession said first by the priest and then by the server (who speaks for the people) near the beginning of Mass. The Confiteor as said by the server is:

I confess to Almighty God, to Blessed Mary ever Virgin, to blessed Michael the Archangel, to blessed John the Baptist, to the holy Apostles Peter and Paul, to all the saints, and to you, Father, that I have sinned exceedingly in thought, word, and deed, through my fault, through my fault, through my most grievous fault. Therefore, I beseech blessed Mary ever Virgin, blessed Michael the Archangel, blessed John the Baptist, the holy Apostles Peter and Paul, all the saints, and you, Father, to pray to the Lord our God for me.

Priest: May almighty God have mercy upon you, forgive you your sins, and bring you to life everlasting.
Server: Amen.

Priest: May the almighty and merciful God grant us pardon, absolution, and remission of our sins.
Server: Amen.

When the priest says the Confiteor, he says "to you, Brethren" instead of "to you, Father." The Confiteor is repeated by the server before Holy Communion.

confraternity An association of the faithful for charitable work or for the advancement of public worship.

congregation   An assembly of persons for religious worship. A
group of Catholics assembled in a parish church for Mass would
make up the congregation at that particular time.

congregation, religious   A religious community bound by a common rule and in which only simple vows are taken. *See* **religious
orders and congregations of men, of women.**

Congregation, Sacred   Twelve agencies in Rome which belong to
the Roman Curia and carry on the affairs of the Holy See. The
congregations are made up of cardinals and officials, and their
decisions must be approved by the Pope. One of the most important of these is the Supreme Sacred Congregation of the Holy
Office, whose business is the protection of faith and morals. The
other eleven sacred congregations are: the Sacred Consistorial
Congregation, the Sacred Congregation for the Discipline of the
Sacraments, the Sacred Congregation of the Council, the Sacred
Congregation for the Affairs of Religious, the Sacred Congregation for the Propagation of the Faith, the Sacred Congregation
of Rites, the Sacred Congregation of Ceremonies, the Sacred
Congregation of Extraordinary Ecclesiastical Affairs, the Sacred
Congregation of Seminaries and Universities, the Sacred Con-
gregation for the Oriental Church, the Sacred Congregation of
the Basilica of St. Peter.

conscience   The judgment of reason which tells whether an act
should be avoided because it is evil or done because it is good.

consecration of the bread   That solemn moment during the Mass
when the priest takes the bread and says over it the words of Our
Lord: "This is my body." At that moment the bread becomes
the body of Christ. After genuflecting, the priest raises the Host
for the people to adore. The bell is rung three times.

When the priest consecrates the bread, he is doing what Jesus
Christ did at the Last Supper. The priest asks God to bless and
approve this offering of bread so that it may become the body and
blood of Jesus Christ.

Who the day before He suffered took bread into His holy and
venerable hands, and with His eyes lifted up to Heaven,
unto Thee, God, His Almighty Father, giving thanks to Thee,
He blessed, broke and gave it to His disciples, saying: Take
and eat ye all of this, *for this is my body.*

consecration of the wine That solemn moment during the Mass when the priest takes the chalice containing the wine in his hands and repeats the words of Our Lord at the Last Supper.

> "Take and drink ye all of this, *for this is the chalice of my blood, of the new and eternal testament: the mystery of faith: which shall be shed for you and for many unto the remission of sins.*"

At that moment the wine becomes the blood of Our Lord. Putting the chalice back on the corporal, the priest adores it, then raises the chalice for the people to adore. The bell is rung three times.

Constitution, Apostolic A document by which the Pope makes and formally proclaims a law.

contemplation Union with God through prayer and meditation. In contemplative orders, religious follow the contemplative rather than the active life and detach themselves from the world to meditate on God's mysteries, to pray for His Kingdom, and to atone for the sins of men.

contrition Sorrow for sin because it offends God, and the intention of sinning no more. Sorrow for sin merely because sin often brings with it unhappiness and loss of position in the world is not contrition. Contrition is perfect when one is truly sorry for his sins because they offend God whom he loves above all things. Perfect contrition comes from an unselfish love of God. By perfect contrition sins are forgiven even before they are confessed. However, one must go to Confession as soon as possible because an act of perfect contrition has in it the desire and intention of confessing the sin. Contrition is imperfect when one is sorry for his sins because they are hateful in themselves or because God's punishment is feared. Imperfect contrition is called attrition. Imperfect contrition is all that is needed to receive the Sacrament of Penance in Confession, but perfect contrition is more pleasing to God.

contrition, act of A form of words which declares sorrow for sins and the resolve to sin no more. The penitent says an act of contrition in the confessional before receiving absolution.

> "O my God, I am heartily sorry for having offended Thee, and I detest all my sins, because of Thy just punishments,

but most of all because they offend Thee, my God, who art all-good and deserving of all my love. I firmly resolve, with the help of Thy grace, to sin no more and to avoid the near occasions of sin."

convent (1) A community of persons in the religious life under a superior. Though a convent is usually considered to be a community of nuns, some religious orders of men call their community a convent. (2) The buildings in which the religious community lives.

Conventual Mass The daily community Mass in churches of priests living in a community according to a rule.

convert, a Catholic One who turns toward the Catholic Church and is received as a member. The form of receiving converts who have been previously baptized in a heretical religion differs from that of receiving converts who have never been baptized.

cope A vestment in the form of a long mantle open at the front and clasped at the breast, with a smaller cape at the back. It is worn in processions and on many other solemn occasions, but never by the celebrant at Mass. It is sometimes worn by cantors, even if they are laymen. *See* **vestments.**

Corinthians I, II Books of the New Testament of the Bible, the First and Second Epistles of St. Paul the Apostle to the Corinthians.

cornet (cornette) A great white cap worn by some nuns. It is a three-cornered headdress made of starched white linen.

corporal A square piece of linen on which the Host and chalice are placed during Mass. It resembles a large handkerchief and is folded into nine squares and carried in the burse when not being used. The corporal is the oldest altar linen. It represents the linen cloth in which Joseph of Arimathaea wrapped the body of Jesus. The corporal is a very sacred cloth and must be washed by the priest or one who is in major orders before it is washed and ironed by anyone else.

Corpus Christi *Corpus Christi* are Latin words meaning the *body of Christ*. The Feast of Corpus Christi is the Feast of the Body of Jesus Christ. It celebrates the institution of the Blessed Sacrament when Jesus Christ gave His body and blood to be the spiritual food of men. Jesus Christ instituted the Blessed Sacrament at the Last Supper on Holy Thursday, the day before He died, but the celebration is left until after Easter. The last days of Lent in memory of the Passion of Our Lord and His death on Good Friday are such sad days that a celebration would be out of place at this time. The feast takes place on the Thursday after Trinity Sunday. The procession of the Blessed Sacrament is held on the following Sunday, though there may also be a procession on the day itself.

councils, church Ecclesiastical meetings for deciding matters of doctrine or discipline. Church councils may be provincial (council of the bishops of a province), plenary (council of the bishops of a nation), or general (representing the whole Church). The Pope or his representative presides at a general council.

Covenant An agreement made between two or more persons. In the Old Testament God promised Noe (Noah) that He would establish a covenant with him and his descendants. God made a covenant with Abram (Abraham), whom He made the father of His chosen people, and with Moses, to whom He gave the tablets of the ten commandments. He promised Moses that He would take care of the Israelites if they would be faithful to Him. These covenants of the Old Testament were sealed with the blood of victims. Moses sent certain young men of the Israelites to offer holocausts (burnt offerings) and to sacrifice young bulls to God. He sprinkled the people with the blood of the victims and told them that this was the blood of the covenant which God had made with them.

Jesus Christ made a New Covenant with His people which was fulfilled at the Last Supper. He promised to give to man a new life of grace which had been lost through the sin of Adam. On Holy Thursday, ready to sacrifice Himself on the Cross the following day for the sins of the world, Jesus Christ gave mankind His own body and blood. He said to the Apostles: "All of you drink of this; for this is my blood of the new covenant, which is being shed for many unto the forgiveness of sins." *Matthew XXVI 27–28*. The Last Supper itself was a true sacrifice because Christ's body and blood were really present and really given to the Apostles. The next day, Good Friday, Jesus Christ was to shed His blood on the Cross.

The Old Covenant is a type of the New Covenant, which partly fulfilled it and partly replaced it. *See* **type.**

covetousness   *See* **capital sins.**

cowl   The hooded garment worn by monks; the hood itself.

creation of the universe   God's bringing into existence out of nothing all created things, including the earth and the heavenly bodies. The Old Testament begins: "In the beginning God created the heavens and the earth." *Genesis I 1.*

creatures   Created persons or things. The creature is the person or thing made, while the creator is he who makes it. Men are all creatures of God, who is the *Creator* of all things.

credence table   A table at the Epistle side of the altar. It is used at Mass to hold a basin, a small linen towel, and two cruets, one containing wine and one water. At a High Mass the chalice, paten, and altar bread are covered by the humeral veil until the Offertory and after the ablutions. *See* **humeral veil.**

credo   Latin word meaning *I believe.* The Apostles' Creed and the Nicene Creed both begin with the word *Credo.*

Credo (at the Mass)   The Nicene Creed is the creed said or sung at Mass on Sundays, feasts of the first class, feasts of Our Lord, of Our Lady, of the Apostles, of Evangelists, of Doctors of the Church, and in Solemn Votive Masses. *See* **Nicene Creed.**

The Credo is that part of the Mass just following the first Gospel, or, on Sundays, following the announcements and the sermon if they are given after the Gospel. It is the last part of the Mass of the Catechumens, for the Mass of the Faithful begins with the Offertory. The priest stands at mid-altar and stretches out his hands, while he says the Credo in a clear voice.

Creed   A list of the chief articles of faith. The Apostles' Creed, the Nicene Creed, the Athanasian Creed, and the Creed of Pius IV are the principal creeds of the Church.

Creed of Pius IV   Profession of faith published by Pope Pius IV in 1564. Pope Pius X added to it in 1910.

crib   Another name for the manger in which Jesus was laid after His birth. At Christmas time a crib scene with its figures is shown in Catholic churches from Christmas Eve until the thirteenth of January. Statues of the Holy Family and the shepherds are shown at the crib. St. Francis of Assisi is said to have begun this custom at Christmas, in 1223, when he set up a crib at Greccia in honor of the mystery of Christmas.

crosier   The staff given to the bishop at his consecration, as a symbol of authority. It is about six feet tall and has a curved top like a crook. It is sometimes called the pastoral staff.

Cross   Symbol of the Christian religion because Christ died upon a cross to save men from their sins. A cross is over every Catholic Church. Everywhere within the church a cross is seen—over the stations, on the holy water fonts, on the altar.

cross, altar   A cross with the image of Christ on it, which must be on the altar during Mass.

cross, pectoral   A cross worn by a bishop, as the sign of his rank. It is also worn by cardinals and other high-ranking clergymen. The pectoral cross is a small cross which contains relics and is worn around the neck on a chain or cord. It is called pectoral from the Latin words *pectoralis* (*pertaining to the breast*), because it is worn on the breast.

Cross, Sign of the   (1) The Sign of the Cross made on one's self is a movement of the right hand to make a cross on the body. It shows belief in Jesus Christ crucified. The words accompanying the Sign of the Cross are: "In the name of the Father, and of the Son, and of the Holy Ghost. Amen." (2) A small Sign of the Cross is made on forehead, lips, and heart by the priest before the Gospel and Last Gospel at Mass. The people make this Sign of the Cross with the priest. (3) In the Mass the priest makes the Sign of the Cross not only over the unconsecrated bread and wine but also over the body and blood of Jesus Christ. (4) A Sign of the Cross is made over persons and things in giving blessings, in absolving, and in anointing.

cross-bearer   The one who carries the Cross at the head of processions.

Crowning with Thorns, the   One of the chief sufferings of Jesus Christ. The Crowning with Thorns is the third Sorrowful Mystery of the Rosary. After Our Lord was scourged by the soldiers, they clothed Him in a purple garment and set a crown of thorns on His head. Putting a reed in His hand, they bowed before Him, mocking Him and saying: "Hail, King of the Jews." *Matthew XXVII 29.*

75

C.Y.O.

crucifix A cross on which the figure of Our Lord crucified is shown.

Crucifixion, the The death of Our Lord by being nailed to the Cross. His death on the Cross, which He accepted willingly, was the supreme act by which He redeemed mankind. The Crucifixion is the fifth Sorrowful Mystery of the Rosary.

cruets Small glass bottles containing wine and water used at Mass.

Crusades Holy wars undertaken by the Christians of Europe in the eleventh, twelfth and thirteenth centuries. The purpose of the Crusades was to recover the Holy Land from the Mohammedans. The Crusaders wore a cross as a symbol of their mission. There were eight Crusades in all, the first of which were successful. However, the Crusaders could not keep the Holy Land, and it fell again into the hands of the Mohammedans.

curate An assistant to the pastor of a parish.

Curia Romana (the Roman court) All the organized bodies which assist the Pope in the government of the Church. *See* **Congregations, Sacred.**

cursing The calling down of some evil on a person, place, or thing. Cursing is forbidden by the second commandment of God. Cursing can be a mortal sin if one deliberately wills a serious evil by a curse.

C.Y.O. Abbreviation for Catholic Youth Organization, an organization of Catholic young people in religious, social, and athletic activities.

D

dalmatic Vestment worn by a deacon. It reaches to the knees and has wide, short sleeves. During Lent and Advent a folded chasuble is worn in place of the dalmatic. Cardinals, bishops, and abbots wear a dalmatic under their chasuble at a Pontifical Mass. *See* **vestments.**

damned Those who are deserving of eternal punishment in Hell.

Daniel A major prophet of the Old Testament. He was one of the captives at Babylon, and he remained with the Jews during their captivity to comfort and cheer them. God protected him through many dangers and kept him unharmed when he was thrown into a lions' den. A book in the Old Testament, *Daniel,* bears his name and tells of his life and visions. Through Daniel God told the people when the Messias would come to save mankind.

David King of Israel after the death of Saul. In his youth he had killed a giant, Goliath, from the army of the Philistines. David reigned in Jerusalem and became well known among the neighboring nations. His many wars were successful, and he brought prosperity to Jerusalem. David sinned grievously and, though he was sorry for his sins and forgiven by God, God did not allow him to build the temple he planned to build. God allowed David's son, Solomon, to build this temple.

Both Mary, the Mother of God, and St. Joseph, His foster father, were descendants of the House of David.

day of recollection A day set aside for special religious exercises.

deacon A cleric in the second of major orders, just below the priest. His chief duty is to assist the priest at the celebration of High Mass.

Dead, Mass for the *See* **Requiem Mass.**

deadly sins, the seven *See* **capital sins.**

death The end of man's life on earth, when his soul leaves his body.

decade The word *decade* means a series of ten. A decade of the Rosary is one Mystery of the Rosary, including one *Our Father,* ten *Hail Marys* and the *Glory Be to the Father* following it.

Decalogue, the The ten commandments of God.

delegate, apostolic A representative of the Pope in a country which has no regular diplomatic relations with the Holy See. There is an apostolic delegate to the United States and to Canada.

Deo gratias Latin words meaning *Thanks be to God* used frequently in the official worship of the Church and taken over into private worship.

deposit of faith The truths which God has revealed and given to the Church to keep and to teach as infallible.

descent into Hell At Christ's death, His soul descended into Limbo where the souls of good people who had died before the Resurrection were waiting to be set free from their prison. At His Ascension, Heaven was opened to these souls.

desecration The act of taking from something which has been consecrated its sacred character. A chalice put to irreverent use or seriously damaged would be said to be desecrated.

despair One of the sins against hope. A person is guilty of the sin of despair when he knowingly and willingly does not believe that God will give him the help which he needs to save his soul. Despair is want of confidence in God, and it destroys the virtue of hope. The first commandment of God forbids the sin of despair.

detraction A sin against charity. In the sin of detraction a person makes known, without a good reason, the hidden faults of another. The eighth commandment of God forbids detraction.

Deuteronomy A book of the Old Testament of the Bible, written by Moses. The word *deuteronomy* means *second law,* and this book is an explanation of the laws given to Moses on Mount Sinai.

devil, the (1) Satan, the leader of those angels who did not remain faithful to God and were cast into Hell. Satan desired to be like God in the power of his own nature. He rebelled against the supernatural order and chose the natural order. Satan tempted Adam and Eve to sin, because he wanted to exclude them from supernatural happiness. (2) Any fallen angel. *See* **angels.**

devil's advocate *See* **advocate, devil's.**

Dialogue Mass   A Low Mass in which the people (the members of the faithful) give aloud in a group the responses which the server alone usually gives.

Dies Irae   The first words of a hymn sung as the sequence at most Requiem Masses. It is sung between the Gradual and the Gospel. The words *dies irae* are Latin for *day of wrath*. The hymn tells of the last judgment and calls on God to spare His children and give them eternal rest.

diocese   The ecclesiastical territory over which a bishop rules. A diocese is divided into parishes.

diptychs   Tablets or leaves bound together by a hinge. The word *diptych* was given to anything folded double, and these tablets could be folded. In the early Church the diptychs were used to inscribe the names of the living and dead to be remembered at the Mass. The names of the living were placed on one tablet and the names of the dead on the other. Today the Commemoration of the living and the dead is called in the Missal the Reading of the Diptychs.

discalced   Barefooted or without shoes. Certain religious orders are called discalced because they wear sandals without stockings instead of ordinary shoes. The Capuchins and Discalced Carmelites are among these orders.

disciple   The word *disciple* comes from the Latin word *discipulus* meaning *a pupil*. The name is sometimes given to each of the twelve Apostles or, more often, to any of the early followers of Our Lord. *Luke X 1* mentions that seventy-two were appointed by Jesus Christ as disciples. "Now after this the Lord appointed seventy-two others, and sent them forth two by two before Him into every town and place where He Himself was about to come."

distraction in prayer   Lack of attention in prayer. This lack of attention may be either voluntary or involuntary. Distraction in prayer is not displeasing to God unless it is willful (voluntary). However, distraction decreases the value of prayer and makes it less perfect.

Divine Office   Certain prayers, psalms, hymns, etc., which all priests or those in major orders must recite every day for the Church and its members. Many nuns and monks also recite the Divine Office in choir. The reading of the Divine Office is dis-

79 DOMINE, NON SUM DIGNUS

tributed among the canonical hours: Matins and Lauds, Prime, Terce, Sext, None, Vespers, and Compline. *See* **canonical hours** and **Breviary.**

Divine Praises, the Words of praise said after Benediction of the Blessed Sacrament before the Host is put back into the tabernacle. In some dioceses, the Divine Praises are included in the prayers after Mass. The Divine Praises are:

> Blessed be God. Blessed be His Holy Name. Blessed be Jesus Christ, true God and true man. Blessed be the Name of Jesus. Blessed be His Most Sacred Heart. Blessed be Jesus in the most Holy Sacrament of the Altar. Blessed be the great Mother of God, Mary most Holy. Blessed be her holy and immaculate Conception. Blessed be her glorious Assumption. Blessed be the name of Mary, Virgin and Mother. Blessed be Saint Joseph, her most chaste spouse. Blessed be God in His angels and in His saints.

Divine Providence God's care and love for man.

divinity of Christ, the The nature of God in Jesus Christ. Jesus Christ has two natures, the nature of God and the nature of man. In His divinity is seen the nature of God. Jesus Christ received His divine nature from the Father as His natural right, because He is the only-begotten Son of God.

Divorce The dissolution (breaking) of the marriage bond. According to the Church law, marriage consummated between baptized persons cannot be dissolved.

Doctor Angelicus Angelical Doctor, the name given to St. Thomas Aquinas because of his great learning and holiness.

Doctor of the Church Title given to those Christian theologians noted for their great learning and sanctity who have been declared Doctors by the Pope or a General Council.

doctrine That which is taught. By Christian doctrine is meant the teachings of the Church.

dogma Truth found in the word of God, either written or unwritten, and taught by the Church.

Domine, non sum dignus A prayer said at Mass just before the priest's Communion and again before the Communion of the people. The prayer begins with the Latin words, *Domine non* *sum dignus* which mean *Lord, I am not worthy.* Holding the Host in his left hand, the priest strikes his breast with his right hand and says three times: "Lord, I am not worthy that Thou shouldst enter under my roof. Say but the word and my soul shall be healed."

This prayer comes from the *Gospel of St. Matthew VIII 5–8.* A Roman centurion approached Our Lord and asked Him to heal his servant who was at home seriously ill with the palsy. Jesus said that He would come to the centurion's home to heal the servant. Believing that he was unworthy to receive Jesus under his roof, the centurion spoke the words of this prayer.

Dominican order *See* **religious orders and congregations of men.**

Dominus vobiscum Latin words meaning *The Lord be with you.* This is said many times during the Mass and is used frequently in the Divine Office. The priest turns to the people with outstretched hands and says, "Dominus vobiscum." The server's answers is "Et cum spiritu tuo" (*And with your spirit*).

Dominus vobiscum was a greeting which the Jews used in their daily life. The word Good-by really means *God be with you,* but it is now seldom thought of in this way.

Doorkeeper *See* **porter.**

Dossal *See* **altar draperies.**

Douay Bible English translation of the Bible done at Douay and Rheims.

double (of a feast) *See* **feasts of the Church.**

dove Symbol of the Holy Ghost, the Third Person of the Blessed Trinity. The Holy Ghost appeared in the form of a dove at the Baptism of Our Lord.

dowry, religious Property or money brought by a postulant when she enters a religious order. A dowry is not always required.

doxology A prayer of praise. The "Gloria in Excelsis Deo" (*Glory to God in the Highest*), first sung by the angels at the birth of Our Lord, is called the greater doxology, and the "Glory Be to the Father" is called the lesser doxology.

E

Easter The name given to the Feast of the Resurrection of Our Lord. It is the chief feast of the Easter season and the greatest feast of the Church. It celebrates Our Lord rising from the dead on the third day after His burial. His glorious triumph over death is the strongest proof of His divinity. Easter is not only a feast of the highest rank, but it also has an octave of the highest rank. *See* **feasts of the Church.** An octave is the eight days, beginning with the feast itself, during which a feast is celebrated. Since Easter has an octave of the highest rank, no other feast may be celebrated during this period of eight days. In the early Church Easter was the day on which the catechumens were baptized. This added to the joy of Easter, for during Easter week the newly baptized rejoiced. Now again since the restoration of the Holy Week Liturgy, baptisms may take place during the Easter Vigil. The joyful character of Easter is shown by the singing of the Vidi Aquam instead of the Asperges before High Mass and the repetition of the Alleluia in the Mass through the season. *See* **Easter Vigil, the restored.**

Easter, date of Easter Sunday is the first Sunday after the first full moon which occurs on or after March 21. Easter always comes some time between March 22 and April 25; that is, it may be as early as March 22 and as late as April 25.

Easter duty The duty or obligation to receive Holy Communion during the Easter time. This is one of the six laws of the Church and must be obeyed by all Catholics who have reached the age of seven. In the United States Easter time begins on the first Sunday of Lent and ends on Trinity Sunday, eight weeks after Easter.

Easter Vigil, the restored The ancient Easter Vigil brought back to its original time, the night before the feast. In 1951 Pope Pius XII brought back the observance of the ancient Easter Vigil on an experimental basis. He allowed bishops to give permission for

81

the Vigil service on Holy Saturday night in place of the morning services of Holy Saturday. When the whole liturgy of Holy Week was restored by a decree of the Sacred Congregation of Rites, November 16, 1955, the celebration of the Easter Vigil was fixed for the evening of Holy Saturday at a time which would permit the Vigil Mass to begin about midnight. The bishop can permit the Vigil service to start earlier.

The restored Easter Vigil has three main parts: (1) the Light Service which includes the blessing of the new fire and the blessing of the Paschal (Easter) candle; (2) the Baptismal Service which includes the solemn blessing of the water for Baptism and the renewal of baptismal vows; and (3) the Eucharistic Service in which Mass is celebrated.

The Solemn Mass of the Easter Vigil begins after the Litany of the Saints has been completed. During the second part of the litany the altar is prepared for the Vigil Mass with flowers and lighted candles. No prayers at the foot of the altar are said at the Mass of the Easter Vigil. After the Kyrie eleison, the first word of the Gloria is sung and the sanctuary bells, silent since Holy Thursday, ring out.

Those present at an Easter Vigil Mass, which is held around midnight, fulfill their obligation of Mass on Easter Sunday.

Eastern Catholic Churches Those Eastern churches which recognize the supremacy of the Pope but are organized under the four major patriarchates of Alexandria, Antioch, Jerusalem, and Constantinople. The Eastern Catholic Churches have their own liturgies, laws, and customs, but they are united with the Western Church because they have the same faith and morals, the same sacraments, and acknowledge the Pope as the supreme head of the Church on earth.

Eastern Churches Those churches, whether in union with the Church of Rome or schismatic (separated by differences in doctrine) which are not a part of the Western or Latin Church. *See* Eastern Catholic Churches.

Ecclesiastes A book of the Old Testament of the Bible. The writer of this book speaks as if he were King Solomon and talks of worldly vanity.

ecclesiastic A member of the clergy.

Ecclesiasticus A book of the Old Testament of the Bible dealing with wisdom.

Eden, the Garden of The garden which was the home of Adam and Eve, the first parents of the human race. After God had formed man out of dust, "The Lord God planted a garden in Eden, to the east, and He put there the man He had formed." *Genesis II 8*. When they sinned, Adam and Eve were driven out of the Garden of Eden. The garden was only part of Eden, so they still lived in Eden.

Egypt, the flight into The flight of Joseph and Mary with the Child Jesus into Egypt. An angel came to Joseph in Bethlehem and told him to take the Child and His mother and go into Egypt in order to escape the anger of Herod, who planned to kill the Child.

ejaculation A prayer of a few words such as "Jesus, mercy." *See* **aspiration**.

elevation of the chalice, the The lifting of the chalice by the priest after he has changed the wine into the blood of Jesus Christ at the consecration.

elevation of the Host, the The lifting of the Host by the priest immediately after its consecration, that is, after it has been changed into the body of Jesus Christ.

elevation, the little The lifting of the Host and the chalice together at the end of the Canon of the Mass. Taking the Host, the priest makes three crosses over the chalice, then two crosses outside the chalice, before he lifts the Host and the chalice together. This is called the little elevation because it follows the separate elevations of the Host and the chalice.

Elias One of the prophets of the Old Testament by whom God chose to send messages to the children of Israel. In the time of Jesus Christ some of the people thought that He might be Elias risen from the grave. Elias, along with Moses, appeared at Our Lord's Transfiguration and spoke with Him concerning His approaching death. *See* **Transfiguration**.

Elizabeth A cousin of Mary, the Mother of Jesus, and the mother of John the Baptist. *See* **Visitation, the**.

Ember days Days of fast and abstinence coming four times a year, near the beginning of each of the four seasons. They fall on Wednesday, Friday, and Saturday after December 13; after the first Sunday in Lent; after Pentecost Sunday; and after September 14. Ember Wednesdays and Saturdays are days of partial abstinence. They are special days of Penance to ask God's blessings on each particular season of the year and on the priesthood. Priests are often ordained on Ember Saturdays.

Emmanuel A name given to Our Lord in prophecy. The word *Emmanuel* is Hebrew for *God with us.*

encyclical A letter written by the Pope to the heads of the Church in all countries or in one particular country. The Pope does not necessarily speak infallibly in the encyclicals, though he might choose to do so. If the Pope should in an encyclical letter or in any other official document purposely pass judgment on a matter up to that time under dispute, then that matter is definitely settled by the word of the Pope. Some of the most well-known encyclicals of the last hundred years are found in the **Appendix.**

end of the world, the That unknown time when the world will end and Jesus Christ will come again in glory to judge the living and the dead.

ends of the Mass, the The four purposes for which the Mass is offered: (1) to adore God; (2) to thank Him for His favors; (3) to ask God's blessings on men; and (4) to satisfy His justice for the sins of the world. In the Mass man is able to give God the adoration and thanksgiving that is worthy of Him. Jesus Christ has allowed the faithful to offer the sacrifice of the Mass with Him so that they may unite their sacrifice to His sacrifice. No other sacrifice could be so worthy. The priest asks God to shower His blessing upon all men, and the Mass, more than anything else, moves God to give His grace. Finally, the Mass is offered to satisfy God's justice for the sins of the world. Man by his sin has set himself apart from God and only by sacrifice can he return to God. Jesus Christ Himself, by His sacrifice in the Mass, makes up to God for the sins of men.

envy *See* **capital sins.**

Ephesians A book of the New Testament of the Bible. It is the Epistle of St. Paul the Apostle to the Ephesians. Ephesus was the capital of the Roman province of Asia and was the center of St. Paul's activity in the East.

Epiphany, the Feast of the An important feast which is celebrated January 6. It is a holy day of obligation in most countries, though not in the United States. The word *epiphany* comes from the Greek and means *a manifestation* or *a showing forth.* The feast is in memory of Our Lord's showing His glory in three different ways. The Infant Jesus showed Himself to the Magi, the Wisemen who had traveled from the East to find Him. The second showing of Himself was the showing of His divinity when John the Baptist baptized Him in the Jordan. At this time the Holy Spirit descended upon Him in the form of a dove, and a voice from Heaven said, "Thou art my beloved Son, in Thee I am well pleased." *Luke III 22.* The third showing of His divinity was the performance of His first miracle at Cana. *See* **Cana, marriage at.** The Feast of the Epiphany is sometimes called Little Christmas and Twelfth Night.

episcopacy The bishops of the Church as a body.

Epistle, the The first of the two lessons (readings from Scripture) of the Mass read just before the Gospel. The lesson is called the Epistle because it is usually taken from the Epistles of the New Testament, though not always. In almost every Mass the Epistle is different.

Epistles, the Twenty-one didactic (teaching) books of the New Testament, letters written by one of the twelve Apostles or by St. Paul, either to some certain person or to Christian communities of the Church. The word *epistle* comes from the Greek word meaning *letter.* St. Paul wrote fourteen of the Epistles of the New Testament. Besides these fourteen Epistles belonging to St. Paul there are seven Catholic Epistles: one of St. James, two of St. Peter, three of St. John, and one of St. Jude. The *Epistles* of the New Testament contain the teachings of Our Lord to the Apostles.

Epistle side The side of the altar at which the Epistle is read.

Esau The son of Isaac and Rebecca and the older brother of Jacob, to whom he sold his birthright.

Esdras The book of the Old Testament of the Bible written by Esdras, Israelite priest. It is concerned with the rebuilding of Jerusalem and the Temple.

Esther Jewish queen of the Persian king, Assuerus. She saved the

Jewish people from death by pleading their cause with the king. The book, *Esther,* in the Old Testament, bears her name.

eternal Lasting forever, without beginning or end, and without change.

eternity The changeless possession of endless life. Defined in this way, eternity belongs only to God.

Eucharist *See* **Holy Eucharist, the Sacrament of.** The word *eucharist* comes from the Greek and means *thanksgiving.* Our Lord gave thanks at the Last Supper at which the Sacrament of the Holy Eucharist was instituted. The word *eucharist* is used both for the sacrament and the sacrifice of Jesus Christ truly present under the appearances of bread and wine.

Eucharistic Congress, the International The gathering of Catholics from all nations, with a delegate from the Pope at its head. The purpose of the Eucharistic Congress is to honor and increase devotion to the Blessed Sacrament. The first International Eucharistic Congress was held in Lille, France, in 1881. Among the thirty-six International Eucharistic Congresses held since that time (through 1955) were those at London, England, in 1908; at Cologne, Germany, in 1909; at Montreal, Canada, in 1910; at Lourdes, France, in 1914; at Rome, Italy, in 1922; at Chicago, United States, in 1926; at Dublin, Ireland, in 1932; at Barcelona, Spain, in 1952; and at Rio de Janeiro, Brazil, in 1955.

evangelical counsels Instructions recommended in the Gospel by Jesus Christ. They are called counsels rather than commandments, because they are undertaken voluntarily. These counsels are voluntary poverty (poverty accepted of one's own free will), perpetual chastity (chastity that lasts throughout life), and perfect obedience. Those taking the vows of religious life take on themselves the obligations of these evangelical counsels. Those who do not take the vows of religious life may observe the spirit of these instructions. Those who are willing to give up needless luxuries in order to help the poor are living in the spirit of voluntary poverty. Those who keep themselves pure in thought and action are living in the spirit of perpetual chastity. Those who are obedient to their lawful superiors are living in the spirit of perpetual obedience.

Evangelists, the The authors of the four Gospels: Matthew, Mark,

Luke, and John. Matthew and John were both Apostles, while Mark and Luke were missionary companions of St. Paul. Because the name *evangelist* at the time of the Apostles was given to those who traveled about teaching the Gospel, the word *evangelist* is now used by some Protestants to mean a traveling preacher.

Eve   The first woman created by God. Eve was tempted by Satan to eat the fruit of the forbidden tree, and she persuaded Adam also to eat of it. Through this sin Adam and Eve lost sanctifying grace which was their greatest gift. Our Lady is called the second Eve because through her Divine Son this grace was to be restored to man. The first Eve had accepted the friendship of Satan, but between Our Lady and Satan there was complete enmity.

Evening Mass   A Mass after four o'clock in the afternoon. *Christus Dominus,* a document issued by Pope Pius XII in January 1953, gave power to the bishops to permit the celebration of Evening Masses on certain days when circumstances required it. An Evening Mass cannot be begun before four o'clock. Communion may be received at an Evening Mass in accordance with the rules for the Eucharistic fast. *See* **fast, Eucharistic.**

evil   The opposite of the good.

examination of conscience   A sincere effort to remember all the sins committed since one's last worthy Confession. *To examine* means *to look into,* and the penitent must look into his conscience before going to Confession to see what sins he has committed. This need not be the only time for an examination of conscience. Many people make an examination of conscience every night to see what sins they may have committed during the day.

excommunication   One form of censure by which a baptized person is deprived of the sacraments and all communion with the Church. *See* **censure.**

existence   State of being.

Exodus   A book of the old Testament of the Bible written by Moses. *Exodus* is the Greek word for *departure,* and this book deals with the departure of the Israelites from Egypt.

exorcism   The driving out of the devil from a person possessed. When a person is possessed by the devil, the devil really enters his body and takes control of his bodily powers. The devil cannot, however, possess his intellect. Permission must be obtained from a bishop before a priest is allowed to exorcise the devil from a person who is possessed. The form of exorcism is found in the Roman Ritual. *See* **Ritual, Roman.**

Lesser exorcisms are performed in the sacrament of Baptism or in the blessing of salt, water, etc.

exorcist (1) A member of the clergy in the third of the four minor orders. (2) The priest who exorcises, drives out the devil. *See* **exorcism.**

exposition of the Blessed Sacrament The public showing of the Blessed Sacrament so that the faithful may adore Christ in the Eucharist. At public exposition the Host is shown in the Monstrance. *See* **Benediction of the Blessed Sacrament** and **Forty Hours Devotion.**

Exsultet *See* **Paschal Proclamation.**

Extreme Unction, the Sacrament of The sacrament of the sick. The word *extreme* means *the very last* and *unction* means *anointing with oil.* Extreme Unction is often the last sacrament to be received, and the sick person receiving this sacrament is anointed with oil by the priest. Anyone who has reached the age of reason and is in danger of death may receive the Sacrament of Extreme Unction.

Only a priest or bishop can give the Sacrament of Extreme Unction. The priest first hears the Confession of the penitent, if he is able to speak, and then gives him viaticum. *See* **viaticum.** He anoints the sick person with blessed oil and says over him prayers for health of soul and body. The eyes, the ears, the nose, the lips, the hands and the feet are anointed. A prayer is said over each of the five senses. Extreme Unction is followed by the papal blessing which gives a plenary indulgence at the moment of death. *See* **Blessing, the Last** (2).

Extreme Unction gives sanctifying grace and takes away venial sins. It takes away mortal sins when the sick person is unconscious but has made an act of imperfect contrition. If a person makes an act of imperfect contrition, he is sorry for his sins because they are hateful in themselves or because he fears God's punishment.

When a priest visits a home to give Holy Communion or Extreme Unction to the sick, these preparations should be made:

In the room there should be a small table covered with a clean
linen cloth. A crucifix, two lighted blessed candles, a spoon, and
holy water should be on the table. If the priest is carrying the
Holy Eucharist, he should be met at the door with a lighted
candle, one of the two from the table.

Ezechiel The book of the Old Testament of the Bible named
after its author, one of the four major prophets. Ezechiel preached
to the exiled Jews in Babylon, where he himself was an exile,
and to those remaining in Jerusalem, the need of repentance so
that the chosen people could return to their worship of God in
the Temple at Jerusalem.

F

faculties Powers granted to bishops or priests by their superiors to allow them to perform acts which they could not otherwise legally perform. For example, a priest may be granted the faculties to hear Confessions and administer the Sacrament of Penance.

faith One of the three theological virtues. *See* **virtues, theological.** It is a supernatural virtue by which, with the help of God's grace, the intellect gives assent to what God has revealed on the words of God revealing it.

faith, act of (1) An act of the intellect which gives assent to what God has revealed. (2) The form of words expressing the assent of the intellect:

> O my God, I firmly believe that Thou art one God in three Divine Persons, Father, Son, and Holy Ghost; I believe that Thy Divine Son became man, and died for our sins, and that He will come to judge the living and the dead. I believe these and all the truths which the Holy Catholic Church teaches, because Thou hast revealed them, who canst neither deceive nor be deceived.

faith, the Catholic The Catholic religion.

faithful, the Those who have been baptized and have professed their faith as members of the Catholic Church.

faithful departed, the Those of the faithful who are dead. *See* **faithful, the.**

Fall of man, the The loss of God's friendship by Adam and the loss to him and his descendants of the supernatural gifts which God had given to him. This loss is called a fall because God by these supernatural gifts had raised man from a natural to a supernatural state. God had given Adam and Eve, the first parents of the human race, sanctifying grace. To sanctify something means to make it holy, and sanctifying grace made Adam and Eve very

90

holy. It made them children of God and gave them the right to
Heaven. God had also given Adam and Eve the supernatural
virtues of faith, hope, and charity, and the seven gifts of the Holy
Ghost. Besides these gifts which were above nature, God had
given them much natural happiness in the Garden of Paradise.
They had been given keen intellectual powers and control of their
passions by reason. Sickness or suffering was unknown to them,
and they were never to die.

If Adam had not sinned, these gifts would have been passed
on to his descendants. But Adam and Eve did sin. Tempted by
Satan, they disobeyed the command of God not to eat the fruit
of the tree of knowledge of good and evil. This was the only tree
in the Garden of Paradise from which they were forbidden to eat.
To eat of it meant death.

Because of their sin Adam and Eve lost sanctifying grace, the
right to Heaven, and their special gifts. It was just as if God had
disinherited Adam, as a displeased father might disinherit his son
who had done wrong and with him his children and his children's
children. Even the gates of Heaven were closed to man until
Jesus Christ, through the Redemption, opened them again.

Family Rosary   Reciting the Rosary in common as a family prayer.

Family Rosary Crusade   A movement begun in 1942 by Father
Patrick Peyton, C.S.C., in Albany, New York, to encourage fami-
lies to pledge the daily recitation of the Family Rosary. The
slogan of Father Peyton's crusade was: "The family that prays
together stays together."

fanon   Hoodlike vestment worn by the Pope when celebrating a
Pontifical Mass. The fanon is made of white silk with red and
gold stripes decorating it. It is put on over the alb and worn
over the shoulders like a collar.

fast, Eucharistic   Fast which must be observed before receiving
Holy Communion. The fast begins at midnight unless one is
receiving at an Evening Mass. *See* Evening Mass.

The *Christus Dominus,* the Apostolic Constitution issued January 6, 1953, relaxed a number of previous regulations for fasting.
See Constitution, Apostolic. Certain concessions were made to
enable more people to receive Holy Communion frequently.
According to the new regulations, natural water (water to which

nothing is added) does not break the Eucharistic fast. Anyone may drink natural water at any time before receiving Holy Communion, and it is not necessary to consult a confessor in order to do this.

Other changes in the law of fasting grant special concessions to the sick, to those engaged in exhausting work, to those receiving Communion at a rather late hour, to those who live far from the church, and to school children. In order to take advantage of these concessions, one must consult a confessor, that is, any priest who has the power to hear Confessions.

The permission of a confessor is not required to take advantage of the regulations for receiving Holy Communion at an Evening Mass. A person may receive at an Evening Mass if he abstains from solid food for three hours before the time of receiving Holy Communion. He may take with his meals on the day of the Evening Mass such beverages as wine and beer but no "hard" liquor. He may not drink any alcoholic beverages outside of his meals, though he may drink other beverages until one hour before Communion.

fast day A day on which only one full meal is allowed. This meal may be taken at noon or in the evening, and at this meal meat may be eaten unless the day is also a day of abstinence. Two other meatless meals sufficient to keep up one's strength may be taken, but together they should be less than one full meal.

Liquids, including milk and fruit juices, may be taken between meals. Days of fasting are: all weekdays of Lent (from Ash Wednesday until Holy Saturday, at midnight); the Ember days and Vigils of Pentecost, Assumption, and Christmas. *See* **Ember days.** Sunday is never a fast day.

The law of fasting obliges all Catholics who are between the ages of twenty-one and fifty-nine, unless they have been excused. The purpose of fasting is to turn the mind towards God through Penance and to strengthen the will.

Father Title in common use given to all priests.

Father, the God and the First Person of the Blessed Trinity.

Fathers of the Church Writers and teachers of the Church who lived in the first twelve centuries and wrote or taught Christian doctrine. They were well-known for their sanctity and learning.

Some of the most famous Fathers of the Church are: St. Ignatius of Antioch, St. Justin the Martyr, St. Athanasius, St. Basil, St. Ambrose, St. John Chrysostom, St. Jerome, St. Augustine, St. Gregory the Great, St. Bernard.

Fatima City in Portugal where Our Lady appeared six times to three young children, Jacinta, Francisco, and Lucy. She made her first appearance to the children on May 13, 1917, and asked the children to say the Rosary daily to obtain peace for the world. At her sixth and last appearance on October 13, 1917, the miracle of the sun occurred in which the sun began to spin like a wheel in the sky.

In her appearances to the children, Our Lady said that peace would come to the world only if reparation were made through Penance, reciting the Rosary, devotion, and consecration of Russia to her Immaculate Heart, and Communion of reparation on five consecutive first Saturdays. *See* **First Saturday.**

Jacinta and Franciso died soon after the appearances of Our Lady, but Lucy stayed on earth, as Our Lady told her she would, to spread devotion to the Immaculate Heart. Lucy entered the Carmelite Convent where she became Sister Mary Lucy of the Sorrows.

feasts of the Church Special days which the Church sets aside in memory of some mystery of the Christian religion or in honor of some saint. Some feast days are holydays of obligation. *See* **holydays of obligation.**

Feasts can be classified as movable or immovable. A movable feast depends on the date of Easter. Pentecost is a movable feast because it comes fifty days after Easter. An immovable feast is always on a fixed day. The feasts of the saints are immovable feasts.

Feasts are also classified according to rank, that is, according to grade or quality. The rank of a feast is the relative degree of solemnity with which it is marked. Feasts may be double or simple. Feasts which are double are further divided into doubles of the first class (the most solemn), doubles of the second class, greater doubles, and ordinary doubles. Easter is a feast of the highest rank, a double of the first class.

feasts of Our Lady Special days set aside in memory of some event in the lift of Our Lady or something connected closely with her. There are seventeen feasts of Our Lady celebrated in the Western Church. These are some of the principal ones: the Immaculate Conception (December 8); the Nativity of Our Lady (September 8); the Annunciation (March 25); the Visitation (July 2); the Seven Sorrows of Our Lady (the Friday after Passion Sunday and September 15); Our Lady of Mount Carmel (July 16); Feast of the Holy Rosary (October 7); the Assumption (August 15); the Queenship of Our Lady (May 31). *See* **Queenship of Mary.**

Of these the Immaculate Conception (December 8) is the only one which is a holyday of obligation throughout the Western Church. The Assumption (August 15) is a holyday of obligation in the United States.

feasts of the Old Law Religious feasts celebrated before the coming of Christ. They were given to Moses by God. *Leviticus XXIII 1–44.* These were: (1) Pasch, in remembrance of the deliverance of the Israelites out of Egypt; (2) Pentecost, seven weeks after the Pasch, in remembrance of the commandments given to Moses; (3) Atonement or Expiation on which the Israelites mortified themselves and made sacrifices to God; and (4) the Tabernacles or Booths, in memory of the years the Israelites spent in the desert.

ferias Weekdays on which no feast of a saint is kept. Ember days, Rogation days, and every feria in Lent have a special Mass. On all other ferias, the Mass of the previous Sunday or a Requiem Mass is said. In a church calendar (*Ordo*), the days of the week from Monday to Friday are called Feria II, III, IV, V, and VI.

fiery furnace, the A furnace of burning fire into which Nabuchodonosor, King of Babylon, threw three young Israelites because they would not adore an idol, a golden statue which he had set up for worship. The three young Israelites walked in the midst of the flames, praising God. God sent an angel to drive the flames out of the furnace, and the Israelites were unharmed. The Canticle of the Three Youths, spoken by the three young men after their deliverance, is sung on certain days in the Divine Office.

Finding of Our Lord in the Temple, the The finding of Jesus Christ by his parents in the Temple at Jerusalem where He was talking with the scholars. Mary and Joseph had taken Jesus, who was twelve years old, to Jerusalem for the Feast of the Passover. On their return journey, they thought that Jesus was with relatives in the caravan, and they had traveled for a whole day before they discovered He was missing. Returning to Jerusalem, Mary and Joseph anxiously searched for Him. After three days they found Him in the Temple, sitting among the scholars, listening and asking questions.

"And when they saw Him, they were astonished. And His mother said to Him, 'Son, why hast thou done so to us? Behold, in sorrow thy father and I have been seeking thee.'

"And He said to them, 'How is it that you sought me? Did you not know that I must be about my Father's business?'" *Luke II 48–49.* These are the first words of Jesus Christ written in the Gospel.

The Finding of Our Lord in the Temple is the fifth Joyful Mystery of the Rosary.

Fire, the Blessing of The first ceremony of the Easter Vigil on Holy Saturday evening. The Blessing of the New Fire takes place before the doors of the church, in the vestibule, or in the church itself, wherever the people can best see what is being done. The priest and other sacred ministers wear violet vestments for the ceremony. Fire is struck from a flint and pieces of charcoal are set burning. The priest blesses this new fire from which the Paschal candle is lighted. *See* **Paschal candle.**

First Friday The first Friday of the month, in honor of the Sacred Heart of Jesus. *See* **Fridays, to make the nine.**

First Saturday The first Saturday of the month set aside to honor the Immaculate Heart of Mary. During one of the appearances of Our Lady to the children of Fatima (July 13, 1917), Our Lady spoke of the communion of reparation which she wanted made on the first Saturday of each month. Later, in 1925, Our Lady appeared to Sister Lucy in her cell at Carmel and made certain promises to those who would receive Holy Communion on five consecutive Saturdays, recite part of the Rosary, meditate for fifteen minutes, and offer reparation.

fish, the One of the earliest symbols of the Church. *See* **symbol.**

five wounds, the The wounds in the hands, side, and feet of Our Lord. These wounds were received during the Crucifixion.

Flood, the Great The flood which, at the command of God, covered the earth and lasted for forty days. *See* ark, Noe's (Noah's). The *Book of Genesis* in the Old Testament of the Bible tells the story of the Great Flood.

flowers, altar Flowers decorating the altar, especially on feast days. They may not be put directly upon the altar table. In Advent, Lent, or at a Requiem Mass flowers are not allowed.

font A basin for holy water. *See* stoup and baptismal font.

Font, the Blessing of the A ceremony which takes place during the Easter Vigil on Holy Saturday evening between the two parts of the Litany of the Saints. After a prayer asking God to be present at the ceremonies, a solemn Preface is read. Prayers accompany each movement of the celebrant. The celebrant divides the water in the form of a cross and touches it with his hand while praying that it be free from evil spirits. He makes the Sign of the Cross three times over the water in honor of the Holy Trinity. He separates the water with his hand and sprinkles some towards the four parts of the earth. He breathes three times on the water in the Sign of the Cross and plunges the Paschal candle into it three times while singing, each time in a higher voice, "May the power of the Holy Spirit come down into this full font." After the Paschal candle is lifted out of the water, part of the water is set aside for the blessing of the faithful and for sprinkling homes and other places. The water intended for Baptism is mixed with a small amount of oil of catechumens and oil of chrism. If there are any people to be baptized, they are baptized at this time. Following the baptisms, the water is carried in procession to the baptistery, where it is poured into the font. The font is incensed, and the procession returns to the sanctuary.

forgiveness of sins Removal of the guilt of sin through the Sacrament of Penance.

fortunetelling Attempting to tell what is going to happen in the future by the reading of the lines on the palms of the hands, looking into a crystal ball, or any such superstitious means. Fortunetelling is forbidden by the first commandment of God, because it gives to a creature (the fortuneteller) the power which belongs to God alone.

Forty Hours Devotion Solemn exposition of the Blessed Sacrament, lasting part of three days and called the devotion of the Forty Hours prayer. The forty hours is in memory of the time Our Lord's body was in the tomb before His Resurrection. Regulations for the Forty Hours Devotion differ somewhat, but usually exposition begins with a High Mass on the first day. A Mass for peace is said on the second day, and another High Mass is said at the end of the exposition. Processions are held at the first and third Masses. Forty Hours Devotion is held once a year and on days appointed by the diocesan bishop in parish churches and other churches where the Blessed Sacrament is reserved.

forum The exercise of jurisdiction (the power to rule) over the faithful. The internal forum concerns the spiritual good of individuals, and this jurisdiction is exercised in the administering of the sacraments and the caring for the spiritual needs of the faithful. The external forum concerns the common good of the faithful and deals with the public welfare of the Church and its members.

fraction of the Host *See* **Bread, the breaking of the.**

Franciscan Order *See* **religious orders and congregations of men.**

free choice *See* **Will.**

free will *See* **Will.**

friar A member of one of the mendicant (begging) religious orders, so called because originally these orders were kept in existence through begging. *See* **mendicant orders.**

Fridays, to make the nine To receive Holy Communion on the first Friday of the month for nine consecutive months. This is a devotion in honor of the Sacred Heart of Jesus. Among the promises made by Our Lord to St. Margaret Mary Alocoque was the promise that those who made the nine Fridays would not die without receiving the sacraments. One is not obliged to believe this promise as it is said to have been given, but may believe it.

frontal *See* **altar draperies.**

fruits of the Holy Ghost Good works inspired by the Holy Ghost. Charity, joy, peace, patience, benignity, goodness, long-suffering, mildness, faith, modesty, continency, and chastity are fruits of the Holy Ghost.

full of grace   Words from the Hail Mary spoken to Our Lady by the Angel Gabriel at the Annunciation. The Angel Gabriel called Our Lady *full of grace* because she was free from original sin. She had been born with sanctifying grace in her soul and had the necessary grace to be the mother of God made man.

Funeral Mass   A Requiem Mass at the burial of a person. *See* **Requiem Mass.**

G

Gabriel, the Archangel One of the three archangels honored by name in the Church. The Angel Gabriel announced to the Blessed Virgin Mary that she was to become the mother of God. *See* **Annunciation, the.** The Feast of Saint Gabriel, Archangel, is March 24, the day before the Feast of the Annunciation. Long before the time of the Annunciation, the Angel Gabriel had appeared to Daniel the Prophet to tell him when Christ would be born. *Daniel IX 21–27.* The Angel Gabriel also appeared to Zachary, the father of John the Baptist, to tell him that his wife, Elizabeth, was to have a son whom he was to call John. When the angel appeared to Zachary, he said, "I am Gabriel who stand in the presence of God." *Luke 1, 19.*

Galatians A book of the New Testament of the Bible. It is the Epistle of St. Paul the Apostle to the Galatians, Gentile Christians who had been converted by St. Paul.

Galilee The northernmost province in Palestine at the time of Jesus Christ. Nazareth was located in this province.

Galilee, Sea of A lake on the western boundary of Galilee. The River Jordan, where Jesus was baptized by John, flows through this lake. The Sea of Galilee was also known as the Lake of Genesareth and the Sea of Tiberias.

Garden of Paradise, the Another name for the Garden of Eden. The word *paradise* comes from a Greek word meaning a *park. See* **Eden, the Garden of.**

Gaudete Sunday The third Sunday of Advent. Gaudete Sunday takes its name from the first word of the Introit, *gaudete,* Latin for *rejoice.* In the Epistle for Gaudete Sunday, St. Paul says, "Rejoice in the Lord always; again I say, rejoice." *Philippians IV 4.* In the Gospel, St. John the Baptist foretells the coming of the Messias. Gaudete Sunday is the one Sunday during Advent when flowers may be put on the altar and the organ played. Vestments may be rose-colored instead of violet.

general Name given to the superior of a religious order. The word *general* here is used as an adjective—as superior general, mother general, minister general, etc.

General Confession, a A confession not only of recent sins, committed since one's last Confession, but of the sins of one's whole life or a large part of one's life. A General Confession is necessary if one has made bad confessions. Sometimes people make General Confessions before entering a new state of life such as marriage, the priesthood, or the religious life. A priest should be consulted before one makes a General Confession.

Genesis The first book of the Bible, written by Moses. The name *Genesis* is the Greek word meaning *origin* or *creation,* and the *Book of Genesis* treats of the creation of the world by God. It is an introduction to the history of the Israelites.

Gentiles, the In the Bible the name *Gentiles* is given to those who are not Jews. St. Paul called himself the Apostle of the Gentiles.

genuflection Bending of the right knee to the floor in reverence to God. The priest frequently genuflects during the Mass. During the Creed both he and the people genuflect when the Incarnation is mentioned. A genuflection is made in reverence to the Blessed Sacrament on entrance into the church and on leaving. A double genuflection (kneeling on both knees and bowing the head before getting up) is made in the presence of the Blessed Sacrament exposed. A genuflection of respect is made before the Pope, a cardinal, or a bishop.

Gethsemani A garden at the foot of the Mount of Olives. It was here that Jesus suffered the Agony in the Garden which is the first of the Sorrowful Mysteries of the Rosary. Here also Jesus was betrayed by Judas and was seized.

gifts of the Holy Ghost, the seven Habits or dispositions which are given to us by God with sanctifying grace. A person who has been baptized receives sanctifying grace and with it the seven gifts of the Holy Ghost: wisdom, understanding, counsel, knowledge, fortitude, piety, and the fear of the Lord. These gifts or dispositions help him listen to the inspiration of the Holy Spirit. In Confirmation the gifts of the Holy Ghost are received more abundantly.

Gloria, the   A prayer of praise beginning with *Gloria in excelsis Deo* (*Glory to God in the highest*). The first words of this hymn were sung by a multitude of angels at the birth of Our Lord. They were first heard by the shepherds in the district of Bethlehem after an angel had come to announce the birth of the Savior. *Luke II 10–14.* The Gloria is said or sung at almost all Masses except those at which black or purple vestments are worn (Masses for the Dead, Masses during Lent, etc.) and ferias (weekdays) not in the Easter season. The Gloria comes just before the Collect in the Mass and is called the greater doxology. *See* **doxology.**

Glorious Mysteries, the   The five Glorious Mysteries of the Rosary:

(1) the Resurrection of Our Lord; (2) the Ascension of Our Lord into Heaven; (3) the Descent of the Holy Ghost upon the Apostles; (4) the Assumption of Our Blessed Mother into Heaven; (5) the Coronation of Our Blessed Mother in Heaven.

The Glorious Mysteries are usually said on Sunday, Wednesday, and Saturday.

Glory be to the Father, the   A short hymn of praise which is used as a prayer. Its most common use is at the end of each decade of the Rosary and at the end of each psalm of the Divine Office. The whole prayer is: "Glory be to the Father, and to the Son, and to the Holy Ghost. As it was in the beginning, is now, and ever shall be, world without end. Amen." This is called the lesser doxology. *See* doxology.

gloves   Silk gloves worn by bishops (or other high prelates) at High Mass. They are removed at the Lavabo.

gluttony   *See* **capital sins.**

Gnosticism   A heresy in the early Church. The Gnostics in the first three centuries after Christ claimed to have a deeper knowledge of natural and supernatural things than the Christians. They taught that the world was eternal and that salvation was through knowledge.

God   The one Supreme Being, infinitely perfect, who made all things and keeps them in existence. God is a Supreme Being because He is above all other things. He is infinitely perfect because He has infinite perfections, that is, perfections without any limit. Perfection is the completeness of goodness and truth.

Some of the perfections of God are: God is eternal, all-good, all-knowing, all-present, and almighty. God is eternal because He always was and always will be the same. Nobody created God because He always existed, and He will never change. He is all-good because He Himself deserves to be loved, and from His love we receive every good thing that we have. He is all-knowing because He knows everything about us, what we have been, what we are now, and what we will be. He is all-present because He is everywhere. He can be in Heaven and on earth at the same time and in every place that is or could be. He is almighty because He can do all things. By His will He can do whatever He wishes. God is also all-wise, all-holy, all-merciful, and all-just.

The difference between human perfections and the perfection of God is that God is not only good; He is goodness. He is not only wise; He is wisdom. He is not only lovable; He is love. No goodness, no wisdom, no love could make Him more perfect, as it can make human beings more perfect, because He is already perfect.

God is a spirit. He has understanding and free will, but no body, and He will never die. God is the only self-existing spirit, and so He is the greatest spirit. Because God is a spirit He cannot be seen with the human eye. Those who attain Heaven will see God in all His perfections.

God the Father The First Person of the Blessed Trinity.

God the Holy Ghost The Third Person of the Blessed Trinity. *See* Holy Ghost.

God the Son The Second Person of the Blessed Trinity. *See* Jesus Christ.

godparents Common name for sponsors in Baptism or those who offer a child to be baptized. The godparents make the act of faith in the child's name and answer, for him, any questions the priest asks. Through his godparents the child promises to renounce the devil and live according to the teachings of Christ and His Church. After the child's Baptism it is the duty of the godparents to see that the child is brought up to be a good Catholic if this is not done by the parents. A godparent forms a spiritual relationship with the godchild which is so close that a child cannot marry his godparent without a dispensation.

Golden Rule, the   The rule by which a man must love his neighbor. Our Lord Himself made the golden rule when He said, "Therefore all that you wish men to do to you, even so do you also to them." *Matthew VII 12.*

Golgotha   Mount Calvary, where Our Lord was crucified. *Golgotha* meant the *place of the skull* in Aramaic.

Good Friday   Friday in Holy Week, the day in memory of Our Lord's Crucifixion. The official name for Good Friday is Friday of the Passion and Death of the Lord. Along with Holy Saturday it is a day of the deepest sorrow. The altar is bare, without Cross, candlesticks, or linen, and the color of the vestments is black.

In the restored liturgy of Holy Week, Good Friday services take place in the afternoon about three o'clock, sometimes later for pastoral reasons, but not after six. Formerly no one but the dying could receive Holy Communion on Good Friday, but now all the faithful may receive. However, Holy Communion may be distributed only during Mass, except for the sick who are in danger of death.

There are four parts to the Good Friday service: (1) the readings from the Scriptures; (2) the Solemn Prayers; (3) the Adoration of the Cross; and (4) Holy Communion. The people share with the priests in venerating the Cross publicly. After the Cross has been venerated by the clergy, it is carried to the altar rail where it is venerated by the people. *See* **Adoration of the Cross, the.**

Goliath   A giant killed by David in a war between the Philistines and the Israelites. *See* **David.**

Good Shepherd, the   Our Lord, the shepherd of the souls of men. Good Shepherd Sunday is the second Sunday after Easter. The Epistle for Good Shepherd Sunday is taken from *I Peter II 21–25,* and speaks of Jesus as the shepherd of the soul. Christ Himself said: "I am the good shepherd. The good shepherd lays down his life for his sheep." *John X 11.*

Good Thief, the   One of the two thieves crucified with Jesus Christ. The good thief repented of his sins and asked Jesus to remember him. Jesus answered, "Amen I say to thee, this day thou shalt be with me in paradise." *Luke XXIII 43.* The Good Thief is called St. Dismas.

good works   Works done by the grace of God. Only works done in the love of God are of spiritual value and deserve a reward from God.

Gospel, the The record of Christ's life and teachings as given in the first four books of the New Testament. These are the Gospels according to Sts. Matthew, Mark, Luke, and John.

The word *gospel* is taken from the Greek word meaning *good news*, and the Gospel is the good news of man's salvation through Jesus Christ. St. Matthew wrote his Gospel in Aramaic (the Hebrew tongue), but the other three Gospels were written in Greek.

Gospel at Mass The reading at the Mass of some part of Sacred Scripture taken from one of the four Gospels. *See* **Gospel, the.** The reading of the Gospel comes soon after the reading of the Epistle. While the priest says a short prayer before reading the Gospel, the server moves the Mass Book to the Gospel side of the altar. The priest makes with his thumb a triple Cross on forehead, lips, and breast before reading the Gospel, and the people do likewise. The meaning of the triple Cross is that the Word of God may penetrate the mind, be spoken by the lips, and remain in the heart.

Gospel, the Last The Gospel read at the end of the Mass and always taken from *John I 1–14,* except at the third Mass of Christmas and on Palm Sunday. It begins: "In the beginning was the Word, and the Word was with God, and the Word was God." The priest moves to the Gospel side of the altar to read the Last Gospel. He makes the Sign of the Cross with his right thumb, first on the altar and then on his forehead, lips, and breast, and he says: "The beginning of the Holy Gospel according to St. John." The server answers: "Glory be to Thee, O Lord." The priest genuflects when he comes to the words, "And the Word was make flesh." The server and the people genuflect with him.

Gospel side The side of the altar at which the Gospel is read.

grace God's greatest gift to the soul. It is a supernatural gift, freely given to rational creatures (angels and men) to help them gain eternal life. Sanctifying grace, or habitual grace, is a habit of the soul and can be lost only through deliberate mortal sin. It was the greatest supernatural gift which God had given to Adam and Eve, as well as to the angels. When Adam sinned, he lost sanctifying grace for himself and his descendants, and those angels who rebelled against God lost grace for themselves.

Because of Adam's sin, everyone in the world is born without sanctifying grace. Sanctifying grace is infused (poured) into the soul through Baptism. Sanctifying grace raises man above his natural condition and makes him a child of God. It gives him the right to Heaven and a share in God's divine life. It is a permanent quality of the soul which is lost only through mortal sin and which is regained through the Sacrament of Penance.

Actual grace is a special help of God which comes to a person when he needs it. Actual grace strengthens the soul and makes it able to perform supernatural acts of virtue. When a person has reached the age of reason—that is, when he is about seven years of age and knows the difference between right and wrong—he needs actual grace. Actual grace is not a permanent quality of the soul. It is not infused into the soul as is sanctifying grace. Anyone can pray for and receive actual grace, even those who are in mortal sin. Actual grace often leads those who are outside the Church to seek Baptism and sanctifying grace which comes with Baptism.

Grace can be attained by prayer and by receiving the sacraments, especially the Holy Eucharist. All the sacraments give sanctifying grace. Each of the sacraments gives a special grace called **sacramental grace** which helps one carry out the particular purpose of the sacrament. All grace comes from God through the merits of Jesus Christ.

grace (at meals) Asking of a blessing on the food before meals and the giving of thanks afterwards. *See* **blessing before meals.**

A form of thanksgiving after meals is: "We give Thee thanks for all Thy benefits, O Almighty God, Who livest and reignest forever; and may the souls of the faithful departed, through the mercy of God, rest in peace. Amen."

Gradual, the The verses from the Psalms or other Scripture said or sung after the Epistle at the Mass. It is called the Gradual because in the early days of Christianity it was sung from the *step* (*gradus* in Latin) of the altar. The Gradual changes with the Proper of the Mass. At certain times during the Easter season it is replaced by the Alleluia.

Greater Litanies, the   The chanting of the Litany of the Saints in procession on April 25, St. Mark's Day. A Rogation Mass follows the procession, though April 25 is not usually called one of the Rogation days. *See* **Rogation days.**

Gregorian chant   *See* **music, liturgical.**

grille   A screen or grating separating the priest from the person making a Confession. The same sort of grating separates cloistered nuns from their visitors and the nuns' choir from the altar of their chapel.

guardian angels   Angels appointed by God to watch over every soul born in the world. From the first moment of life, each human being has an angel assigned to look after him. The guardian angels protect the bodies of men as well as their souls, warn them of danger, and encourage them when they are in trouble.

The Feast of the Holy Guardian Angels is October 2.

H

Habacuc The book of the Old Testament of the Bible written by Habacuc, a minor prophet.

habit An inclination toward a certain kind of act and an ease, gained by constant practice, at doing it. Habits may be either good or bad. Many good habits are natural virtues. *See* **virtue.**

habit, religious The clothing worn by members of a religious congregation or order. The clothing included in most men's religious habits are the tunic, belt (or girdle), hood (or cowl), and scapular. Women's religious habits usually include a veil, coif, headband, and belt.

In September, 1952, Pope Pius XII, speaking to members of the First International Congress of Mothers General for Religious Congregations, urged them to be willing to modify their habits according to modern demands and hygiene.

Hail, Holy Queen A prayer to the Blessed Virgin Mary. This prayer in Latin is called *Salve Regina.* It is the fourth of the antiphons of Our Lady and is said after Divine Office at certain times of the liturgical year. The Hail, Holy Queen is included in the prayers said at the foot of the altar after Low Mass. The words of the prayer are:

> Hail, Holy Queen, Mother of Mercy; hail, our life, our sweetness, and our hope! To thee do we cry, poor banished children of Eve; to thee do we send up our sighs, mourning and weeping in this vale of tears. Turn, then, most gracious advocate, thine eyes of mercy toward us; and after this our exile, show unto us the blessed fruit of thy womb, Jesus. O clement, O loving, O sweet Virgin Mary!

When the prayer is said at the foot of the altar, both the priest and the people say the prayer together. At the end of the prayer the priest says: "Pray for us, O holy Mother of God." The people answer: "That we may be made worthy of the promises of Christ."

Hail Mary, the The most well-known prayer to the Blessed Virgin

107

Mary. It is called the Angelical Salutation because the first part of it is the greeting (salutation) which the Angel Gabriel gave to Our Lady when he told her that she was to become the Mother of God.

> Hail Mary, full of grace! the Lord is with thee; blessed art thou among women, and blessed is the fruit of thy womb, Jesus. Holy Mary, Mother of God, pray for us sinners, now and at the hour of our death. Amen.

Hallowe'en The eve of All Saints' Day which at one time was called All Hallows' Eve in England. Halloween would therefore be the evening before All Hallows.

halo A circle of light pictured around the head of a sacred person to show holiness. A person must be beatified to have a halo pictured around his head. Our Lord is usually shown with a halo which has a cross on it.

Hanc igitur The offering prayer of the Canon of the Mass. This prayer follows the Communicantes. The bell is rung once as a sign that the consecration is near. The priest spreads his hands over the offering to show that Jesus Christ sacrifices Himself on the altar in the place of every human being in the world. He asks God to accept this offering and to give peace, safety of soul, and final perseverance. *Hanc igitur* are Latin words meaning *This therefore.* The prayer in English begins: "This oblation, therefore, of our service and that of Thy whole family we beseech Thee, O Lord, graciously to accept."

happiness, celestial *See* **beatitude.**

hear Mass, to To be present at Mass. *See* **assist at Mass.**

Heart of Mary, Immaculate The physical heart of the Blessed Virgin Mary venerated because it was the seat of her love for her Divine Son and because it was immaculate. Devotion to the Immaculate Heart of Mary was begun by St. John Eudes in the seventeenth century. In the third appearance of Our Lady to the children of Fatima, Our Lady told Lucy that Our Lord wanted devotion to the Immaculate Heart of Mary spread in the world. On October 31, 1942, Pope Pius XII consecrated the world to the Immaculate Heart of Mary. On August 22, 1945, he instituted the Feast of the Immaculate Heart of Mary.

heathen, the Those who are not Christians, Jews, or Moham-
medans. Under Christians are included both Catholics and non-
Catholics. Christians, Jews, and Mohammedans worship the One
God and so cannot be called heathen.

Heaven Place of perfect happiness lasting forever. The blessed
in Heaven see God and understand better the mysteries that they
could not understand on earth. Heaven is the reward of those
who die in the state of grace.

Hebrews, the Epistle to the A book of the New Testament of
the Bible. It is the Epistle of St. Paul the Apostle to the Hebrews
and tells of the advantages of Christianity over Judaism.

Hell Place and state of eternal punishment for those who die
in mortal sin. The devils or evil spirits are in Hell, where they
were cast by God when they lost their angelic state. Those who
are in Hell are deprived forever of the sight of God.

Help of Christians Title of the Blessed Virgin Mary given to her
after the battle of Lepanto. During the sixteenth century when all
Christian countries were threatened by the Turkish power, Pope
Pius V appealed to the nations of Europe. Under Don John of
Austria, the Spanish and Italian navies met the Turks at Lepanto
near Greece and destroyed their forces.

In gratitude to Our Lady, to whom the Christian forces had
prayed, Pope Pius V added this new title *Our Lady Help of
Christians* to the Litany of Loreto. The Feast of Our Lady Help
of Christians is May 24.

heresy The refusal of a baptized person to believe one or more
truths of the Catholic faith. If this refusal is willful (that is, if the
baptized person deliberately decides not to believe), then the
heresy is called formal heresy. If this refusal is made through
ignorance—that is, through lack of knowledge—the heresy is called
material heresy. Formal heresy is a serious sin.

Heresy differs from schism which is a separation from the
authority of the Pope and communion with the Church. *See*
schism.

For early heresies in the Church, *see* **Arianism, Gnosticism,
Manicheism, Pelagianism, and Sabellianism.**

hermit One who lives alone in a life of religious retirement.

Herod, King Roman King of the Jews during whose reign Jesus Christ was born. Herod feared the words of the prophet that Jesus would be "a leader who shall rule my people Israel" (*Matthew II 6*), and he plotted to kill Jesus. He asked the Magi to bring him news concerning the Child, but the Magi, who had been warned in a dream not to return to Herod, went back to their own country by a different route. Herod was responsible for the murder of the Holy Innocents, those baby boys of Bethlehem whom he ordered his soldiers to kill in the hope that Jesus would be among them. Jesus, however, was safe with His mother and foster father, on the way to Egypt. After the death of Herod, Mary and Joseph brought Him back to Israel. Another King Herod, Herod Antipas, executed John the Baptist and was in charge of the trial of Jesus Christ.

hierarchy of angels *See* **choirs of angels**.

High Mass A Mass sung by one priest assisted by a deacon and subdeacon. A choir, a certain number of servers, and incense are common to the High Mass.

holiness (1) Closeness to God through the presence of sanctifying grace in the soul. Only mortal sin can take holiness away from the soul. (2) One of the marks of the Catholic Church. *See* **marks of the Church, the.**

Holiness, Your (His) Title of respect given to the Pope. The Pope is addressed as Your Holiness and spoken of as His Holiness.

Holy Coat The seamless garment said to have been worn by Jesus Christ at the time of His passion. It is kept at the Cathedral of Treves in Germany.

holydays of obligation Days on which a Catholic must assist at Mass in obedience to the law of the Church, *to assist at Mass on all Sundays and holydays of obligation.* A Catholic must also refrain from servile work on holydays, as on Sunday. The holydays of obligation in the United States are these six: Christmas Day (December 25); the Circumcision (January 1); Ascension Thursday (forty days after Easter); the Assumption (August 15); All Saints' Day (November 1); the Immaculate Conception (December 8).

   In Canada, the Epiphany (January 6) is a holyday of obligation, while the Assumption (August 15) is not.

Holy Eucharist, the Sacrament of the   The sacrament by which Our Lord is received in Holy Communion under the appearances of bread and wine. *See* **Communion, Holy.** The Holy Eucharist is both a sacrament and a sacrifice. As a sacrament it is the true body and blood of Jesus Christ under the appearances of bread and wine. Christ instituted the Sacrament of the Holy Eucharist at the Last Supper the night before He died. He took bread, blessed and broke it and, giving it to His Apostles, said: "Take and eat; this is my body." Then He took a cup of wine, blessed it, gave it to them, and said: "All of you drink of this; for this is my blood of the new covenant which is being shed for many unto the forgiveness of sins." Then He said to His Apostles: "Do this in remembrance of me."

Holy Face, the   The face of the suffering Lord. Devotion to the Holy Face has been widespread since the Middle Ages. *See* **Veronica's veil.** The Confraternity of the Holy Face was founded in 1850 to spread this devotion.

Holy Family, the   Jesus, Mary, and Joseph. In Nazareth the Holy Family practiced all the virtues of home life—charity, respect, obedience. The Holy Family is the model of family life. The Feast of the Holy Family is the first Sunday after the Epiphany. The Gospel for the Feast of the Holy Family tells the story of the Child Jesus in the Temple.

Holy Father   A title of the Pope.

Holy Ghost, the   God and the Third Person of the Blessed Trinity. He is called the Holy Ghost because He is breathed forth by the Father and the Son. The word *ghost* here means *spirit*. He came down upon the Apostles on Pentecost and gave them the courage to go out to preach the Gospel. In the Sacrament of Confirmation, the Holy Ghost comes to the person confirmed in a special way and gives him the courage to defend the Catholic faith.

Holy Hour   A devotion to the Blessed Sacrament. The Blessed Sacrament is exposed for an hour while the people pray before it. Hymns are often sung and special prayers said. Exposition ends with Benediction of the Blessed Sacrament.

Holy House at Nazareth   The house in which the Holy Family is said to have lived and which is preserved within the basilica at Loreto, Italy.

Holyland, the Palestine, the land at the eastern end of the Mediterranean Sea. This is the land which God first gave to His chosen people and which Jesus Christ made holy through His life, suffering, death, and Resurrection. *See* **Palestine.**

Holy Name of Jesus The name of Jesus which means *Jehovah is salvation. Jehovah* was the name given to God in the Old Testament, and the word *salvation* means the act of being saved. It was through Jesus, the Son of God, that man was saved from his sins. The Feast of the Holy Name of Jesus is the Sunday following January 1, unless the first Sunday is the 1st, 6th, or 7th of January. Then the feast is observed January 2.

Holy Orders, the Sacrament of The sacrament through which men receive the power and grace to carry out the sacred duties of bishops, priests, and other ministers of the Church. The word *order* comes from the Latin word meaning *order* or *rank,* and the words Holy Order or Orders mean the rank or ranks of the clergy.

Jesus Christ Himself instituted the Sacrament of Holy Orders when He gave His Apostles spiritual power in such a way that others would receive it from them. He breathed on His Apostles and said: "Receive the Holy Spirit; whose sins you shall forgive, they are forgiven them; and whose sins you shall retain, they are retained." *John XX 22, 23.*

The Apostles, after the death of Jesus Christ, administered the Sacrament of Holy Orders—ordaining priests and consecrating bishops. They did this by the imposition of hands. St. Paul said to St. Timothy in *I Timothy IV 14:* "Do not neglect the grace that is in thee, granted to thee by reason of prophecy with the laying on of hands of the presbyterate." The laying on of hands (the imposition of hands) is the external sign of the Sacrament of Holy Orders.

The Apostles were the first bishops of the Church, and they were the first after Jesus Christ to consecrate other bishops and to ordain priests. The bishop is the minister of Holy Orders, and he himself has received the fullnes of Holy Orders. Below the bishop are the major orders of priest, deacon, and subdeacon and the minor orders of acolyte, exorcist, lector, and porter (or doorkeeper).

To receive the Sacrament of Holy Orders a man must (1) be in the state of grace and be of excellent character; (2) be of the necessary age and have the required education; (3) have the intention of spending his life in the sacred ministry; and (4) be called to Holy Orders by his bishop.

The Sacrament of Holy Orders imprints a character or spiritual mark on the soul which can never be blotted out. This sacrament, like that of Baptism and Confirmation, can be given only once.

holy places Places in Palestine connected with the life, death, and Resurrection of Our Lord. *See* **Holyland, the.**

Holy Saturday The Vigil of Easter, the day on which the Church waits at the tomb of Our Lord until His Resurrection. *See* **Easter Vigil, the restored.**

Holy See The seat of authority at Rome, under the Sovereign Pontiff (the Pope) and those associated with him in the government of the Church.

Holy Thursday Thursday of Holy Week, sometimes called Maundy Thursday from the ceremony of the Washing of the Feet (Mandatum). See *Maundy Thursday* and *Washing of the Feet.* It is the day in memory of the Last Supper. On Holy Thursday Jesus Christ instituted the Holy Eucharist both as a sacrament and a sacrifice. As a sacrament He gave His Apostles His own body and blood in Holy Communion. As a sacrifice He said the first Mass. He was preparing His Apostles for the priesthood when He said, "Do this in remembrance of me."

Except for the bishop's Morning Mass at the cathedral (Mass of the Chrism) at which the holy oils are consecrated, Mass for Holy Thursday is celebrated only in the evening. The Mass must begin no earlier than 5:00 P.M. and no later than 8:00 P.M. Holy Communion is distributed only during the Evening Mass or immediately after it, except to those in danger of death. Ordinarily priests may not offer private Masses on Holy Thursday. They receive Communion at the Solemn Evening Mass from the celebrant. The bishop can permit one or two Low Masses on Holy Thursday evening in individual churches and public oratories, besides the Solemn Mass, if it is found necessary, or one Low Mass in the chapels of hospitals, convents, etc.

White vestments are worn, the symbol of joy, and the Crucifix is veiled in white. The Gloria is sung for the first time since the beginning of Lent, and the church bells ring out. After the Gloria of the Mass the bells are not rung again until the Mass of the Easter Vigil.

At the Solemn Evening Mass of Holy Thursday hosts are consecrated for the general Communion of Thursday and Friday. After Mass the Blessed Sacrament is carried in procession to the repository where it is adored at least until midnight.

holy water Water in which salt has been mixed and which is blessed by a priest. Holy water is a sacramental. *See* **sacramentals.** It has been used by the Church since the time of the Apostles. Holy water fonts are placed at the entrance of the church so that a person entering may make the Sign of the Cross on himself. Holy water is used at blessings given by the Church and at the Asperges before High Mass on Sunday. *See* **Asperges.** Holy water may be kept in the home to be used in times of trouble or temptation.

Holy Week The week between Palm Sunday and Easter. It is a week of special services in memory of the last days of Our Lord's life on earth and His passion. Palm Sunday shows Our Lord's triumphal entry into Jerusalem. Holy Thursday marks the institution of the Holy Eucharist, and Good Friday marks Our Lord's death on the Cross. There are special services for every day of Holy Week. The new Holy Week order, by a decree of November 16, 1955, has restored the services of Holy Week to the evening hours, hours at which the events, in memory of which the services are held, really took place. The changes in the order of Holy Week were made so that the people could more easily and more devoutly take part.

Holy Year *See* **Jubilee Year.**

hood *See* **cowl.**

hope The supernatural virtue by which one firmly trusts that God, who is all-powerful and who always keeps His promises, will, because He is merciful, give eternal happiness and the means to obtain it. When a person hopes for something, he desires it and in a sense expects it, but he does not feel certain of obtaining it. He knows that he must do his part to obtain it. God is willing and able to give eternal salvation to everyone in the world, but each person must make use of the means he has been given to obtain salvation. Hope is one of the three theological virtues. *See* **virtues, theological.**

hope, act of   Words expressing the hope for eternal happiness through God's help and one's own co-operation with it.

> O my God, relying on Thy almighty power and infinite mercy and promises, I hope to obtain pardon of my sins, the help of Thy grace, and life everlasting, through the merits of Jesus Christ, my Lord and Redeemer.

Hosanna   A shout of joy taken from the Psalms and meaning "Save us, pray." The Jews used it on joyful occasions such as the Feast of the Tabernacles, which came to be known by the name Hosanna. The Jews shouted, "Hosanna in the highest!" when Jesus entered the city of Jerusalem on Palm Sunday. Hosanna is said at Mass during the Sanctus, and is also said during the blessing of the palms and the procession on Palm Sunday.

Host   A round, flat piece of bread made from pure flour and water without yeast. It is sometimes called altar bread or wafer bread. When it is consecrated at Mass, it becomes the body and blood of Jesus Christ under the appearance of bread.

hours, canonical   *See* **canonical hours.**

house, the blessing of a   A special blessing which a priest may give to a house. The form of blessing is taken from the Roman Ritual. *See* **Ritual, Roman.**

humanism   Any point of view that is especially devoted to the appreciation of human nature. The term is often used to express interest in art and literature. *Christian humanism* is an expression intended to show the deep interest of Christianity in all aspects of human life. In the modern world there are people who call themselves humanists, by which they mean that they believe in nothing beyond human nature.

humanity of Christ, the   The human nature which Jesus Christ, the Second Person of the Blessed Trinity, took at His Incarnation. Jesus Christ, in His humanity, had a body and a soul like ours.

humeral veil   A silk veil, decorated with embroidery, worn by a priest over his shoulders at Benediction of the Blessed Sacrament, when he blesses the people with the Host or when he carries the Blessed Sacrament in procession. It is also worn by a subdeacon at a High Mass, when he carries the sacred vessels from the credence table to the altar and when he holds the paten. The humeral veil is also called the velum.

hymn A song in honor of God, Our Lady, or the saints.

hypostatic union The union of the two distinct natures of God and man in Jesus Christ.

I

idolatry Worshipping anyone or anything that is not God. The sin of idolatry is a sin against the first commandment of God: "I am the Lord thy God; thou shalt not have strange Gods before me." To pray before the Crucifix, relics, or sacred images is not idolatry because one does not pray to the Crucifix, relics, or images but to the persons they represent.

ignorance Absence of knowledge in one who could acquire it. Ignorance can be vincible or invincible. The word *vincible* means able to be overcome, and the word *invincible* means not able to be overcome. Vincible ignorance is ignorance which can be overcome. If a person knows he can find the truth by looking for it but does not make any effort to look for it, then he is guilty of vincible ignorance. Invincible ignorance is ignorance that cannot be easily overcome. A person brought up in a non-Catholic religion would probably have invincible ignorance of many truths of the Catholic Faith.

IHS The first three letters of the Holy Name of Jesus in Greek. IHS, the Latin form, is taken from the contraction of the Greek for Jesus. IHS is sometimes called a sacred monogram. It was chosen by the Jesuits as their badge.

image (of God) Man's likeness to God in intellect and reason. This likeness to God is chiefly in the soul. The soul is like God because it is a spirit which has understanding and free will and will never die. God Himself said in *Genesis I 26*: "Let us make mankind in our image and likeness." *Genesis I 27* continues: "God created man in His image. In the image of God He created him." Some of this original likeness to God was, of course, lost for man by Adam because of his sin. Through His merits, Jesus Christ restored to man some of this likeness to God.

images, sacred Pictures or statues of Our Lord, Our Lady, or the saints. One does not pray to the images but to the persons they represent.

images, veiling of The covering of pictures, statues, and crosses in the church with purple veils on Passion Sunday, as a sign of grief. The Stations of the Cross are not covered. The Cross is unveiled on Good Friday, and the other pictures and statues are unveiled on Holy Saturday.

Immaculate Conception, the The privilege by which the Blessed Virgin Mary was free from original sin from the very moment of her conception. Her soul was filled with sanctifying grace at its creation. The word *immaculate* means free from any stain, that is, perfectly pure. The Blessed Virgin Mary was perfectly pure from her first moment of being. The Feast of the Immaculate Conception is December 8 and is a holyday of obligation in most countries. Our Lady Immaculate is the patron saint of the United States of America. The Immaculate Conception, which refers entirely to Our Lady, should not be confused with the Virgin Birth. *See* **Virgin Birth.**

impediments to marriage *See* **marriage, laws concerning.**

imposition of hands The ceremony of laying hands upon a person especially in the sacraments of Baptism, Confirmation and Holy Orders, to give grace and power. The imposition of hands was known in the Church from the time of the Apostles. *See* **Holy Orders, the Sacrament of.**

imprimatur The permission to print or publish a book dealing with a Catholic subject of a religious nature. The word *imprimatur* comes from the Latin word of the same spelling which means *let it be printed.* When a bishop or someone chosen by the bishop puts his *imprimatur* on a book, it is his word that the book may be printed.

Improperia *See* **Reproaches.**

Incarnation The taking of a human nature by God the Son, the Second Person of the Blessed Trinity. At the time of His Incarnation, Jesus Christ, keeping His divine nature, took also a human nature, a true body, and a true human soul. He was conceived and made man on Annunciation Day. *See* **Annunciation.** He was conceived and made man by the power of the Holy Ghost in the womb of the Blessed Virgin Mary. When the Blessed Virgin Mary gave her consent to the message of the Angel Gabriel with the words, "Behold the handmaid of the Lord; be it done to me according to thy word," that was the moment of the Incarnation. *Luke I 38.*

Incense   Sweet-smelling resin burned at various services in the Church. The incense is put in a censer (also called a thurible) when it is being burned. *See* **censer.** Before burning, the incense is kept in an incense boat resembling a small coal scuttle and is lifted out with an incense spoon. Incense is a symbol of Christian zeal, the odor of virtue, and the rising of prayer to God.

indefectibility   One of the three chief attributes (characteristics) of the Catholic Church. The word *indefectible* means *unfailing.* By the indefectibility of the Catholic Church is meant that the Church, as Christ founded it, will last until the end of time.

Index (of forbidden books)   A list of books (title and author) which Catholics may not read because they are heretical, dangerous to morals, or objectionable in some other way. The Congregation of the Holy Office publishes this list of books. The Pope himself is the prefect (president) of this Congregation. Permission to read these books may be given under certain conditions.

indulgence   The remission granted by the Church of the temporal punishment due to sins already forgiven. The Church has the power to take away, in whole or in part, the temporal punishment which a person, who is sorry for his sins and has been absolved from them by the priest, has still to suffer, either in this life or in Purgatory. A plenary (full) indulgence is the taking away of *all* the temporal punishment due to sins. A partial (incomplete) indulgence is the taking away of *part* of the temporal punishment due to sins.

To gain an indulgence one must be in the state of grace. One must have at least a general intention of gaining the indulgence. Such a general intention may be made each day with the morning offering: "I wish to gain all the indulgences attached to the prayers I shall say and to the good works I shall perform this day." One must also perform the works required by the Church. The conditions for gaining a plenary indulgence are Confession, Communion, a visit to the church, and prayers for the intentions of the Pope. *See* **Jubilee indulgence** and **Portiuncula.**

Whenever a time-period is attached to an indulgence prayer (a certain number of days or years) that means the remission of as much temporal punishment due to sin as could have been obtained by that number of days or years of Penance in the early Church. In the early days of Christianity many days or years of heavy Penance were exacted from the penitent for grievous sins. Sometimes these were cut short if the penitent showed himself truly sorry for his sins. This was the beginning of the doctrine of indulgences. God alone, of course, knows just how much temporal punishment is taken away by an indulgence.

The Church offers many opportunities to gain plenary indulgences. Saying the Rosary before the Blessed Sacrament, making the Stations of the Cross, and saying the Indulgence Prayer before the Crucifix after receiving Communion are some of the ways given by the Church to gain a plenary indulgence. A partial indulgence may be gained by reciting certain prayers. Indulgences may also be gained by reading the Bible.

A person can gain indulgences for the souls in Purgatory as well as for himself, but no one can gain indulgences for any other living person. On All Souls' Day, November 2, a plenary indulgence can be gained for the poor souls under the usual conditions by visiting the church at some time between noon on November 1 and midnight on November 2. Certain privileged altars have plenary indulgences attached to them which may be applied to the souls in Purgatory.

The Church through Jesus Christ has the power to grant indulgences. In giving to St. Peter and the Apostles the power to forgive sins, Jesus Christ also gave them the power to take away the eternal and temporal punishment due to sins. The Pope has the power to grant indulgences in the whole Church. Bishops have the power to grant indulgences in their own dioceses. The Church draws from her spiritual treasury to grant indulgences. *See* treasury of merits.

indwelling (of the Holy Ghost)　The presence of the Holy Ghost in the Church and in the soul of one who is in the state of grace. The Holy Ghost began to live in the Church on Pentecost Sunday and will live in the Church until the end of the world. God the Holy Ghost dwells in a special way in a soul which is in the state of grace.

infallibility of the Church　Inability to teach what is not true.

By the infallibility of the Catholic Church is meant that the Church, by the special help of the Holy Ghost, is protected from making mistakes when it teaches or believes a doctrine of faith or morals. A doctrine of faith or morals is any truth which God has revealed concerning what one must believe or what one must do in order to be saved. The Church teaches infallibly when it explains, through the Pope or through the Pope and the bishops, a doctrine of faith or morals which the members of the Catholic Church must believe. Infallibility is one of the three supernatural attributes (characteristics) of the Catholic Church.

infallibility, papal The Pope's inability to make mistakes when he speaks on matters of faith and morals with supreme authority as the head of the Church on earth. Infallibility is attached to the teaching office of the Pope and is a result of the assistance of the Holy Ghost. When the Pope speaks *ex cathedra* (when he speaks to the Church as a teacher of faith and morals), then he is infallible. *See* **Cathedra.** When the Pope speaks as an ordinary human being he does not, of course, speak infallibly. Even when he speaks as a teacher in his encyclical letters he does not necessarily teach infallibly. *See* **encyclical.** He speaks infallibly only when he speaks concerning a doctrine of faith and morals to be held by all the faithful.

infidel One who is not baptized.

infinite Perfection without limit. Only God is infinite because He has perfections without limit.

infused virtue *See* **virtue.**

innocence, original Man's freedom from sin before the Fall. *See* **Fall of man, the.** God had given Adam and Eve sanctifying grace. They lost sanctifying grace and their original innocence when they sinned.

Innocents, the Holy The children slain at the command of King Herod. When the Wise Men did not return to King Herod as he had asked them to do, he sent out the command to kill all baby boys two years old and under in Bethlehem and bordering districts. The Feast of the Holy Innocents is kept December 28. Vestments are violet for mourning unless the Feast falls on a Sunday, when they are red, the color for the feasts of martyrs.

From earliest time the Church has considered the Holy Innocents as martyrs.

Inquisition A court of justice to inquire into and punish heresy. Such tribunals existed in the Church in the thirteenth century, with Dominicans at the head. The Spanish Inquisition was a branch of one of these early courts and was founded by Ferdinand and Isabella of Spain. Much has been written about its cruelty, but it existed at a time when penalties for small offenses were severe in all countries. It often acted independently and not in accord with the Pope at Rome.

The Congregation of Cardinals of the Holy Inquisition was formed in 1542. This has become the Congregation of the Holy Office, the most important of the Sacred Congregations with the Pope as its prefect. Its purpose is to protect faith and morals, to judge heresy, to examine impediments to marriage, and to examine books for heresy.

I.N.R.I. First letters of the Latin words, Jesus of Nazareth, King of the Jews. Pontius Pilate placed this inscription on the Cross at the Crucifixion of Jesus Christ.

intellect The spiritual power of the human soul by which man knows, understands, thinks, and reasons. The intellect in man is also called *reason* from the fact that it needs to go through a *reasoning* or inquiring process to reach most of the truths it knows.

intercession The praying of one person for another. To intercede means to beg something for another. There are a number of prayers of intercession in the Mass. In the first remembrance prayer before the consecration the priest prays for the whole Church Militant and all its living heads and members. *See* **Commemoration** regarding prayers of intercession for the faithful on earth and for the souls in Purgatory. In the *Communicantes* the priest joins with the saints in Heaven in honoring the Church Triumphant.

intercession of Christ, of the saints The pleading of Christ or the saints in behalf of men.

Introit The first prayer read by the priest when he ascends to the altar after the prayers at the foot of the altar. It is read at the Epistle side of the altar. The word *introit* comes from the Latin word meaning *entrance*. It is the entrance to or the beginning of the Mass. The Introit is the first Mass prayer which changes with the day. It is usually made up of an antiphon, a verse of a Psalm, the Gloria Patri, and the antiphon said again. The Introit was originally a chant sung by the choir as the bishop or priest made his entrance into the church.

Isaac   The son of Abraham and Sara. Isaac married Rebecca and had two sons, Esau and Jacob.

Isaias   One of the most famous of the major prophets of the Old Testament. Isaias is mentioned in the Mass when the priest asks God to prepare him for the reading of the Gospel: "Cleanse my heart and my lips, O almighty God, who didst cleanse the lips of the prophet Isaias with a burning coal." The book *Isaias* in the Old Testament was written by him and is a collection of prophecies. Isaias was especially the prophet of the Messias.

Israel, the children of (Israelites)   The family of Jacob who was called Israel. Jacob had twelve sons and they were to be the leaders of the twelve tribes of Israel. After King Solomon's rule, the tribes were divided, the ten northern tribes forming the kingdom of Israel and the two southern tribes, the kingdom of Judah. The Israelites were conquered by the Assyrians and the ten tribes were taken away. They are called the Ten Lost Tribes of Israel. The two tribes of Judah, with Jerusalem as its capital, kept alive the faith in God. The Israelites were later known as Hebrews or Jews.

Ite, Missa Est   Latin words meaning, *Go, it is the dismissal*. These words are said by the priest to the people after the Postcommunion. The *Ite Missa Est* used to be dismissal time at Mass. In the early days of the Church these words were said at the end of the Mass of the Catechumens, and also at the end of the Mass of the Faithful. Now they are said near the end of the Mass, though three prayers have been added: the Placeat, the Last Blessing, and the Last Gospel. It is thought that the word *Mass* comes from the word *missa*. At Masses of ferias (weekdays on which no feast of a saint is kept) and Sundays during Advent and Lent, *Benedicamus Domino* (*Let us bless the Lord*) is said instead of *Ite Missa Est,* and *Requiescant in pace* (*May they rest in peace*) is substituted in Masses for the Dead.

Iudica Psalm   *See* Psalm XLII.

J

Jacob The second son of Isaac and Rebecca, and the grandson of Abraham. Jacob was his mother's favorite, and his brother Esau was jealous of him. Jacob went into his mother's land, Haran, to stay with his mother's brother, Laban. Here he married, first Lea and then Rachel. On his return to his own land, he made peace with his brother Esau. God changed Jacob's name to Israel and told him that many nations would spring from him.

Jacob's Ladder The ladder, reaching from earth to Heaven, which Jacob saw in a dream. The Lord was leaning on the top, and angels were climbing upon it.

Jairus, the daughter of The daughter of a ruler named Jairus, whose faith in Jesus was so great that he asked Jesus to bring back to life his daughter who had just died. Jesus went to the ruler's house and took the dead girl by the hand, and she arose.

James, Epistle of St. A book of the New Testament of the Bible. It is the Epistle of St. James the Apostle (St. James the Less) and is addressed to the entire Church.

Jehovah The sacred name of God in the Old Testament. Jahveh is probably the correct form.

Jeremias One of the four major prophets. Jeremias had warned the Jews that Jerusalem would be destroyed. The *Prophecy of Jeremias* and the *Lamentations of Jeremias* are books written by him in the Old Testament.

Jerico An ancient city of Palestine. When the Israelites, led by Josue, entered the Promised Land, the walls of Jerico fell.

Jerusalem The Holy City of God and the capital city of the Jews. The city of Jerusalem is of great importance in the Old Testament. King Solomon built a temple to the Lord in Jerusalem and it was here that the Ark of the Covenant was carried from Mount Sion. This temple was destroyed, and the Jews were carried into captivity in Babylon. The Jews returned from their captivity about 500 years before the birth of Jesus Christ. The temple was rebuilt, but it was not so beautiful as the one Solomon had built.

Just outside the city of Jerusalem Jesus Christ was crucified and rose from the dead. On the day which is now celebrated as Palm Sunday, Jesus entered Jerusalem in triumph. Branches from palm trees were spread before Him while the people cried: "Hosanna! Blessed is He who comes in the name of the Lord. Blessed is the kingdom of our father David that comes! Hosanna in the highest!" *Mark XI 10*. Long before this, Zacharias the prophet had predicted Christ's entrance into Jerusalem when he said: "Rejoice greatly, O daughter of Sion, shout for joy, O daughter of Jerusalem: Behold thy King will come to thee, the just and savior; he is poor, and riding upon an ass, and upon a colt the foal of an ass." *Zacharias IX 9*.

Jesuits   *See* religious orders and congregations of men.

Jesus   Name given to Our Lord. When the Angel Gabriel told the Blessed Virgin Mary that she was to be the Mother of God, he said to her: "Behold, thou shalt conceive in thy womb and shalt bring forth a son; and thou shalt call his name Jesus." *Luke I 31*. The name *Jesus* in Hebrew means "the Lord is salvation."

Jesus Christ   The son of God made man and the Second Person of the Blessed Trinity. As God He was born of the Father existing from all eternity. As man He was born in Bethlehem, Palestine, during the reign of Augustus, Emperor of Rome. The Blessed Virgin Mary was His mother, and her spouse, St. Joseph, was His foster father.

The first thirty years of His life were spent quietly in Nazareth, Israel. At the age of thirty He began His public life, preaching in Jerusalem and Judea and working miracles. He gathered about Him many disciples of whom He picked twelve, called Apostles, to carry on His work. His public life lasted only three years. Shortly before His death He founded the Church and gave to it the Blessed Sacrament. He was crucified by the Jews, was buried, and rose from the dead by His own power on the third day. For forty days He remained on earth, appearing to His Apostles and others. Forty days after His Resurrection He led His Apostles out to Bethany, where He ascended into Heaven from the top of the Mount of Olives.

Jews   The Israelites, God's chosen people; also called Hebrews.

Job   Principal character of the *Book of Job* in the Old Testament of the Bible. In Hebrew the name *Job* means *one persecuted*, and the story of Job is the story of his many trials. Among the misfortunes of Job were the loss of his possessions, the death of his children, and the affliction of his body with sores from head to foot. Through all this suffering Job remained faithful to God. God rewarded him by giving him good fortune in his later years.

The expression "to have the patience of Job" means to accept misfortune in the same patient way that Job did. It was Job who said: "The Lord gave and the Lord hath taken away; as it hath pleased the Lord so is it done; blessed be the name of the Lord." *Job I 21.* Parts of the Office of the Dead are taken from the *Book of Job.*

Joel   The book of the Old Testament of the Bible written by Joel, one of the minor prophets.

John, Epistles of St., I, II, III   Books of the New Testament of the Bible. They are three Epistles written by St. John the Apostle.

John (the Gospel of St.)   The fourth and last Gospel of the New Testament of the Bible. John, called "the beloved disciple," was the last to write his Gospel. His Gospel differs from the other three in that his main theme is to show the divine nature of Jesus Christ.

John the Baptist, St.   The son of Zachary and Elizabeth who was the cousin of the Blessed Virgin Mary. John the Baptist was filled with the Holy Ghost while still in his mother's womb. His birth was foretold by an angel to his father, Zachary, a priest in the Temple. John the Baptist was the forerunner of Jesus Christ. He said to the people: "I indeed baptize you with water. But one mightier than I is coming, the strap of whose sandals I am not worthy to loose. He will baptize you with the Holy Spirit and with fire." *Luke III 16.*

Jesus Christ Himself was baptized by John in the River Jordan. A new feast commemorating this baptism is the thirteenth of January.

The last part of John's life was spent as a prisoner of Herod, who finally had him beheaded at the desire of a cruel woman. The feast of the birthday of St. John the Baptist is June 24. Another feast commemorating the beheading of John the Baptist is August 29.

Jonas   Minor prophet of the Old Testament. The *Prophecy of Jonas* in the Old Testament of the Bible bears his name. The Lord had a great whale swallow Jonas, who remained in the whale for three days. When Jonas cried to God for help, God set him free. Jonas is an Old Testament type of Jesus Christ, who remained in the tomb for three days. *See* **type.**

Jordan, the river   The river which the Israelites had to cross in order to enter the Promised Land. When the priests carried the Ark of the Covenant into the river Jordan, the waters divided. Many years later John the Baptist was to baptize people in the river Jordan. Jesus Himself was baptized by John in the river Jordan.

Joseph   One of the twelve sons of Jacob, and the favorite among all his sons because he had been born in his old age to his wife Rachel. Joseph had a beautiful coat of many colors. Joseph's brothers were jealous of him because of the favors his father showed him, and they sold him to some merchants from Israel who were going into Egypt. Joseph's brothers took his coat from him, dipped it in the blood of a goat, and took it to Jacob to make him believe that his favorite son was dead. In the meantime the merchants had sold Joseph to one of Pharoah's officers, a captain of the guards. Joseph became governor of Egypt and was able to help his brothers when famine came to Chanaan. In this way God took care of the chosen people during the famine. When Jacob learned that Joseph was safe in Egypt, he was eager to go to him, but he feared the journey into Egypt. In a vision the Lord told Jacob not to be afraid to leave Chanaan and go into Egypt. When Jacob died, Joseph took his body back into Chanaan to be buried, as he had promised. Joseph then returned to Egypt, where he remained till his death.

Joseph of Arimathea   A member of the Jewish council from Arimathea, a town of Judea. He himself was interested in finding the Kingdom of God, and he had nothing to do with the sentencing of Jesus Christ. He asked Pilate for the body of Jesus, which he wrapped in a linen cloth and laid in the tomb.

Joseph, St.   The spouse of the Blessed Virgin Mary and the foster father of Jesus. St. Joseph was closer than any other human being to Our Lady and her Divine Son, for it was he who was chosen by God the Father to be their protector. St. Joseph was of the royal family of David, a carpenter by trade and a man who was both just and gentle. He was a man to whom the angels spoke. It was an angel who told Joseph to take Mary as his wife when he was filled with doubt at the time of the Annunciation. Soon after the birth of the Holy Child, an angel told Joseph to take Jesus and His mother and fly into Egypt. An angel made known to Joseph when it was time to return to Israel. St. Joseph spent his life in obscurity, working in his carpenter shop, watching over the Holy Child and His mother during those years of Our Lord's hidden life. St. Joseph must have died some time before Our Lord began His public life. Because Jesus was probably with him when he died, St. Joseph is known as the patron saint of a happy death. He is also known as the patron saint of carpenters and woodworkers. He was given as patron to the universal Church by Pope Pius IX and as patron of workmen by Pope Benedict XV in 1920. St. Joseph has two feast days: the Feast of St. Joseph, on March 19; and the Feast of St. Joseph the Workman, May 1. Bishops of the United States and Canada have been given the permission to celebrate the Mass of the feast on their Labor Day, which is the first Monday in September. The Solemnity of St. Joseph has been dropped. *See* **Solemnity.**

Josue One of the twelve men chosen by Moses to examine the Promised Land. Josue became the leader of the Israelites after the death of Moses. The book *Josue* of the Old Testament of the Bible bears his name. It is a record of the settlement of the land of Chanaan.

Joyful Mysteries The five Joyful Mysteries of the Rosary: (1) the Annunciation; (2) the Visitation; (3) the Birth of Our Lord; (4) the Presentation of Our Lord in the Temple; (5) the Finding of Our Lord in the Temple. The Joyful Mysteries are usually said on Monday and Thursday.

Jubilee indulgence An extraordinary plenary indulgence granted by the Pope during the Jubilee Year.

jubilee year A year in which the Pope grants the Jubilee indulgence to the faithful who fulfill the necessary conditions for gaining it. The Church took the name *jubilee* from the Jewish church which, in accordance with ancient law, every fiftieth year proclaimed a jubilee year. An ordinary jubilee is granted by the Church every twenty-five years at Rome, from one Christmas to the next, and is given to the Church the following year from one Christmas to the next. The jubilee year begins and ends with the opening and closing of the holy door in Rome.

Jude, Epistle of St.   A book of the New Testament of the Bible. It is the Epistle of St. Jude the Apostle (the brother of James).

Judea   The largest of the three provinces of Palestine at the time of Jesus Christ. Its chief city, Jerusalem, was the center of Jewish political and religious life.

Judges   The book of the Old Testament of the Bible telling the deeds of twelve heroes of Israel. The judges were military leaders sent by God to help the Israelites.

judgment, general   The decision of God which will be passed on all men immediately after the final resurrection at the end of the world. In this judgment the body will share in the reward or punishment of the soul. At the time of the general judgment all creation will be able to see the justice, wisdom, and mercy of God.

judgment, particular   The decision of God which will be passed on each individual immediately after death. At the particular judgment God will look into everything that a human being has ever said, done, or thought and judge his soul accordingly. If the soul is without sin, it will go immediately to Heaven. If the soul is in the state of grace but needs to be purified before entering Heaven, it will be cleansed in Purgatory. If the soul is guilty of mortal sin it will descend to Hell.

Judith   A widow who delivered the Jewish people by saving Bethulia, a town in Palestine, from the Assyrians. The book of *Judith* in the Old Testament tells of her deeds.

jurisdiction   (1) The power of the Catholic Church to govern the faithful for their supernatural good. (2) Ordinary jurisdiction is that power of administration which is attached to an office. Delegated jurisdiction is that power of administration which is given to a person and not attached to an office. A priest or bishop may be granted the delegated jurisdiction to hear Confessions and administer the Sacrament of Penance. *See* **faculties.**

K

keys of the Kingdom *See* **power of the keys.**

King of the Jews Title first given to Jesus by the Magi when they came from the East to Jerusalem, saying: "Where is he that is born king of the Jews?" *Matthew II 2.* The soldiers who scourged Jesus before His Crucifixion used the title to mock Him. The soldiers put a purple garment on Him because purple was the color worn by kings. They put a crown of thorns on His head and a reed in His hand for a scepter, crying: "Hail, King of the Jews!" At His Crucifixion Pilate put above His head the charge against Him: "This is Jesus, the King of the Jews."

Kingdom of God, the In the Old Testament, this referred to the Jewish people who were ruled over by God. The Jewish people began to look forward to another Kingdom of God to come. John the Baptist preached that the Kingdom of God was at hand. In the New Testament the Kingdom of God is sometimes referred to as the Kingdom of Heaven. It may mean the Kingdom of God in this world—that is, the spiritual rule of God, through His Church—or the Kingdom of God in the next world. The Kingdom of God, as spoken of by Jesus Christ, began with His Incarnation.

Kings, Books of Four books in the Old Testament of the Bible—I Samuel, II Samuel, III Kings, and IV Kings—that tell the history of the Jewish people from about 1039 to 587 B.C.

kiss of peace A mark of brotherly love given at Solemn High Masses after the Agnus Dei. When the kiss of peace is given, each person bows the head forward so that their left cheeks almost touch. The one giving the kiss says: "Pax tecum" (Peace be with you). The other answers: "Et cum spiritu tuo" (And with your spirit).

Knights of Columbus Roman Catholic society of laymen engaged in doing good work, both religious and civic. The society was founded in 1882 in the United States.

Kyrie Eleison   Prayer for mercy said at the middle of the altar immediately after the Introit of the Mass. *Kyrie eleison* is Greek and means *Lord, have mercy on us.* It is the only part of the Mass said in Greek instead of Latin.

"Lord have mercy on us" is said three times to God the Father. "Christ, have mercy on us" is said three times to God the Son. "Lord, have mercy on us" is said three times again to God the Holy Ghost.

L

Laetare Sunday The fourth Sunday of Lent. It takes its name from the first word of the Introit, *Laetare*, Latin for *Rejoice*. On Laetare Sunday flowers may be placed on the altar and the organ played. Rose-colored vestments may be used, and the dalmatic and tunic, which are replaced by the folded chasuble during Lent and Advent, are worn.

laity, the Members of the Church who do not belong to the clerical or the religious state. Religious brothers and sisters are actually members of the laity although they enjoy the privileges of the clergy under canon law. In common usage the word laity refers to laymen and laywomen.

lamb Symbol of Our Lord as the victim of sacrifice. *See* **Agnus Dei.**

Lamentations of Jeremias The book in the Old Testament of the Bible following the *Prophecy of Jeremias*.

lamp, sanctuary *See* sanctuary lamp.

La Salette A shrine at La Salette, a mountain in southeastern France, where Our Lady appeared to two children, Melanie Matthieu and Maximin Girard, in 1846. Our Lady, who was weeping bitterly, urged the children to tell the people that they would suffer punishment if they kept their evil ways, but that they would be shown divine mercy if they repented. The day after the appearance of Our Lady, a fountain appeared on the spot where she had sat weeping.

Last Sacraments, the The Sacrament of Extreme Unction and viaticum (Holy Communion given to those in danger of death).

Last Supper, the The meal which Jesus Christ took with His Apostles in Jerusalem the night before He died. At the Last Supper He instituted the Sacrament of the Holy Eucharist and said the first Mass. *See* **Holy Thursday.**

last things, the four Death, Judgment, Heaven, and Hell.

Latin The language of the Roman rite of the Church. Latin was once the language of ancient Rome.

Lauds The second hour of the Divine Office. *See* **canonical hours.**

132

It takes its name from the word *Laudate* (*Praise*) used frequently in the Psalms which make up part of this hour.

Lavabo, the The washing of the hands after the offering of the bread and wine. The washing of the hands is a symbol of the spiritual purity one must have in offering Mass. The Lavabo is a part of the Offertory of the Mass. The priest goes to the right side of the altar where the server pours water from the cruet over the priest's forefingers and thumbs. During the washing of the hands the priest says the prayer which begins with the word *Lavabo* (Latin word meaning *I shall wash*). This prayer is taken from *Psalm XXV 6–12*. The priest washes his fingers because he soon will touch the Sacred Host and chalice. During the Lavabo, priest and people pray for purity of heart.

Lavabo bowl A bowl held under the hands of the priest at the Lavabo. The water poured over his fingers falls into this bowl.

Law, Canon The body of laws which the Church has made. These are contained in *The Code of Canon Law* which is an official collection of ecclesiastical laws binding the Latin Church.

lay brothers and sisters Those who have taken religious vows but have not received the Sacrament of Holy Orders or who do not say the Office in choir. Lay brothers and sisters are engaged in many kinds of work, depending on the community to which they belong.

layman or laywoman A member of the laity. *See* **laity.**

Lazarus of Bethany Brother of Mary and Martha and friend of Jesus Christ. Jesus raised him from the dead after he had been buried for four days. Jesus had known that Lazarus, His friend, was sick, but He did not come to him until after he had died and had been buried in the tomb for four days. Jesus asked that the stone against the door of the tomb be taken away. After praying, He cried: "Lazarus, come forth." Lazarus, though his feet and hands were bound with bandages, came out of the tomb. This miracle is told in the Gospel of *St. John XI 1–14.*

lector A member of the clergy in the second of the four minor orders. The order of the Lector is a very ancient order, and originally the duty of the lector was to read the lessons of the Church.

legate, papal A messenger from the Holy See. Such a messenger is a member of the clergy sent by the Pope and having some authority from him. A papal legate is addressed as Your Excellency. *See* **nuncio** and **delegate, apostolic.**

Legion of Mary, the Society of lay people whose purpose is to help the clergy in their work of saving souls. Members engage in such work as visiting the sick, distributing reading material, giving religious instruction. The society was founded in Dublin in 1921 and took the name *Legion* because it is organized according to a Roman legion.

Lent The period of forty days from Ash Wednesday to Holy Saturday during which by prayer and fasting the Church makes itself ready for the Passion, Death, and Resurrection of Our Lord. Lent is the second part of the Cycle of Easter and follows Septuagesima. The time of Lent is six and a half weeks, but the Sundays are not counted so that the period is considered forty days.

After Our Lord had been baptized by John the Baptist in the Jordan, He fasted for forty days and nights in the desert. Here He was tempted three times by the devil and resisted him. In Lent the faithful follow the example of Our Lord in fighting against the devil through prayer and fasting.

Lent is divided into two parts: the beginning of the Holy Forty Days, from Ash Wednesday to Passion Sunday, and Passiontide, from Passion Sunday to Holy Saturday. Each day has its special Mass, and there are few feasts. Violet vestments are used except on Laetare Sunday, when rose-colored vestments may be worn. During Lent the organ is not played, and the altar is not decorated. The Gloria and Alleluia, both prayers of rejoicing, are not said.

Lesser Litanies The chanting of the Litany of the Saints in procession on the Rogation days. *See* **Rogation days.**

lesson (at Mass) A reading from Scripture—the Epistle and the Gospel of the Mass. Sometimes there is a third lesson taken from the Old Testament, and on certain days there are several lessons read before the Gospel.

Leviticus A book of the Old Testament of the Bible, written by Moses. It deals with the laws which the priests of the tribe of Levi were to follow.

lie a A statement made which is not true and which the person who makes it does not believe to be true. A lie in jest is not wrong if everyone knows that it is not true. A lie which is a serious sin is one told with the desire to injure someone. If real harm is meant, the lie may be a mortal sin. Lies are forbidden by the eighth commandment: "Thou shalt not bear false witness against thy neighbor."

Limbo (1) Limbo of the Fathers: the place or state of rest where the soul of Christ descended after He died. Here the souls of the good people who had died before Christ's Ascension remained until He should reopen Heaven to them. The soul of Christ descended into Limbo to tell these souls that Heaven was now reopened to mankind. (2) Limbo of Children: a state of perfect and natural happiness which unbaptized children and unbaptized adults free from serious actual sin enjoy when they die.

litany A prayer of devotion consisting of short invocations followed by responses. In the invocations, Our Lord, Our Lady, or the saints are called upon for help. The response is usually *Pray for us* or *Have mercy on us*. Five litanies approved for public worship are: the Litany of the Saints, the Litany of the Blessed Virgin (Litany of Loreto), the Litany of the Most Holy Name of Jesus, the Litany of the Sacred Heart, and the Litany of St. Joseph. All the litanies begin: "Lord, have mercy on us." Other litanies may be used privately.

Litany of the Blessed Virgin Prayer of devotion to Our Lady. *See* **Litany**. In this litany Our Lady is given some very lovely titles, such as: Mirror of Justice, Seat of Wisdom, Cause of Our Joy, Mystical Rose, Tower of David, Tower of Ivory, House of Gold, Morning Star, Queen of Angels. The Litany of Our Lady is also called the Litany of Loreto. It is sometimes sung at Benediction of the Blessed Sacrament.

Litany of the Saints Prayer of devotion to the saints. *See* **Litany**. In this litany the saints are invoked. It is sung on the three Rogation days. *See* **Rogation days**. It is also sung on St. Mark's Day (April 25) and on other special occasions, such as at the Forty Hours Devotion, when certain verses are added. On Holy Saturday the Litany of the Saints is sung after the lessons or prophecies from the Old Testament.

Little Christmas A name sometimes given to the Feast of the Epiphany. *See* **Epiphany, the Feast of.**

Little Flower, the A name given to St. Thérèse of the Child Jesus. *See* **Appendix, Saints, St. Thérèse of the Child Jesus, October 3.**

Little Office of the Blessed Virgin Mary Short Office, consisting of Psalms, lessons, and hymns in honor of the Blessed Virgin Mary, arranged in seven hours.

liturgical art *See* **art, liturgical.**

liturgical colors Five colors used by the Church in her vestments and altar drapes: white, red, green, purple or violet, and black. Rose-colored vestments are also used on two occasions, Gaudete Sunday in Advent and Laetare Sunday in Lent, both days of rejoicing in the midst of penance. In Spain blue vestments are sometimes used in honor of the Blessed Virgin.

White, the color of purity, is used for most of the feasts of Our Lord—Christmas, New Year's (the Feast of the Circumcision), Ascension Thursday, and the Feast of Christ the King. It is also used for feasts of the Blessed Virgin and for saints who were not martyrs.

Red, the color of blood, is used for the feasts of the saints who were martyred for the Catholic faith, and also for the feasts of the Apostles because they too suffered for the faith in the early days of Christianity. It is used on Pentecost Sunday to represent the Holy Ghost coming down upon the Apostles in the form of tongues of fire, and on the Feast of the Precious Blood (July 1).

Green, the color of hope, is often used on Sunday. *See* **Time after Pentecost** and **Time after Epiphany.** Purple or violet, showing penance, is used during Advent and Lent. Black, the color of sorrow, is used on Good Friday and in Masses for the Dead.

liturgical language Latin is the official language of the Western Church. In the Eastern Church Mass is said in Greek, Arabic, Slavonic, Syriac, Rumanian, Armenian, Coptic, and Georgian, all of which are dead languages or old forms of languages not generally understood by people today.

On June 3, 1954, Pope Pius XII gave permission for the use of English in administering the sacraments. The sacraments of Baptism, Matrimony, and Extreme Unction may now be administered in English speaking countries with most of the words in English. The Pope gave this permission so that those receiving the sacraments might understand them better.

liturgical movement A movement whose purpose is to encourage the faithful to take a more active part in the official worship (the liturgy) of the Church. Catholics who use their Missals at Mass and who attend and take part in solemn liturgical services, such as those of Holy Week, are helping the liturgical movement.

liturgical music *See* music, liturgical.

liturgical seasons, the The seasons or times which make up the ecclesiastical year. *See* year, the ecclesiastical. The two chief liturgical seasons are Christmas and Easter. The Time after Pentecost, however, which comes at the end of the Easter cycle and closes the ecclesiastical year, is usually considered a separate cycle.

The Christmas season or cycle celebrates the Incarnation and includes the time from Advent to Lent. The Christmas cycle is divided into Advent, Christmas, and the Time after Epiphany.

The Easter cycle celebrates the Redemption. It is made up of the nine weeks leading up to Easter (Septuagesima, Lent, and Passiontide, which is the last two weeks of Lent) and the Easter season or Paschaltide itself. This cycle ends with the Feast of Pentecost.

The Time after Pentecost, which is from twenty-three to twenty-eight weeks long, shows the development of the Church, strengthened by the coming of the Holy Ghost on Pentecost Sunday. The Time after Pentecost is closely connected to the Easter cycle because in this cycle the work of the Redemption, which was celebrated in the Easter cycle, is continued by the Church through the inspiration of the Holy Ghost.

liturgy Forms of public worship arranged by the Church. The offering of the Mass, the singing of the Divine Office, and the administration of the sacraments are the main forms of public worship. Processions, public prayers, and the ceremonies used in the official public worship of the Church belong to the liturgy.

Lord's Day, the Sunday, the Christian Sabbath, observed in memory of the Resurrection of Jesus Christ. Among the Jews, Saturday, the seventh day of the week, was the day of rest and religious observance. This day is still observed by the Jews and by some Protestant groups (Seventh-Day Adventists). The early Church changed the day of worship from Saturday to Sunday, because on Sunday Jesus Christ rose from the dead and on Sunday the Holy Ghost descended upon the Apostles. Christians in general observe Sunday, the first day of the week, as the Lord's Day.

Lord's Prayer, the   The *Our Father,* the prayer taught by Our Lord to His Apostles in the Sermon on the Mount (*Matthew VI 9–13*). Jesus Christ taught His Apostles to pray: "Our Father who art in heaven, hallowed be Thy name; Thy kingdom come; Thy will be done on earth as it is in heaven. Give us this day our daily bread; and forgive us our trespasses as we forgive those who trespass against us; and lead us not into temptation, but deliver us from evil. Amen." The *Our Father,* called in Latin the *Pater Noster,* is said by the priest at Mass after the little elevation. It is the best of all prayers, given to us by Jesus Christ Himself.

Loreto   Town in Italy where the most sacred shrine of Our Lady is located. The House of Nazareth, in which Jesus lived with Mary and Joseph, is said to be preserved here.

Lost Tribes of Israel, the Ten   *See* Israel, the children of.

Lourdes   Town in France where Our Lady appeared to a peasant girl, Bernadette Soubirous, now St. Bernadette, in 1858. At Lourdes, on the very spot where a spring arose at the time of Our Lady's appearance, is the well-known shrine of Our Lady, most famous pilgrim shrine in the world. Here over a million pilgrims a year come to do honor to Our Lady. Many cures have been brought about at this famous shrine. A special medical bureau has been set up at Lourdes to examine the sick who claim to have been cured. Some of these cures have been declared miraculous by the Church. The feast of the appearance of Our Lady at Lourdes is February 11.

love   The virtue of charity. *See* charity.

Low Mass   Simplest form of Mass and the most common way in which Mass is celebrated. The priest reads rather than sings the prayers. There is no choir.

Low Sunday   Another name for the first Sunday after Easter. It is probably called Low Sunday in contrast to the great feast of Easter.

Lucifer   Another name for Satan, the chief fallen angel, or the devil. The name *Lucifer* is Latin for *light-bearer*. *See* **devil, the.**

Luke, the Gospel of St.   The third Gospel of the New Testament of the Bible. It was written by St. Luke who was a physician and the missionary companion of St. Paul. In the prologue St. Luke addresses his words to a certain Theophilus, but the Gospel was intended for the teaching of the Gentile converts.

lunette   Double circle of gold which holds the Host securely in the Monstrance.

lust   *See* **capital sins.**

lustral water   Another name for holy water.

M

Machabees I, II Two books of the Old Testament of the Bible concerning the persecution of the Jewish people. They tell the story of the Holy Machabees, seven young Jewish boys who were slain with their mother because they would not break God's laws. They are martyrs whose feast is commemorated August 1, and they are the only saints of the Old Testament liturgically honored.

Madonna Italian name meaning *My Lady*. Pictures or statues of the Blessed Virgin Mary are sometimes called Madonnas, especially if the Child Jesus is pictured with His mother.

Magi, the The Wise Men who saw the star in the East and came to visit the Infant Jesus. A legend handed down from the Middle Ages gave the names of the three Wise Men as Gaspar, Melchior, and Balthasar. They brought gifts of gold, frankincense, and myrrh.

magic, black Recourse to the devil in order to accomplish marvels.

magisterium The divine authority of the Church to teach. *See* **authority of the Church.**

Magnificat, the The canticle or song of the Blessed Virgin Mary, the first word of which is *magnificat,* Latin for *magnify* or *praise.* The hymn begins: "My soul magnifies the Lord." The words of the Magnificat are taken from the Gospel according to *St. Luke I 46–55.*

THE MAGNIFICAT

My soul magnifies the Lord,
   and my spirit rejoices in God my savior,
Because he has regarded the lowliness of his handmaid,
   for behold, henceforth all generations shall call me blessed,
Because he who is mighty has done great things for me,
   and holy is his name;
And his mercy is from generation to generation
   toward those who fear him.

He has shown might with his arm;
   he has scattered the proud in the conceit of their heart.
He has put down the mighty from their thrones
   and has exalted the lowly.
The hungry he has filled with good things,
   and the rich he has sent empty away.
He has given help to Israel his servant,
   mindful of his mercy,
As he promised our fathers,
   toward Abraham and his descendants forever.

Mary spoke these words soon after the Annunciation, when the Angel Gabriel told her that she was to become the mother of God. Mary had gone to visit her cousin Elizabeth, and Elizabeth cried out to her: "Blessed art thou among women, and blessed is the fruit of thy womb." Mary answered with the words of the Magnificat in which she praised God for all His gifts. The Magnificat is said daily in the Roman Office.

major orders The sacred orders conferred on bishops, priests, deacons and subdeacons. Bishops have the fullness of Holy Orders. *See* **Holy Orders, the Sacrament of.**

Malachias The book of the Old Testament of the Bible concerning the prophecy of Malachias (messenger of the Lord). Malachias was the last of the minor prophets and promised a new sacrifice and another priesthood.

mammon Worldly goods. The word comes from the Aramaic *mammon,* meaning *riches.* Jesus Christ says in *Matthew VI 24:* "You cannot serve God and mammon."

man A created being composed of body and soul and made in the image and likeness of God. *See* **image.**

Mandatum The ceremony of the Washing of the Feet which takes place on Holy Thursday. *See* **Washing of the Feet, the.**

Manichesism (Manichaeanism) The heresy of the Manichees or Manichaeans. Their founder, Manes, who lived in the third century, taught that there were two eternal principles, one good, the other bad, which were equal to each other.

maniple A short band of cloth worn on the priest's left forearm and pinned just below the elbow. The maniple once served as an

official handkerchief used by the Roman officers to start their
games. It is the special vestment of the subdeacon and may not
be worn by those in lower orders. The maniple signifies penance
and sorrow. *See* **vestments.**

manna Miraculous bread which was given to the Israelites by
God during the forty years they were in the desert. The bread
tasted like flour and honey and looked like dew or frost. It is
called manna because when the Israelites saw it they cried out:
"Man-hu!—What is this?" Manna is a figure of the Holy Eucharist.
See **type.** Jesus Himself said: "I am the living bread that has
come down from heaven." *John VI 51.*

manuterge The small linen towel used at the Lavabo.

Marian Year, the A special year of devotion to the Blessed Virgin
Mary (December 8, 1954 to December 8, 1955) to mark the 100th
anniversary of the day on which belief in the Immaculate Conception was proclaimed as part of the dogma of the Church.
Pope Pius XII announced the Marian Year in an encyclical (a
letter to the heads of the churches) on September 8, 1954. The
year was officially opened by His Holiness December 8, 1954, the
Feast of the Immaculate Conception. The purpose of the Marian
Year was to bring men closer to God through devotion to the
Blessed Virgin Mary. Pope Pius XII wrote a Marian Year Prayer
for the occasion and granted special indulgences for acts of devotion to the Mother of God.

Mark (the Gospel of St.) The second Gospel of the New Testament of the Bible. St. Mark wrote his Gospel in Greek for the
gentile converts. St. Peter has an important place in his narration.

marks of the Church, the Qualities or characteristics of the
Catholic Church which declare that it is the true Church established by Jesus Christ. These marks or characteristics are unity,
holiness, catholicity, and apostolicity.

By the unity of the Catholic Church is meant that it is one,
that it is not divided. All its members have the same faith, the
Catholic faith. All its members have the same sacrifice and sacraments, that is, the Mass and the seven sacraments. The Church
has one government, for all its members are united under one
invisible head, Jesus Christ, and under one visible head, the Pope.

The Catholic Church is holy because it was founded by Jesus

Christ who is all-holy. The Holy Spirit was promised to the Church to dwell in it forever. The Church teaches holy doctrines, the doctrines taught by Jesus Christ Himself, and, through the sacraments, gives to the faithful the means of living a holy life.

By the catholicity of the Catholic Church is meant its universality. The Church teaches, because God commanded it to do so, all nations all the truths revealed by God. Jesus Christ said to the Apostles: "Go, therefore, and make disciples of all nations, baptizing them in the name of the Father and of the Son and of the Holy Spirit." *Matthew XXVIII 19.*

By the apostolicity of the Catholic Church is meant that Jesus Christ founded the Church on the Apostles, and it is ruled by the successors of the Apostles. Jesus Christ gave the commission of teaching and baptizing all nations to the Apostles just before He ascended into Heaven. The successors of the Apostles are the Popes, bishops, and priests who came after the Apostles.

marriage, Christian   The natural contract between a man and a woman which Jesus Christ made a sacrament.

marriage, laws concerning   Laws made by the Church concerning Christian marriage. The Catholic Church has the right to make laws regulating the marriage of baptized persons because marriage is a sacrament and the Church has authority over the sacraments. The sixth commandment of the Church is: "To observe the laws of the Church concerning marriage." The Church has made many laws concerning Christian marriage. Here are a few of them:

(1) The Catholic Church requires that a Catholic be married in the presence of the parish priest or the bishop of the diocese, or a priest chosen by either of them, and before two witnesses; (2) a Catholic may not marry a person who is not a Catholic; (3) a Catholic may not marry a second cousin or a relative closer than a second cousin; (4) if a Catholic is married during Lent or Advent, the marriage must take place quietly and without a Nuptial Mass; (5) a boy not sixteen years of age or a girl not fourteen years of age may not contract marriage; (6) a godchild may not marry his godparent; (7) a widow or widower may not marry a close relative of the wife or husband who has died. Dispensations from some of these laws are sometimes granted for serious reasons.

Martha and Mary Sisters of Lazarus and friends of Jesus Christ. *See* **Lazarus.** When Jesus visited their home at Bethany Martha was busy serving Him, while Mary seated herself at His feet and listened to His words. Martha asked Jesus to tell Mary to help her. "But the Lord answered and said to her, 'Martha, Martha, thou art anxious and troubled about many things, and yet only one thing is needful. Mary has chosen the better part, and it will not be taken from her.'" *Luke X 41.*

Martinmas (St. Martin's Summer) Old English name for the Feast of St. Martin, November 11. The name comes from the words Martin and Mass. Warm weather around this time is sometimes called St. Martin's Summer.

martyr The word *martyr* means "witness." A martyr is one who suffers death for the cause of Jesus Christ. *The Martyrs* usually refers to those Christians who suffered death from the Romans during the first three hundred years of the Church. *See* **North American Martyrs.**

martyrdom Suffering death for the cause of Jesus Christ. Two conditions are necessary for true martyrdom: (1) the martyr must be killed because of his Christianity; (2) the martyr lets himself be killed for his faith.

martyrology List of the martyrs and other saints for every day of the year. The *Roman Martyrology* is used in the Western Church.

Mary *See* **Blessed Virgin Mary, the.**

Mass, different kinds of High Mass, Low Mass, Pontifical Mass, and Sung Mass (Missa Cantata) are the four main types of Masses. Other Masses, such as Parochial Mass, Conventual Mass, Requiem Mass, Month's Mind Mass, Memorial Mass, Nuptial Mass, Private Mass, Public Mass, Votive Mass, belong under these four types.

Mass, Sacrifice of the The sacrifice of the New Law in which Jesus Christ offers Himself to God in an unbloody manner under the appearances of bread and wine. Sacrifice has always been a way of worship. Before the coming of Jesus Christ, sacrifices were offered to God in the form of food and drink (fruits, wine) or animals. These offerings, the sacrifices of the Old Law, were destroyed when they were offered in order to show the power of God. Christ's offering Himself on the Cross for all mankind was the sacrifice of the New Law. Every day in the Sacrifice of the Mass He renews that sacrifice.

The Mass is the same sacrifice as the Sacrifice of the Cross, because Jesus Christ is the innocent victim and at the same time He is the principal priest, offering Himself to God for men. The difference between the Sacrifice of the Mass and the Sacrifice of the Cross is that the Sacrifice of the Mass is not a bloody sacrifice. Christ does not physically shed His blood as He did on the Cross. On Calvary He shed His blood for men, and in the Mass He renews that sacrifice in an unbloody manner.

The first Mass was said by Jesus Christ at the Last Supper the evening before His death. At the Last Supper He spoke the words of consecration that made ordinary bread into His body and ordinary wine into His blood. He gave His own body and blood to His Apostles in Holy Communion.

The word *mass* comes from the Latin word *missa* meaning dismissal. When the Church was first established, the catechumens, who were not as yet members of the Church, left at the end of the Gospel and sermon, but those who were baptized remained until the sacrifice was completed. At the end of the sacrifice, *Ite Missa Est* (Go, it is the dismissal) was said. Perhaps the early Christians thought that *missa* was the name of the sacrifice. We still have the *Ite Missa Est* in the Mass today. *See* Ite Missa Est.

Mass Book   The book on the Missal stand. The priest reads most of the Mass prayers from this book. *See* Missal.

Mass of the Catechumens, the   The first part of the Mass from the beginning of the Mass to the Offertory. In the early days of Christianity, catechumens were those who were preparing to become Christians, and they were allowed to stay only for the Mass of the Catechumens.

Mass of the Faithful, the   The sacrifice Proper of the Mass from the Offertory to the end. In the early days of Christianity, only the baptized were allowed to stay for the Mass of the Faithful.

Mass of the Presanctified   A eucharistic service without a consecration in which the priest receives in Communion the Host consecrated at a previous Mass. The Mass of the Presanctified was formerly a part of the morning Office of Good Friday. The

Mass of the Presanctified is quite common in the Eastern Church during Lent.

Mass, principal parts of The Offertory, the Consecration, and the Communion are the principal parts of the Mass. In order to fulfill the precept of the Church to be present at Mass on Sundays and holydays of obligation, one must be present at these three principal parts of one Mass.

master of ceremonies One in charge of solemn religious ceremonies. A layman, wearing cassock and surplice, may be the master of ceremony. When a bishop officiates at a solemn ceremony, he has two masters of ceremonies, both of whom are usually priests.

master (or mistress) of novices Religious appointed by the superior of a monastery or convent to take care of the training of the novices.

Matins The longest hour of the Divine Office. *See* **canonical hours.**

Matrimony, the Sacrament of The sacrament by which a baptized man and a bapitzed woman bind themselves for life in a lawful marriage and receive the grace to discharge their duties. The man and woman administer the sacrament to one another, but a priest must be the official witness of the ceremony.

Matthew (the Gospel of St.) The first Gospel of the New Testament of the Bible. Its author, St. Matthew, was one of the twelve Apostles. He wrote in Aramaic, similar to the Hebrew language, and his Gospel is the only Gospel not originally written in Greek. However, it was soon translated into Greek. St. Matthew wrote for Jewish Christian converts, and he shows Jesus Christ as the long-awaited Messias.

Maundy Thursday Another name for Holy Thursday, Thursday in Holy Week. The word *maundy* comes from the Latin word *mandatum* which is the first word of the ceremony of the Washing of the Feet. *See* **Washing of the Feet, the.**

May devotions Devotions in honor of Our Lady during the month of May.

medal A piece of metal with a religious image such as Our Lord, Our Lady, or one of the saints on it. A medal is a sacramental. *See* **sacramentals.**

mediator One who comes between two persons to bring peace between them. Christ is the only mediator between God and man, because He came into the world to bring peace between God and man. He came to win back for man the right to Heaven which Adam had lost. The Blessed Virgin and the saints are also sometimes called mediators, because they will intercede for those who pray to them. *See* **Mediatrix of All Graces.**

Mediatrix of All Graces   A name for Our Lady, who through her intercession helps to dispense the graces which come from the Holy Ghost through the merits of Jesus Christ. The Feast of Our Lady, Mediatrix of All Graces, is May 31. *See* **Queenship of Mary.**

meditation   Mental prayer in which one's thoughts are directed to a certain subject in order to increase one's love of God. Meditation makes use of memory, understanding, and will. A person meditating on a mystery of the Rosary recalls the mystery through memory, considers the mystery through understanding, and keeps his attention by means of will.

Melchisedech   The King of Salem and a priest at the time of Abram (Abraham). He offered bread and wine as the sacrifice of the Old Law. *Genesis XIV 18.* Melchisedech is mentioned in the Mass when the priest recalls the sacrifices of the Old Testament.

Memento for the Dead, for the Living   *See Commemoration* and *diptychs.*

Memorial Mass   Requiem Mass for the repose of the soul of a dead person, said on a particular day.

Memorare, the   A prayer to Our Lady named after its first word in Latin, *memorare* (*remember*). It is generally considered to have been composed by St. Bernard:

Remember, O most gracious Virgin Mary, that never was it known that anyone who fled to thy protection, implored thy help, and sought thy intercession, was left unaided. Inspired with this confidence, I fly to Thee, O Virgin of virgins, my Mother. To Thee I come: before thee I stand, sinful and sorrowful. O Mother of the Word Incarnate, despise not my petitions, but graciously hear and answer me.

mendicant orders   Religious orders that originally lived by begging since their rule did not permit them to own property even in common. The Dominicans, Franciscans, Carmelites, and Augustinians were the first mendicant orders, but since then certain other orders have taken the name. All of these orders do not actually live by begging, but the friars (brothers or members of these orders) stress Christian poverty in their rule.

mensa The latin word for *table* is the name given to the top of a fixed altar or the portable altar stone in a movable altar. When the portable altar stone has been placed in an unconsecrated alter, the whole top is also referred to as *mensa*. *See* **altar** and **altar stone.** The mensa is supported by stipes. *See* **stipes.**

mercy, the works of Works of Christian charity performed for the good of one's neighbor's soul and body. The spiritual works of mercy are for the good of his soul, and the corporal works of mercy are for the good of his body. There are seven chief spiritual and seven chief corporal works of mercy.

The seven chief spiritual works of mercy are: (1) to admonish the sinner; (2) to instruct the ignorant; (3) to counsel the doubtful; (4) to comfort the sorrowful; (5) to bear wrongs patiently; (6) to forgive all injuries; and (7) to pray for the living and the dead.

The seven chief corporal works of mercy are: (1) to feed the hungry; (2) to give drink to the thirsty; (3) to clothe the naked; (4) to visit the imprisoned; (5) to shelter the homeless; (6) to visit the sick; and (7) to bury the dead.

merit, supernatural The right to a reward for good work done freely for the love of God. *See* **treasury of merits.**

Messias (Messiah) Word meaning in Hebrew *the anointed one.* The expected Redeemer (Jesus Christ) was spoken of by the Israelites as the Messias. *See* **Christ.**

Michaelmas English name for the Feast of St. Michael, September 29. It is also used in English schools and universities to designate the fall term (Michaelmas term).

Micheas The book of the Old Testament of the Bible concerning the prophecy of Micheas. Micheas was a minor prophet active both in Judea and Israel. He promised to the people a Prince of Peace who would be born in Bethlehem.

midnight Mass The first Mass of Christmas Day, said at midnight. A priest may say three Masses on Christmas, each with a different Proper. A midnight Mass is now permitted on Holy Saturday. *See* **Easter Vigil.**

minor orders   The lower ranks of ministers of the Church: the orders of acolyte, exorcist, lector, and porter (or doorkeeper).

miracle   Something brought about in nature by God and not according to the usual course of nature. God is the principal cause of a miracle. Jesus Christ worked many miracles during His public life, and He promised that miracles would continue in His Church. Catholics are bound to accept this as a matter of faith. However, the worth of each miracle must be settled by evidence; that is, something that appears to be a miracle must be proved to be a real miracle before it is accepted by the Church.

miracles of Jesus Christ, the   The miracles performed by Jesus Christ when He was on earth. The Gospels record about thirty-eight miracles. Jesus Christ performed them by His own power because He is God. In this way the miracles of Christ differ from the miracles of the angels or saints. The miracles of the angels or saints are done not by their own power but by the power of God. God is only using the saint as His instrument when a miracle is performed through a saint. Jesus Christ raised the dead, healed the sick, and drove the devil out of those who were possessed. He also worked a number of nature miracles, such as changing water into wine at the marriage of Cana and the miracle of the loaves and the fishes. See *John XI 1–44* (Jesus Christ raises Lazarus from the dead); *Matthew IX 18–25* (He heals the daughter of Jairus); *Mark I 30–31* (He cures Peter's mother-in-law); *Luke V 18–25* (He heals at Capharnaum a paralyzed man who had been lowered through the roof on his pallet); *Matthew VIII 28–32* (He drives the devils out of two possessed men into a herd of swine); *John II 1–11* (He changes water into wine at the marriage feast at Cana); *Matthew XIV 15–21* (He feeds over five thousand people with five loaves of bread and two fishes).

Miraculous Medal, the   A medal, oval in shape, with an image of Our Lady on one side and on the other the initial M, a cross, and an emblem of the hearts of Jesus and His mother. Our Lady is shown standing on a globe with rays of light coming from her hands. The words, "O Mary conceived without sin" surround her image. The design for this medal is said to have been revealed by Our Lady to St. Catherine Labouré, a Sister of Charity of St. Vincent de Paul, in 1832. The Miraculous Medal is the badge of the Children of Mary.

Missa cantata *See* **Sung Mass.**

Missal The book from which the priest reads the prayers of the Mass. In the Missal is a calendar of the Church year, the Proper of the Seasons and of the Saints, the Common of the Saints, Votive Masses, Masses for the Dead, the Ordinary of the Mass, and the Canon and the prayers to be said by the priest before and after Mass.

Missal stand A stand on the altar for holding the Missal.

Missale Romanum The official Mass book for the Roman Rite.

Mission, a A territory not organized as a diocese under a bishop. A mission is cared for by a priest appointed by the Congregation for the Propagation of the Faith. *See* **Congregations, Sacred.**

missions, foreign Missions to the heathen and Mohammedans. The Congregation for the Propagation of the Faith is in charge of foreign missions. Secular clergy are supplied by special schools for mission work. Many religious orders also do some foreign missionary work. The object of the foreign missions is to convert the heathen to the faith of Jesus Christ.

Missions, popular Series of special religious services conducted by missionary priests visiting a parish. A Mission usually lasts a number of days and consists of sermons, instructions, and religious exercises. The time of the Mission is often divided into a number of day for men, a number for women, and a special mission for children. The purpose of a mission is to instruct the faithful, to revive religious fervor, and to convert sinners. The Mission usually ends with a renewal of baptismal vows.

Mitre Tall pointed hat worn by bishops, cardinals, abbots, etc., at Church services.

mixed marriage, a A marriage between a Catholic and a non-Catholic. *See* **marriage, laws of.**

monastery The place where monks live. The word *monastery* is sometimes applied to a convent, just as the word convent is sometimes applied to a monastery.

monasticism The word *monasticism* comes from the Greek and means *a life lived in solitude.* The first *monastics* or *monks* were hermits. Christian monasticism began in Egypt in the third century, and St. Anthony of the Desert was its most successful founder. Under the influence of St. Pachomius, in the fourth century, and St. Benedict of Nursia, in the sixth century, monasticism became established in the Western world as a community life of divine service under a common religious rule.

monk A member of a religious community of men who take solemn vows of poverty, chastity, and obedience, and live according to a religious rule in a monastery separated from the world. St. Anthony of the Desert is the patron saint of monks.

Monsignor Title of honor given to certain priests on whom the Pope has bestowed an office which gives him a right to this title.

Monstrance A large vessel in which the Host is exposed through a glass-covered opening in the center. The Monstrance is used at Benediction and Exposition of the Blessed Sacrament and is carried in procession on such feasts as the Feast of Corpus Christi. *Ostensorium* is another name for *Monstrance*.

Month's Mind Mass Requiem Mass said on the 30th day (a month) after a death or burial, or at monthly intervals thereafter.

morning offering A prayer which is said the first thing in the morning and in which God is offered the works, prayers, and sufferings of the day. There are various forms of morning offering, but here is one that includes a good many things:

> O my God, I offer Thee all my prayers, works, and sufferings in union with the Sacred Heart of Jesus, for the intentions for which He pleads and offers Himself in the Holy Sacrifice of the Mass, in thanksgiving for Thy favors, in reparation for my offenses, and in humble supplication for my temporal and eternal welfare, for the wants of our holy Mother the Church, for the conversion of sinners, and for the relief of the poor souls in Purgatory. I wish to gain all the indulgences attached to the prayers I shall say and to the good works I shall perform this day.

mortification The performance of acts of self-discipline to strengthen the will.

Moses A prophet of the Old Testament. At the command of God, Moses led the Israelites out of Egypt towards the Promised Land.

God showed them the way by means of a column of cloud in the day and a column of fire at night. Moses was the leader of the Israelites during the years they stayed in the desert. Moses did not lead the Israelites into the Promised Land, although the Lord let him see it from Mount Nebo.

God gave to Moses the Covenant of the Old Law on Mount Sinai. He gave Moses two tablets of stone, on which were written the ten commandments, and told him how the Israelites were to worship God. Moses is often spoken of as a type or symbol of Jesus Christ. *See* **type.** He gave the Old Law to the Jews while Jesus Christ gave the world the New Law. Moses confirmed the Old Law with the blood of animals, while Jesus Christ confirmed the New Law with His own blood.

Moses is the author of the first five books of the Old Testament: *Genesis, Exodus, Leviticus, Numbers, and Deuteronomy.*

mother church The cathedral or principal church of a diocese.

mother-house The chief convent of a congregation of nuns. Other convents look to the mother-house for guidance. The mother general of the congregation usually lives in the mother-house.

Mother of God The Blessed Virgin Mary, the mother of Jesus Christ. She is the mother of the Second Person of the Blessed Trinity.

music, liturgical Music suitable for use in the official and public worship of the Church. Gregorian chant is the official music used in the ritual of the Roman Catholic Church. It is called "Gregorian" because it is believed to have been perfected by St. Gregory the Great. Church music, however, does not belong to any one age or come from any one country. It began as far back as the first century and came from Hebrew, Syrian, Roman, and Gallic sources. Other music besides Gregorian chant is allowed in the ritual under certain circumstances. The Church attempts to protect sacred music against anything that might lessen its dignity.

mysteries of the Rosary The fifteen mysteries of the Rosary—five Joyful, five Sorrowful, and five Glorious, which are the subjects of meditation in the recitation of the Rosary. *See* **Glorious, Joyful,** and **Sorrowful Mysteries.**

mystery of faith A truth which cannot be fully understood but which is believed on the word of God.

mystic A person whose life is exclusively directed to an interior union with the Divine Being. The word *mystic* comes from the Greek and means *one who has been initiated into religious mysteries*. Christian mystics, such as St. Bernard of Clairvaux, St. Teresa of Avila, and St. Thérèse of Lisieux, followed and taught ways of spiritual perfection leading to greater and more intimate union with God.

Mystical Body of Christ, the A spiritual body in which the members of the Church are united by supernatural bonds with Christ as their head. Christ is the head of the Church because the supernatural life of grace flows from Him. The faithful on earth are members of this spiritual body through this supernatural life of grace (sanctifying grace) which is received in Baptism. Through the mystical body of Christ they are united not only with Him but with one another in Him.

mysticism The way of life, the practice, and the teaching of the mystics. *See* **mystic.**

N

Nahum The book of the Old Testament of the Bible concerning the prophecy of Nahum. Nahum, a minor prophet, foretold the destruction of Ninive, capital of Assyria.

Name day The feast of the saint whose name one bears. In religious orders this feast is celebrated rather than the real birthday of the religious. A nun's feast day will be the feast day of the saint whose name she has taken in religious life. In certain European countries, people not in religious life celebrate their saints' feast days rather than their own birthdays. Sometimes they celebrate both.

Nativity, the Feast of the Christmas, the birthday of Jesus Christ, kept on December 25. *See* **Christmas.**

Nativity, Feasts of the The three birthdays kept by the Church: that of Our Lord, December 25; of Our Lady, September 8; and of St. John the Baptist, June 24.

Nativity of Our Lady, the The feast of Our Lady's birthday, kept on September 8.

nave That part of the church in which the people assist at Mass. The nave extends from the main door to the Communion railing.

Nazarene (1) One who lives in Nazareth. The name Nazarene is sometimes given to Jesus Christ because He lived in Nazareth. (2) A member of an early Christian group who continued to observe the Mosaic Law.

Nazareth A town in Galilee, the home of Mary and Joseph. The Annunciation, the announcement of the Angel Gabriel to Our Lady that she was to become the mother of God, took place at Nazareth. Jesus was born in Bethlehem but, after the flight into Egypt, Mary and Joseph brought Him back to Nazareth where He lived for the first thirty years of His life.

Nabuchodonosor King of Babylon who besieged Jerusalem and carried away many of the most talented of the Israelites and some of the sacred vessels from the Temple.

Nehemias A book of the Old Testament of the Bible, sometimes called the Second Book of Esdras.

neighbor, our Everyone else in the world. In the second great commandment of God, He said: "Thou shalt love thy neighbor as thyself." By this He meant that every human being should love with the love of charity everyone else in the world, no matter of what race, creed, or color, and that everyone should love his enemies as well as his friends. Jesus Christ Himself answered the question, "Who is my neighbor?" for a certain lawyer who was trying to test him.

> "A certain man was going down from Jerusalem to Jericho, and he fell in with robbers, who after both stripping him and beating him went their way, leaving him half dead. But, as it happened, a certain priest was going down the same way; and when he saw him, he passed by. And likewise a Levite also, when he was near the place and saw him, passed by. But a certain Samaritan as he journeyed came upon him and, seeing him, was moved with compassion. And he went up to him and bound up his wounds, pouring on oil and wine. And setting him on his own beast, he brought him to an inn and took care of him. And the next day he took out two denarii and gave them to the innkeeper and said, 'Take care of him; and whatever more thou spendest, I, on my way back, will repay thee.'
>
> "Which of these three, in thy opinion, proved himself neighbor to him who fell among the robbers?" And he said, "He who took pity on him." And Jesus said to him, "Go and do thou also in like manner." *Luke X 30–37.*

neophyte Name given to a newly baptized member of the early Church.

Nestorianism The heresy of Nestorius. In the fifth century, Nestorius, Bishop of Constantinople, held that there were two persons as well as two natures in Jesus Christ. He said that the Blessed Virgin Mary was the mother of Jesus Christ but not the mother of God.

New Law, the *See* Covenant.

New Testament, the   The second part of the Bible, the twenty-seven books written since the Incarnation of Our Lord. The New Testament is divided into Gospels, Epistles, Acts, and the Apocalypse. The four Gospels were written by Sts. Matthew, Mark, Luke, and John. The Acts of the Apostles were written by St. Luke. The Epistles were written by Sts. Peter, Paul, John, and Jude. The Apocalypse was written by St. John.

Nicene Creed   A confession of faith, said at Mass on all Sundays, feasts of the first class, feasts of Our Lord, of Our Lady, of the Apostles, of Evangelists, of Doctors of the Church, and in Solemn Votive Masses. See *Credo*. It was compiled in the year 325 at the Council of Nice (City of Nicaea in Asia Minor) from which it takes its name; there have been some slight additions since then.

> I believe in one God, the Father almighty, maker of heaven and earth, and of all things visible and invisible. And in one Lord Jesus Christ, the only-begotten Son of God. Born of the Father before all ages. God of God, light of light, true God of true God. Begotten, not made; being of one substance with the Father; by whom all things were made. Who for us men, and for our salvation, came down from heaven. *And was incarnate by the Holy Ghost of the Virgin Mary: and was made man.* He was crucified also for us, suffered under Pontius Pilate, and was buried. And the third day He rose again according to the Scriptures. And ascended into heaven. He sitteth at the right hand of the Father. And He shall come again with glory to judge both the living and the dead; of whose kindgdom there shall be no end. And I believe in the Holy Ghost, the Lord and giver of life; Who proceedeth from the Father and the Son. Who together with the Father and the Son is adored and glorified. Who spake by the Prophets. And in one holy, catholic, and apostolic Church. I confess one Baptism for the remission of sins. And I look for the resurrection of the dead. And the life of the world to come. Amen.

The priest genuflets at the words: "And was incarnate by the Holy Ghost of the Virgin Mary: and was made man." The people genuflect with him.

Nicodemus A member of the Jewish Council who was interested in Christianity. When he asked Jesus what he must do to be saved, Jesus told him that he must be born again of water and the Holy Ghost. Later Nicodemus, along with Joseph of Arimathea, claimed the body of Jesus for burial.

Nihil Obstat Latin words meaning *nothing hinders,* that is, nothing hinders a book from being printed. The *Nihil Obstat* granted by the censor states that the book contains nothing in it that is against faith and morals. The granting of the Nihil Obstat does not mean that those who have granted it agree with the contents or opinions expressed.

Noah See *Noe.*

Noe Early Biblical patriarch who, at the command of God, built an ark for the safety of himself and his family during the Great Flood which covered the earth. *See* ark, Noe's.

Nobis quoque peccatoribus Latin words meaning *and also to us sinners.* This prayer, said towards the end of the Canon of the Mass, follows the Memento for the Dead. The priest and the people ask God for fellowship with the saints, a number of whom are mentioned by name. In this way the Church Militant (the faithful on earth) and the Church Triumphant (the saints) are remembered along with the souls in Purgatory (Memento for the Dead). The first words of the prayer, *Nobis quoque peccatoribus,* are the only words spoken aloud during the Canon of the Mass.

None The hour of the Divine Office said at the ninth hour. It takes its name from the Latin word *nonus* (*ninth*). *See* canonical hours.

North American Martyrs, the Sts. Isaac Jogues, Jean de Lalande, René Goupil, John Brébeuf, Anthony Daniel, Gabriel Lalemant, Charles Garnier, and Noel Chabanel, all of whom were martyred by the Indians between 1642 and 1649. All were Frenchmen by birth and worked for the conversion of the Indians. The first three were martyred in territory which is now the United States, and the other five were martyred in Canada. The feast day of the North American Martyrs is September 26.

novena The practice of devoting nine successive days to a special prayer or devotion. The word *novena* comes from the Latin word *novenus* meaning ninth. Public novenas are often held in a church before some particular feast day. For example, a novena to St. Thérèse (The Little Flower) might be held beginning September 25 and ending on her feast day, October 3. Novenas before Pentecost are common in parish churches. The novena to the Holy Ghost for the Feast of Pentecost was the first of all novenas. Private novenas may be made at any time.

novice   One received into a religious order for a period of probation before taking vows. Before becoming a novice he (or she) is usually a postulant. *See* **postulant.** The postulant becomes a novice by being clothed with the habit of the order.

novitiate   (1) The period during which a religious is a novice. (2) The separate house or part of a house in which novices live.

Numbers   The book of the Old Testament of the Bible continuing the story told in *Exodus* and *Leviticus* of the Israelites on their way to the Promised Land. The book is called *Numbers* from two censuses taken of the Hebrew people. The book of *Numbers* was written by Moses.

nun   A woman who is a member of a religious congregation or order. According to Canon Law, a *nun* is one belonging to an institute whose members take solemn vows, and a *sister* is one belonging to an institute in which only simple vows are taken. However, in common speech the word *nun* or *sister* is used for either. There are contemplative and active orders of nuns. Contemplative orders spend their time mainly in prayer and contemplation. Active orders engage in teaching, care of the sick, bringing up of orphans, and other charitable work. Nuns take vows of poverty, chastity, and obedience.

Nunc dimittis   The canticle (song) of Simeon when he took the Child Jesus into his arms on the day of the Presentation in the Temple. The first two words of the canticle *Nunc dimittis* are Latin for *Now you dismiss.* Simeon had been promised by the Holy Ghost that he would not die until he had seen Christ the Lord. Joyfully he cried, "Now you dismiss your servant, O Lord, according to your word, in peace, Because my eyes have seen your salvation which you have provided in the sight of all the peoples: A light of revelation for the Gentiles, and the glory of your people Israel." *Luke II 29-31.*

nuncio Title given to an ambassador of the Pope, representing the Holy See at a foreign government. An internuncio is a papal ambassador of lower rank.

Nuptial Blessing Blessing which the priest gives the bride and groom at the Nuptial Mass. The blessing is given from the Epistle side of the altar after the *Our Father*. The Nuptial Blessing is never given during Lent or Advent or if either of the parties is not a Catholic.

Nuptial Mass Mass offered for the bride and groom at their wedding.

O

O salutaris hostia *O Saving Victim.* The opening words of a Latin hymn sung at Benediction of the Blessed Sacrament. This hymn is the last two verses of the longer hymn, *Verbum supernum* written by St. Thomas Aquinas and sung at Lauds on the Feast of Corpus Christi.

oath An appeal to God to witness the truth of what is said. An oath is lawful if one has a good reason for taking it, sincerely believes that what he says is true, and does not take an oath to do what is wrong.

obedience One of the moral virtues. Obedience is that habit which helps one to do the will of his superiors, that is, those who have the right to command him.

obedience, vow of *See* **vows, religious.**

Oblates (1) Members of certain religious congregations who offer themselves to the bishop for whatever work he wants them to do (Oblates of St. Charles, Oblates of Mary Immaculate). (2) Lay persons who are associated with a particular Benedictine monastery and share in the good works.

oblation The act of offering a victim to God.

obligation The duty, imposed by the laws of God, of doing good and avoiding evil.

obligation, day of *See* **holydays of obligation.**

occasions of sin Any persons, places, or things that may easily lead a person into sin.

occurrence of feasts The happening of two feasts on the same day. Since the Proper of the Season and the Proper of the Saints move forward at the same time, each in its own cycle, a feast of the one cycle may fall on the same day as the feast of the other cycle. When this happens, the lesser feast gives place to the greater.

octave The eight-day period during which Christmas, Easter, or Pentecost is celebrated. The eighth day is called the *octave*, and days in between are said to be within the octave.

offering of Holy Communion Offering one's own reception of Holy Communion for the benefit of others. The person receiving Communion really receives the benefit of his Holy Communion, but he can pray for others at this time and so, in a sense, offer his Communion for their welfare.

Offertory That part of the Mass which follows the Gospel or Creed and in which the offering of bread and wine is made by the priest. The priest says the offertory prayer for the Mass of the day. He then removes the veil and pall from the chalice, takes the paten on which the altar bread lies and, holding it up, makes the offering of the bread. He says a prayer which begins, "Accept, O holy Father, almighty eternal God, this spotless Host." The priest lowers the paten and makes the Sign of the Cross. He goes to the Epistle side of the altar where he pours wine into the chalice, adding a few drops of water. The water represents the human nature of Jesus Christ mingling with His Divine nature and also our human nature sharing in the divine life of God. Going to the middle of the altar, the priest offers the chalice with the prayer beginning: "We offer unto Thee, O Lord, the chalice of salvation."

Office, Divine An official daily prayer service consisting of prayers, hymns, readings, and instructions arranged by the Church and found in the Roman Breviary. *See* **Breviary.** All clerics in major orders and all religious who have Office in choir must say the Divine Office daily for the Church and its members. These prayers, hymns, etc., are taken from the Old and the New Testaments of the Bible, from the lives of the saints, and other religious writings. The Divine Office is divided into eight hours, all of which have Latin names. *See* **canonical hours.** On March 23, 1955, the Sacred Congregation of Rite issued a decree simplifying the rules governing the recitation of the Divine Office.

oils, holy Oil of catechumens, oil of the sick, and chrism. These are blessed by the bishop on Holy Thursday at the Mass of the Chrism. The oil of the sick is the first to be blessed, just before the Pater Noster of the Mass. The bishop blesses the sacred chrism and the oil of catechumens after the ablutions. Oil of catechumens is olive oil, while chrism is olive oil with which balsam has been mixed.

Oil is used for anointing, that is, putting oil on persons or things in a church ceremony. This was a custom in the Church from early times. Oil is used in the sacraments of Baptism, Confirmation, Holy Orders, and Extreme Unction. In Baptism both the oil of catechumens and chrism are used. The priest anoints the head and shoulders of the child with a blessed oil called the oil of catechumens. Later the priest anoints him with chrism. Chrism is also used in Confirmation, in the consecration of a bishop, in the consecration of churches, altars, chalices, and in the blessing of bells. Oil of catechumens, besides being used in Baptism, is used at the ordination of priests, and with holy chrism is used for the blessing of the baptismal font and the consecration of altars. Oil of the sick is used in the Sacrament of Extreme Unction and in the blessing of church bells.

Old Testament The first part of the Bible, the books written before the coming of Jesus Christ. These books tell the history of the Jewish people before the coming of Christ. There are forty-five books in the Old Testament. Some texts give forty-six books, but the content is the same. Twenty-one books of the Old Testament are historical, seventeen are prophetical, and seven are didactic (intended for instruction).

omission (sin of) A sin in which an obligation due to God is neglected. Missing Mass on Sunday or a holyday of obligation is a sin of omission.

omnipotence of God God's power to do all things. He can do anything that is not opposed to His perfection.

omnipresence of God God's presence everywhere. God is everywhere in the sense that all things are under His dominion, nothing is hidden from Him, and He is in all things because He is the cause of their being.

omniscience of God God's knowledge of all things.

Orate Fratres Latin words meaning, *Pray, brethren.* They are the first words of a Latin prayer said by the priest just before the Preface at Mass. This prayer is part of the Offertory of the Mass. The priest faces the people and says: "Pray, brethren, that my and your sacrifice may be acceptable to God the Father almighty." The server answers: "May the Lord accept this sacrifice from your hands, to our own benefit also as well as for the good of His entire Holy Church." In the Orate Fratres the priest invites the people to join with him in prayer so that the sacrifice may be pleasing to God.

oratory A chapel which is public, semi-public, or private, but which is not intended for the general public. *See* **chapel.**

Order of Preacheresses *See* **religious orders and congregations of women.**

order, religious A religious community, bound by a common rule and in which solemn vows are taken. The difference between a religious order and a religious congregation is that in a religious order the vows taken are solemn, while in a religious congregation the vows are simple. *See* **religious orders and congregations of men, women, and vows, religious.**

Ordinal of Holy Week A book printed at the Vatican, giving the new order for Holy Week. This Ordinal replaces the Missal for Holy Week.

ordinary Name given to a diocesan bishop.

Ordinary (of the Mass) Those parts of the Mass which do not change. Certain prayers of the Mass are almost always the same, while other prayers, which make up the Proper of the Mass, change according to the seasons and particular feasts. Some of the prayers which belong to the Ordinary of the Mass and do not change are the Kyrie Eleison, Gloria, Credo, Offertory prayers, Sanctus, Canon, Pater Noster, Agnus Dei and Last Gospel. The Ordinary of the Mass is sometimes called the Common of the Mass.

Ordination The ceremony in which the Sacrament of Holy Orders is conferred. Ordination always takes place at a Mass, usually in an important church of the diocese. Holy Orders are conferred on a priest by the bishop through the imposition of hands, a symbol of giving grace and power. *See* **imposition of hands.** The imposition of hands takes place three times during the Ordination of a priest.

The bestowal on the one receiving Holy Orders of the symbol of his office is also a part of the ceremony. The bishop invests each deacon with a chasuble, and, after anointing the hands of those being ordained with oil of catechumens, he gives each a chalice and paten.

At the last laying on of hands, the bishop says the words which Our Lord said to His Apostles after His Resurrection: "Receive the Holy Ghost. Whose sins you shall forgive, they are forgiven them; and whose sins you shall retain, they are retained." *John XX 22, 23.*

Ordo A book giving directions for the recitation of the Divine Office and the celebration of Mass according to the calendar of the year. It is published annually and every diocese, religious order, and congregation has its own particular directions either in an edition of its own or in a supplement to the regular edition.

Oremus Latin word meaning *let us pray.* It is an invitation to pray used in the Mass before Collects, Postcommunions, and other prayers.

original sin A state of sin which came down to man through his origin or descent from Adam. It is a lack of sanctifying grace due to the sin of Adam. Adam, in losing sanctifying grace for himself, lost it for the whole human race.

Osee The book of the Old Testament of the Bible concerning the prophecy of Osee, one of the minor prophets.

Ostensorium *See* Monstrance.

Our Father, the *See* Lord's Prayer, the.

Our Lady A name given to the Blessed Virgin Mary. Many of her titles begin with Our Lady: Our Lady of Sorrows, Our Lady of Ransom, Our Lady of Lourdes, etc.

Our Lord Our Lord Jesus Christ.

outward sign The matter of the sacraments. *See* sacraments, the.

P

pagan   One who is not a Christian, Jew, or Mohammedan. *See* heathen, the.

Palestine   Country on the Mediterranean Sea. This was the land which God gave to His chosen people and which Jesus Christ made holy through His life, sufferings, death, and Resurrection.

pall   Square of cardboard, covered with linen. It is placed on top of the chalice during many parts of the Mass.

pallium   Band of white wool marked with black crosses and worn over the chasuble. The Pope wears the pallium, and he sends it to other high ecclesiastics, such as archbishops, as a symbol of full episcopal power. The pallium is the special insignia of an archbishop. *See* **Appendix, Saint Agnes, January 21.**

Palm Sunday   The second Sunday of Passiontide, the Sunday before Easter. Palm Sunday is in memory of Our Lord's triumphant entry into Jerusalem. Riding upon an ass, Jesus entered Jerusalem while the people strewed the road with branches and cried out: "Hosanna to the Son of David! Blessed is he who comes in the name of the Lord! Hosanna in the highest." *Matthew XXI* 9.

In the new Holy Week order, the ritual for Palm Sunday has been simplified. The rite of the blessing of the palms, which takes place before the principal Mass, has been shortened. The faithful who already have palms hold the palms in their hands during the blessing, though they do not hold them during the Passion read at the Mass as formerly required. The newly blessed palms are distributed to those who do not have them, immediately before the procession. The Gospel story of Jesus Christ's triumphal entry into Jerusalem is read. The procession of the palms follows and, where it is possible, the congregation is invited to join the procession. In this way, the people are taking an active part in the ceremony. Antiphons are sung during the procession, as well as the Hymn to Christ the King which the people join in singing. The Mass of Palm Sunday follows the procession.

Vestments worn for the blessing of the palms and the procession are red, but violet vestments are put on before the beginning of Mass.

papal flag The flag of Vatican City. It is half yellow and half white with the Pope's tiara (triple crown) sewn upon it. The keys crossed below the crown are the sign of authority.

papal knight A person whom the Pope has honored with one of the six orders of knighthood.

parable Short story told to illustrate some religious truth. Over thirty parables are recorded in the Gospels. Our Lord told these parables to His Apostles while He was teaching them. The seven parables of the Kingdom of God are: the Parable of the Sower (*Matthew XIII 3–9*); the Parable of the Cockle, sometimes called the Parable of the Weeds (*Matthew XIII 24–30*); the Parable of the Mustard Seed (*Matthew XIII 31–32*); the Parable of the Leaven (*Matthew XIII 33*); the Parable of the Treasure (*Matthew XIII 44*); the Parable of the Pearl (*Matthew XIII 45–46*); and the Parable of the Good and Bad Fishes (*Matthew XIII 47–50*). Other very well known parables told by Our Lord are: the Parable of the Good Samaritan (*Luke X 30–37*); the Parable of the Lost Sheep (*Luke XV 3–7*); the Parable of the Prodigal Son (*Luke XV 11–32*); the Parable of the Unjust Steward (*Luke XVI 1–8*); the Parable of the Ten Foolish Virgins (*Matthew XXV 1–13*); the Parable of the Talents (*Luke XIX 12–27*); and the Parable of the Rich Man and Lazarus (*Luke XVI 19–31*).

Paraclete Name given to the Holy Ghost, the Third Person of the Blessed Trinity. The word *paraclete* means *comforter* and is used in St. John's Gospel.

Paradise (1) Another name for Heaven. (2) Another name for the Garden of Eden. *See* **Heaven** and **Eden, Garden of.**

Paralipomenon I, II Books of the Old Testament of the Bible telling the religious history of the Hebrew people from Saul to the Babylonian Exile. The first nine chapters deal with an account of the genealogy (record of the family tree) from Adam to Saul. In Protestant versions of the Bible these books are called Chronicles.

parents, duties of Obligations of parents toward their children.

Parents must provide for the spiritual and bodily welfare of their children. They must love them, care for their health, keep them from occasions of sin, and give them a Christian education.

parish   Division in a diocese with a priest, assigned by the bishop, at its head as pastor. Within this division the priest has the right to govern the faithful in spiritual affairs and to administer the sacraments.

parish church   A particular church in the parish in which the pastor says Mass and administers the sacraments. Baptisms, marriages, and funeral services should take place in the parish church.

parish priest   The pastor of a parish church or his assistants.

parochial   Relating to a parish.

Parochial Mass   The principal Mass said on Sundays and holydays in the parish church.

particle   The small, consecrated Host which is received by the faithful in Holy Communion.

Pasch   Once the Jewish feast of the Passover, now the Christian feast of Easter. *See* **Passover.** Jesus and His Apostles were observing the Passover on the Thursday before His death. This Thursday, now known as Holy Thursday, was the day of the Last Supper and the day on which Jesus Christ said the first Mass. The law of Moses said that a Paschal lamb must be sacrificed during the Pasch. Jesus Christ was the true Paschal Lamb, put to death on Good Friday.

Paschal Candle   The Easter Candle. A large candle blessed on Holy Saturday and placed in a special candlestick on the Gospel side of the altar until Ascension Day. The Paschal Candle is a symbol of Christ who rose from the dead and remained on earth for forty days after His Resurrection. After the Blessing of the New Fire, the Paschal Candle is brought to the celebrant by one of the servers. The celebrant cuts a cross on the candle. Then he cuts the letters Alpha and Omega at the top and the bottom of the candle. *See* **Alpha and Omega.** The celebrant cuts the four numbers of the current year on the candle, from the upper left hand angle of the cross to the lower right hand angle of the cross. He then inserts five grains of incense in the candle. These represent the five wounds received by Jesus Christ on the Cross.

The Paschal Candle is lighted from the new fire. *See* **Fire, the Blessing of.**

Paschal Proclamation A hymn of praise in honor of the risen Christ. It is sung on the Vigil of Easter (Holy Saturday) after the Paschal Candle has been placed on a stand. This hymn is called the *Exsultet* from its first word *Exult*. It begins: "Now let the angelic heavenly choirs exult; let joy pervade the unknown beings who surround God's throne; and let the trumpet of salvation sound the triumph of this mighty King."

Paschaltide That season of the ecclesiastical year belonging to the Easter cycle and extending from Holy Saturday to the Saturday after Pentecost. During Paschaltide the Church celebrates three great feasts: Easter (the Resurrection), the Ascension, and Pentecost.

Passion of Jesus Christ Our Lord's suffering and death through which He redeemed mankind. On Good Friday Jesus Christ died on the Cross for the sins of men. The Passion of Our Lord as told in the Gospels is read at Mass on Palm Sunday, and on Tuesday, Wednesday, and Friday of Holy Week. The Gospel read on Palm Sunday is *St. Matthew XXVI, 36–75* and *XXVII, 1–54.* A shorter Gospel, taken from the same chapters, may be read by a priest who says a second or third Low Mass on Palm Sunday.

Passion Play The Passion of Our Lord acted out in drama. The most famous passion play is the one at Oberammergau, a village in southern Germany.

Passion Sunday The first Sunday of Passiontide, the Sunday before Palm Sunday. Passion Sunday begins the last period of the Easter cycle. On Passion Sunday the images in the church are covered with veils.

Passiontide The last two weeks of Lent, between Passion Sunday and Holy Saturday. The Church puts on mourning and thinks of the sufferings of Jesus Christ.

Passover, the Jewish feast in memory of the Lord passing over (sparing) the Israelites and striking down the Egyptians. On the night that the Israelites left Egypt, an angel of God struck down the first born in the house of each Egyptian but passed over the houses of the Hebrews. In return for this deliverance, in each Hebrew house a lamb was to be slain and its blood sprinkled on the doorposts. Later the lamb was to be eaten with unleavened bread.

pastor A priest who is head of a parish. The word *pastor* comes from the Latin word meaning *shepherd*.

pastoral letter A letter addressed by a bishop to the faithful of a diocese. The letter is read at Mass on Sunday.

paten (1) A small plate usually made of gold or silver and consecrated by a bishop. If the paten is made of another metal, it must at least be plated with gold. The paten is used to hold the consecrated Host at Mass. (2) The plate held beneath the chin of a person receiving Communion is called a communion paten.

Pater Noster *See* **Lord's Prayer, the.**

patriarch (1) A bishop holding the highest rank below the Pope. The Pope is sometimes called the Patriarch of Rome. *See* **Eastern Catholic Churches.** (2) Name given to such Biblical men as Abraham, Isaac, and Jacob, who were rulers of a family. Abraham is referred to as *our patriarch* in the Canon of the Mass.

patron saint Saint chosen to be the special advocate for a person, country, diocese, or church, or for a particular occupation in life. One's own patron saint is usually the saint whose name has been given to him in Baptism or whose name he has taken in Confirmation.

Some of the patron saints of countries are: the United States, Our Lady Immaculate; Canada, St. Ann; Mexico, Our Lady of Guadelupe; England, St. George; Ireland, St. Patrick; France, St. Joan of Arc; Italy, St. Francis of Assisi and St. Catherine of Siena; China, St. Francis Xavier.

Some of the patron saints of occupations are: fishermen, St. Andrew; housewives, St. Anne; musicians, St. Cecilia; travelers, St. Christopher; medical doctors, St. Luke; carpenters, St. Joseph; teachers, St. Thomas Aquinas.

Paul, St. The Apostle of the Gentiles and the author of fourteen Epistles in the New Testament. The story of his life is told in the *Acts of the Apostles.* His miraculous conversion on the road to Damascus made him a new creature in Jesus Christ. A special feast of his conversion is celebrated on January 25. His principal feast is shared with St. Peter. *See* **Sts. Peter and Paul, the Feast of.**

Pauline privilege The privilege by which a marriage can be dissolved if one of two unbaptized persons united in a consummated marriage desires to become a baptized Christian and the other refuses to be converted or will not live in peace with the Christian partner. The circumstances in such a case are always carefully examined. The name *Pauline* comes from St. Paul who discusses such a case in *I Corinthians VII 12–16*.

pectoral cross *See* cross, pectoral.

Pelagianism The heresy of Pelagius begun in the fifth century. Pelagius, who denied original sin, claimed that grace was not a supernatural gift of God but a natural gift. St. Augustine wrote against Pelagianism.

penance Prayers or good works required of the penitent by the priest who has heard his confession. This penance satisfies in part for the sins confessed. *See* satisfaction for sin.

Penance, the Sacrament of The sacrament by which sins committed after Baptism are forgiven through the absolution of the priest. To receive the Sacrament of Penance worthily a person must, first, examine his conscience; second, be sorry for his sins; third, have the firm purpose of not sinning again; fourth, confess his sins to the priest; and fifth, perform the penance the priest gives him.

Jesus Christ Himself instituted the Sacrament of Penance on Easter Day. Before His death He had said to Simon to whom He gave the name of Peter: "And I will give thee the keys of the Kingdom of Heaven; and whatever thou shalt bind on earth shall be bound in Heaven, and whatever thou shalt loose on earth shall be loosed in Heaven." *Matthew XVI 19*. When He appeared to His Apostles on the evening of the day of His Resurrection, He breathed on them and said: "Receive the Holy Spirit; whose sins you shall forgive, they are forgiven them; and whose sins you shall retain, they are retained." *John XX 22*. Only a priest or a bishop possessing the proper faculties can give the Sacrament of Penance. *See* faculties.

Pentecost The feast in memory of the coming of the Holy Ghost upon the Apostles. The word *pentecost* in Greek means *fiftieth day*, and the Feast of Pentecost is fifty days after Easter. Like Easter it is a feast of the highest rank, and no other feast may be celebrated during the octave. *See* octave. Vestments are red at

Pentecost because the Holy Ghost is symbolized as tongues of fire. Pentecost is sometimes known as Whitsunday.

per dominum nostrum Jesum Christum Latin words meaning *Through Our Lord, Jesus Christ*. Collects in the Mass frequently end with these words.

perfection The state of being perfect. Only God is infinitely perfect, because He only has all perfections without any limit. *See* **God**. Jesus Christ called all men to perfection. In the Sermon on the Mount, He said to the people, "You therefore are to be perfect, even as your heavenly Father is perfect." *Matthew V 48*. The ideal of Christian perfection consists in loving God and loving one's neighbor. Everyone, no matter what his vocation, is able to seek this ideal of perfection. A special kind of perfection (religious perfection) may be attained by those who leave the world and take the vows of religion.

perpetual adoration Continual adoration of the Blessed Sacrament, night and day, by certain congregations of nuns and priests. The watchers take turns kneeling in adoration before the altar.

persons (in God) *See* **Blessed Trinity.**

Peter I, II, Epistles of St. Two books of the New Testament of the Bible. They are the Epistles of St. Peter the Apostle and are addressed to Christian communities in Asia Minor.

Peter's Pence Money given for the support of the Holy See by Catholics from all over the world. One Sunday a year is appointed as the day for this contribution which is entirely voluntary. The money is sent to the Pope through the bishops. The name *Peter's Pence* comes from a small penny tax during the Middle Ages which was collected in the summer (on St. Peter's Day) and paid to the Holy See.

pew A bench-like seat, usually with a kneeling rack, used by the people in church for sitting and kneeling.

Pharisees, the Jewish religious group of Our Lord's time who observed all the rules of the law without observing its true spirit. The Pharisees were extremely proud, and Our Lord rebuked them several times.

Philemon A book of the New Testament of the Bible. It is the Epistle of St. Paul the Apostle to Philemon, a wealthy Christian.

Philippians A book of the New Testament of the Bible. It is the Epistle of St. Paul the Apostle to the church at Philippi.

philosophy The word *philosophy* comes from the Greek and means *the love of wisdom.* Philosophy is the study of all existing things in order to discover their nature, origin, and purpose. In Catholic thought, philosophy differs from theology because theology depends on revelation, while philosophy develops under the light of reason. *See* **theology.**

Pilate *See* **Pontius Pilate.**

pilgrimage Journey to a holy place as an act of devotion. Sometimes a person makes a pilgrimage to ask for some particular gift or to perform an act of penance. Many pilgrimages are made to the shrine of Our Lady of Lourdes to seek cures of bodily ills.

placeat, the A prayer said at Mass after the *Ite Missa Est* and before the Last Blessing. In this prayer the priest asks that the sacrifice which has been made may be acceptable to God. The Latin word *placeat* means *let it be pleasing.*

plenary indulgence *See* **indulgence.**

polygamy The possession of more than one wife at a time. Polygamy is forbidden by divine law and natural law.

pontiff A bishop. The sovereign or supreme pontiff is the Pope.

Pontifical Mass A solemn Mass offered by a cardinal or bishop. A Papal Mass is a special form of this Mass.

Pontius Pilate Roman governor of Judea at the time of the Crucifixion of Jesus Christ. Pilate was a weak man, and although he believed that Jesus was innocent of the wrongs of which He was accused, he did not dare oppose the people who wanted to crucify Him. He finally delivered Jesus to the people. Hoping to ease his conscience, he took a basin of water and washed his hands in front of the crowd, saying: "I am innocent of the blood of this just man; see to it yourselves." *Matthew XXVII 24.*

Poor Clares *See* **religious orders and congregations of women.**

Poor Souls The souls in Purgatory.

Pope The head of the Catholic Church on earth. He is Bishop of Rome, the successor of St. Peter, and the ruler of all Christians. He is infallible when he speaks concerning a doctrine of faith and morals to be held by all Christians. *See* **infallibility, papal.** The Pope is elected by the College of Cardinals in a solemn conclave. *See* **College of Cardinals and conclave.** Fifteen days are allowed after the death of a Pope to allow the cardinals in other countries to come to Rome. Absolute secrecy is kept concerning the election. Usually election is by all the members of the conclave voting, and one vote more than two-thirds of the number present elects the new Pope. The Pope can be deposed only for heresy, but this has never happened.

porter A member of the clergy in the lowest of the four minor orders. This minor order is also called that of doorkeeper.

Portiuncula (1) The chapel of St. Mary of the Angels which the Benedictines gave to St. Francis of Assisi and which was the first church of the Franciscan Order. (2) The Portiuncula indulgence is a plenary indulgence first attached to the chapel of the Portiuncula. This indulgence may be gained for the dead as often as one visits the chapel from noon of August 1 until midnight of August 2 under the usual conditions for gaining indulgences. This indulgence has been extended for the same date to all Franciscan churches. A similar indulgence (also called Portiuncula indulgence) has been extended to the principal churches of some other orders but for different dates.

Postcommunion The last prayer read on the Epistle side of the altar. It is read from the Missal after the Communion of the Mass and changes every day.

postulant A novice before the clothing ceremony. He or she wears ordinary clothes or a cassock (if a man) and studies under a novice master or mistress. Six months is the ordinary time for one to remain a postulant.

postulator The official at Rome who presents the cause of beatification or canonization of a saint. He must be a priest and reside at Rome.

poverty, vows of *See* **vows, religious.**

power of the keys The ecclesiastical power given by Jesus Christ to St. Peter and his successors. Jesus said to Peter: "And I will give thee the keys of the kingdom of heaven; and whatsoever thou shalt bind on earth shall be bound in heaven; and whatsoever thou shalt loose on earth shall be loosed in heaven." *Matthew XVI 19.* This power includes that of forgiving sins, and the expression "the power of the keys" is often used to refer only to this power to forgive sins.

powers of the priest The chief supernatural powers of the priest are: to change bread and wine into the body and blood of Jesus Christ in the Holy Sacrifice of the Mass, and to forgive sins in the Sacrament of Penance.

Prague, Infant Jesus of Statue brought by a Spanish princess to Bohemia and given to a Carmelite monastery in Prague. The statue of the Infant Jesus of Prague is an image of the Divine Infant wearing a royal mantle and a jeweled crown. This statue is called "The Miraculous Infant Jesus of Prague" because of the many graces and cures that have been received through devotion to the Infant.

Prayer The lifting of one's thoughts to God. Prayer may be either mental or vocal. Mental prayer is speaking to God through thought and meditation, while vocal prayer is an expression of these thoughts in words. Many prayers are the prescribed prayers of the Church, but these need not be the only prayers offered to God. Prayers offered in one's own words are particularly pleasing to God. God wants men to pray to Him. In the Sermon on the Mount He said to His disciples: "Ask and it shall be given you; seek, and you shall find; knock, and it shall be opened to you." *Matthew VII 7*. The Apostles taught the importance of prayer. St. Paul in his first Epistle to the Thessalonians said: "Pray without ceasing." *I Thessalonians V 17*. Without prayer one cannot be close to God.

prayer book A book of prayers for personal use. Such a book usually contains morning and evening prayers, a method of hearing Mass, preparations for Confession, and other devotions.

preaching The instruction of the people by a priest in a sermon.

Preces et Pia Opera *See* **Raccolta.**

Precious Blood, the The blood of Our Lord shed for the sins of men. The blood of Our Lord is received with His body, soul and divinity, in the Sacrament of the Holy Eucharist in the form of bread. The Feast of the Most Precious Blood is July 1.

predella The platform or footpace on which the priest stands before the altar.

Preface of the Mass Prayer of praise and thanksgiving to the

Blessed Trinity said at Mass as an introduction to the Canon, the most solemn part of the Mass. The Common Preface is said at all Masses which have no Proper Preface. There are Proper Prefaces for certain seasons of the year, for certain feast days, and for the Mass for the Dead. The Preface ends with the Sanctus. *See* **Sanctus, the.**

prelate A cleric who has ordinary jurisdiction in the external forum. *See* **forum.** There are some honorary prelates who do not have jurisdiction. The principal prelates are the bishops.

presumption A sin against hope. A person sins by presumption when he believes that he can be saved by his own efforts without any help from God, or by God's help without his own efforts.

Presentation of the Blessed Virgin Mary Presenting of Mary by her parents, Joachim and Anne, to God in the Temple. November 21 is the Feast of the Presentation.

Presentation in the Temple (of our Lord) The presentation of Our Lord by Mary and Joseph to God in the Temple at Jerusalem forty days after His birth. The Presentation in the Temple is the fourth Joyful Mystery of the Rosary. *See* **Candlemas Day.**

pride *See* **capital sins.**

prie-dieu Kneeling bench with a rest above for the prayer book or elbow. *Prie-dieu* is French and means *pray God.*

priest One who has received the sacrament of Holy Orders and may offer the Sacrifice of the Mass. The priesthood is the first of the major orders below the bishop. Besides offering the Sacrifice of the Mass, the priest administers the Sacraments of Baptism, Penance, Holy Communion, and Extreme Unction, and solemnizes marriages. In order to give absolution in the Sacrament of Penance and to solemnize marriages, the priest must have jurisdiction—that is, the power to administer—which is attached to a certain office or delegated to an individual or a group. *See* **faculties.**

primacy (of the Pope) The supreme power of the Pope to teach, sanctify, and rule the Universal Church as the Vicar of Christ on earth.

Prime That part of the Divine Office which is said at the first hour in the morning. *See* **canonical hours.**

Private Mass A Mass offered by a priest privately, as opposed to a Public Mass which is celebrated in a place open to the public. The priest must always have a server at a Private Mass to represent the people.

Prince of the Apostles Name given to St. Peter, chief of the Apostles.

Prince of the Church Name given to a cardinal.

prior One in charge of a monastery, or second in command to the abbot.

prioress The assistant to the abbess of a convent or the one in charge of a convent.

prisoner of the Vatican A name given the popes from the capture of Rome in 1870 until the Treaty of the Lateran in 1929. In protest against the seizure of Rome by the Piedmontese king, for fifty-nine years the reigning popes remained within the Vatican and its gardens. By the Treaty of Lateran in 1929 the Pope received recognition of his sovereign independence.

privileged altar An altar at which a plenary indulgence may be gained for a soul in Purgatory when a Mass is said for the dead. On All Souls' Day all altars are privileged.

procession, divine The word *procession* comes from the Latin word *procedere*, meaning *to go forth*. Divine procession is the way in which the Holy Ghost, the Third Person of the Blessed Trinity, goes forth from the Father and the Son. The Holy Ghost proceeds not from the Father alone but from the Father and the Son.

procurator An official who is appointed to act for another or for a group of persons. The word *procurator* comes from the Latin word *procurare*, meaning *to look after*. A *procurator* of a religious order lives permanently at Rome and looks after the affairs of the Order at the Holy See. A *procurator* in a monastery, convent, or seminary looks after the practical affairs of the house, such as the feeding and the clothing of the members.

profession, religious The promise freely given by which a person of the required age devotes himself or herself to the religious life after completing the novitiate.

profession of faith Declaration of acceptance of religious belief. Profession of faith is usually made by reciting the Creed; a special and longer form is used for converts and for those who are appointed to various offices in the Church, such as that of a religious superior.

Promised Land, the Chanaan, the land promised by God to Abraham. The Israelites had left the Promised Land to go into Egypt, where they lived for many years, but Moses led them back to Chanaan.

promoter of the faith An official of the Sacred Congregation of Rites. *See* **advocate, devil's.**

Proper of the Mass The parts of the Mass which change according to the day or feast. The prayers which belong to the Proper of the Mass are the Introit, the Collects, the Epistle, the Gradual and Alleluia (or the Tract), the Gospel, the Offertory verse, the Secret, the Communion verses, and the Postcommunion prayers.

Proper of the Saints Division of the Missal and Breviary in which are given the Proper for feasts of the saints and of Our Lord and Our Lady. The Proper of the Saints begins on November 29 (about the beginning of Advent).

Proper of the Season Division of the Missal and Breviary in which is given the Proper for the Sundays of the season and other days of the liturgical season. The Proper of the Seasons begins with the first Sunday of Advent.

prophecies, the four Four lessons from the Old Testament read after the Paschal Proclamation on Holy Saturday (the Vigil of Easter). After the second, third, and fourth lessons, a canticle is sung. Formerly twelve lessons or prophecies were read. The original purpose of the prophecies was to instruct those who were to be baptized.

prophecy The gift of foretelling the future.

prophets Messengers of God in the Old Testament who foretold the future. Isaias, Jeremias, Ezechiel, and Daniel are spoken of as the major prophets.

Protestant, a One who belongs to any of the Christian groups which separated from the Catholic Church at the time of the Reformation in the 16th century. The word *protestant* means *one who protests.*

Proverbs The book of the Old Testament of the Bible said to have been written by Solomon and containing the sayings of the wise men of Israel.

Providence *See* **Divine Providence.**

province (1) District over which an archbishop rules, usually made up of several dioceses or his archdiocese with one subordinate diocese. (2) Particular division of a religious order. A province is made up of the religious houses in that district.

provincial Head of a province or district of a religious order. A provincial is responsible to the superior general of the order or congregation.

psalm A song of praise from the *Book of Psalms* of the Old Testament. The Psalms are used in the Divine Office of the Church.

Psalm XLII Psalm said by the priest and server at the foot of the altar after the priest has made the Sign of the Cross at the beginning of Mass and has said the first antiphon taken from the psalm. "I will go in to the altar of God." The server answers: "To God, the joy of my youth." The psalm begins: "Judge me, O God, and distinguish my cause against an ungodly nation. O deliver me from the unjust and deceitful man." This is sometimes called the *Iudica Psalm.* It is omitted during Passiontide and at Masses for the Dead.

Psalms The book of the Old Testament of the Bible containing 150 Psalms or religious songs of praise. David is said to have written about half of them, but many have no author's name attached to them. Their subject matter is varied. There are songs of supplication, hymns of thanksgiving, songs of praise, and songs that point out a moral or teach a lesson.

Public Mass A Mass celebrated in a place open to the public.

public procession of the Blessed Sacrament The carrying of Holy Communion publicly to the sick, as in a hospital, college, or convent. The priest wears surplice, white stole, and humeral veil, and a small canopy should be carried over the Blessed Sacrament.

publican Jewish tax collector generally despised by the other Jews. The Parable of the Publican and Pharisee showed that Jesus did not despise anyone. To Him the humility of the publican, who said: "O God, be merciful to me, the sinner!" was more worthy than the false pride of the Pharisee. *Luke XVIII 13.* Matthew, one of the Apostles, was a publican.

pulpit Enclosed platform from which the priest gives his sermons.

punishment Suffering inflicted for wrongdoing. The Church has the right to inflict spiritual and temporal penalties on those guilty of offenses.

Purgatory Place and state of punishment in which the soul suffers for a time in order to be cleansed before going to Heaven. In Purgatory venial sins and mortal sins, which have been confessed but for which full satisfaction has not been made, must be removed by purification before the soul is ready for Heaven. The word *purgatory* comes from the Latin word *purgare,* meaning *to cleanse.*

purification (of the chalice) The cleansing of the chalice with wine and water after the priest has received Communion.

Purification of our Lady Feast of Our Lady on February 2. This feast is in memory of Our Lady's purification in the Temple after the birth of Jesus. According to the Jewish law, a mother, after the birth of a child, went to the Temple to present her child and to be purified after childbirth. The Presentation in the Temple is commemorated in the fourth Joyful Mystery of the Rosary. The Feast of the Purification is also called Candlemas Day. See *Candlemas Day.*

purificator Small piece of linen used to clean the chalice and paten during the Mass and to dry the priest's fingers. The purificator, like the corporal, is a very sacred cloth and must be washed by the priest or one who is in major orders before it is washed and ironed by anyone else.

purity Freedom from sin against chastity. *See* **chastity.** Purity is a moral virtue.

pyx Small metal container in which the priest carries the Blessed Sacrament to the sick.

Q

Quadragesima Word meaning the fortieth. It is used to indicate the whole season of Lent (forty days).

quarantine The word *quarantine* was once used in granting indulgences to denote forty days of penance. *See* **indulgence**.

Queenship of Mary The Feast of the Queenship of Mary, proclaimed by Pope Pius XII on the Feast of All Saints, November 1, 1954. The feast is kept May 31, a date already belonging to Our Lady, Mediatrix of All Graces. The idea of the queenship of Our Lady is not a new one. The fifth decade of the Glorious Mysteries is dedicated to the crowning of Our Lady in Heaven. The *Hail Holy Queen* is, next to the *Hail Mary*, the best-known prayer to Our Lady. In the Litany of Loreto Our Lady is addressed as Queen of Angels, Queen of Patriarchs, Queen of Prophets, Queen of Apostles, Queen of Martyrs, Queen of Confessors, Queen of Virgins, Queen of All Saints, Queen Conceived Without Original Sin, Queen Assumed into Heaven, Queen of the Most Holy Rosary, and Queen of Peace.

Quinquagesima The Sunday before Lent. The word *quinquagesima* means *fiftieth*, but Quinquagesima Sunday is not exactly the fiftieth day before Easter.

R

rabbi (1) A Jewish minister. (2) Hebrew name for master. In the Gospels Jesus is often called *Rabbi*.

Raccolta The official book of indulgenced prayers of the Catholic Church. *Raccolta* is an Italian word meaning *collection*. The Latin title of the same book is *Preces et Pia Opera* (*Prayers and Acts of Devotion*).

rash judgment Judging another person without sufficient knowledge. One who thinks evil of another person without good reason is guilty of rash judgment. The eighth commandment of God forbids rash judgment.

Real Presence, the doctrine of the The teaching of the Church that in the Sacrament of the Holy Eucharist, after the consecration of the bread and wine, Jesus Christ is truly, really, and substantially present under the appearances of bread and wine. There is no bread and wine when Jesus Christ is present, only the outward appearances of bread and wine. Because of the words said at the consecration, the bread and wine are no longer bread and wine but are changed into the whole body and blood of Jesus Christ. Jesus Christ, whole and entire, body and blood, soul and divinity, is present under the appearances of bread and wine.

reason *See* **intellect** and **age of reason**.

rector, a Title often used for a priest who is the head of a place of learning (college, university, or seminary). It is sometimes used for a priest appointed head of a church.

Redeemer One who saves. Jesus Christ, the Son of God, is the Redeemer of the whole human race because He died for the sins of men. Adam had lost for man his right to Heaven and his special gifts. Jesus Christ, as the Redeemer, paid the price of His own death on the Cross in order to gain back for man his right to Heaven. The Redeemer had been promised by God long before He came. In the Old Testament God kept renewing this promise to man through Sem, Abraham, Isaac, and Jacob. The Jews were waiting for the Messias who was to save the people of Israel. At the Incarnation, the long-awaited Redeemer came into the world.

Redemption, the The word *redemption* really means *buying back*. Jesus Christ, by His sufferings and death on the Cross, bought back for men the right to be children of God and heirs of Heaven. Because Jesus Christ was God, He was able to give infinite satisfaction for the sins of men.

red hat, the The scarlet hat of a cardinal. It has a broad brim, a flat crown, and two clusters of fifteen tassels. The Pope confers the red hat on the cardinal at the first public consistory (assembly of cardinals) after his appointment to the office of cardinal. The red hat is the symbol of the office of cardinal, but it is not worn after it is bestowed by the Pope.

Red Mass A Votive Mass of the Holy Ghost celebrated for judges and lawyers.

refectory Dining room in a monastery of men or women.

Reformation, the Protestant A religious revolt in Western Europe, during the sixteenth century, against the Catholic Church. This revolt led to the establishment of the Protestant churches.

Regina Coeli Latin words meaning *Queen of Heaven*. This is a title given to Our Lady and is also the title of one of the antiphons sung in the Divine Office. *See* **antiphons of Our Lady.** The Regina Coeli is said or sung instead of the Angelus during the Easter season.

> Queen of heaven, rejoice, Alleluia!
> For He whom thou didst deserve to bear,
>   Alleluia!
> Hath risen as He said, Alleluia!
> Pray for us to God, Allelulia!

> V. Rejoice and be glad, O Virgin Mary!
>   Alleluia!
> R. Because Our Lord is truly risen,
>   Alleluia!

Let Us Pray

O God, who by the resurrection of Thy
Son, Our Lord Jesus Christ, hast vouchsafed
to make glad the whole world, grant, we
beseech Thee, that, through the intercession
of the Virgin Mary, His Mother, we may
attain the joys of eternal life. Through the
same Christ Our Lord.   Amen.

Registers, Parochial   Books, kept by a parish priest, which contain
entries of baptisms, confirmations, marriages, and deaths in the
parish.

regular clergy   Priests living in a community under a rule and
bound by vows.

relic   The body or part of the body of a saint or something associated with his person, such as his clothing. First-class relics are
parts of the body of a saint; second-class relics are the clothing
or possessions used by a saint during his lifetime; third-class
relics are objects which have been touched to the tomb or body
of a saint. The veneration of relics is allowed and encouraged
in the Catholic Church. *See* **veneration.** An altar must contain
the relics of at least two saints who were martyrs.

religion   Man's way of worshiping God in his thoughts and in
his acts. A religion is a particular system by which a group of
people worship God. The Catholic religion is that way of worshiping God which God Himself taught to the first Apostles and
handed down through His Church.

religious, a   A person who is a member of a religious order or
congregation.

religious orders and congregations of men   While, according to
Canon Law, the name, religious order, is restricted to religious
institutes in which solemn vows are taken, the name is commonly
used for both religious congregations and religious orders. The
word *order* in this sense was first used in 1119 when the *Cistercian
Order* was organized.

There were certainly religious orders before that time. In the
third century St. Anthony of the Desert, who is called the father
of monastic life, organized religious communities throughout the

East (Egypt, Palestine, Syria, Greece). In the West St. Benedict founded monasteries. His monastery at Monte Cassino in Italy was famous as a place of piety and learning. Later the name Benedictine Order was given to monasteries under the same rule.

The three great orders of the Middle Ages were the Benedictine, Dominican, and Franciscan. St. Dominic was a Spanish priest who in 1215 established the religious order called the *Dominican Order of Preachers*. St. Francis of Assisi established the Franciscan Order in 1209. The Dominican and Franciscan orders are known as mendicant orders because begging was part of their religious life. *See* **mendicant orders.**

Two other religious orders, the Order of Carmelites and the Augustinian Friars, were also known as mendicant orders. The *Servites* became a fifth. The Carmelite Order was founded in the twelfth century and took its name from Mount Carmel, where a monastery was built. The Carmelites regard the prophet Elias as their spiritual founder. The Order of Augustinian Hermits (or Friars) was founded in 1256 from several other congregations under the Rule of St. Augustine. The Order of Servites (Order of the Religious Servants of the Holy Virgin) was founded by seven merchants of Florence in 1233 and flourished under St. Philip Benizi, who saved it from being suppressed.

At the time of the Reformation other religious orders sprang up. Some of these were: the *Theatines* (1524) founded by St. Cajetan in Italy; the *Capuchins* (1528), a branch of the Franciscan Order; and the *Barnabites* (1533). The *Society of Jesus* (the *Jesuits*) was founded by St. Ignatius Loyola in 1534. The first aim of this Society is to be at the call of the Pope for whatever work he might want its members to do. The Father General of the Society, who lives in Rome, is subject entirely to the Pope. When the Jesuits take their final vows, they add a fourth vow, to go on missions wherever sent by the Holy See. The Jesuits are engaged chiefly in education and in foreign missions.

There are over eighty religious congregations and orders of priests with houses in the United States. A list of these orders and congregations may be found in the *Official Catholic Directory* published annually by J. P. Kenedy and Sons, New York.

religious orders and congregations of women Some of the early religious congregations and orders of women sprang from similar religious orders of men. St. Francis, with St. Clare, founded the *Poor Clares* in the thirteenth century. St. Dominic founded the Order of *Preacheresses* (Second Order of St. Dominic) in 1218. The Order of *Carmelite Nuns* was founded in 1542, and the Order of *Discalced Carmelites* (a Reform Order) was founded in 1563 by St. Teresa of Avila. The Discalced Carmelites are enclosed and live in poverty. They engage in prayer and manual work. The *Cistercian Nuns,* like the Cistercian monks, lead cloistered, contemplative lives. This order was founded in France in 1125 by St. Stephen Harding.

There are over half a million women in religious congregations and orders in the United States alone. They belong to over 200 different religious congregations and orders. A list of these congregations and orders may be found in the *Official Catholic Directory,* published annually by J. P. Kenedy and Sons, New York.

remission (of sin) The forgiveness of sins through Baptism, Penance, or an act of perfect contrition. When an older person is baptized, any actual sins are also taken away by Baptism. After Baptism, actual sins are taken away through the Sacrament of Penance or an act of perfect contrition. This perfect sorrow for sin, while it blots out sin, must carry with it the intention of going to Confession as soon as possible. In the remission (forgiveness) of sins, the guilt of sins is blotted out.

Renaissance The word *renaissance* comes from the Latin and means *rebirth.* The name is applied to a period in history during which there was a noticeable revival of interest in literature, painting, music, architecture, etc.: the fifteenth and sixteenth centuries in Europe, especially in Italy.

reparation Making amends for a wrong or injury done. To make reparation is to try to repair the harm done another. If one has stolen or damaged something belonging to another, then his reparation is called restitution, that is, giving back another's property in good condition.

repentance Sorrow for sins and the intention of not sinning again.

Reproaches, the The reproaches of Jesus Christ spoken to the Jews and meant for all men. The *Reproaches* are part of the Good Friday Office and are sung by the choir during the Adoration of the Cross. The Latin name for Reproaches is *Improperia.*

Requiem Mass A Mass for the Dead. In a Requiem Mass the first word of the Introit is *Requiem* (*Rest*): "Eternal rest give unto them, O Lord; and let perpetual light shine upon them." Vestments are always black at a Requiem Mass. The Iudica, Gloria, and Creed are not said, and a blessing is not given at the Gospel. The Agnus Dei is changed. Instead of "Have mercy on us," "Grant them rest" is said twice, and instead of the last "Grant us peace," "Grant them eternal rest" is said. There is no Last Blessing. The Proper of the Requiem Mass deals with death.

Requiescant in pace Latin words meaning *May they rest in peace.* These words are said instead of the *Ite Missa Est* at the close of a Requiem Mass.

repository The side altar or chapel where the Sacred Host, consecrated on Holy Thursday, is kept until Good Friday. The altar is beautifully decorated, and the faithful keep constant watch and adoration before the Blessed Sacrament.

reredos *See* **altar draperies.**

response An answer to the priest given by the server, choir, or people during Mass or other services in the church.

Resurrection (of Christ) The greatest of Christ's miracles, His coming back to life three days after His death. This miracle proved His divinity beyond all doubt. His body and soul were joined together again by His own power, the power of God. Jesus Christ had foretold His own Resurrection when He said to the Jews: "Destroy this temple, and in three days I will raise it up." *John II 19.* Easter is the Feast of the Resurrection. *See* **Easter.**

resurrection (of the body) The uniting of man's dead body with his immortal soul at the end of the world.

retreat A period of withdrawing from one's ordinary work in the world to spend a number of days in prayer, meditation, and religious study. All members of the clergy and religious communities make a retreat at least once a year. A number of religious orders give retreats for laymen, and some of them have special houses for this purpose. The nuns of the Institute of Our Lady of the Retreat in the Cenacle open their convents to women and children who are making retreats. *See* **Cenacle, the.**

revelation, supernatural   Truth which God Himself has revealed to man. Man cannot know revealed truth by his own nature. Supernatural revelation is found in the Scriptures or in Divine Tradition. *See* **Tradition, Divine.** A private revelation is truth made known by God to a certain individual, as the revelations made to some of the saints.

revenge   The desire to return injury for injury. Revenge is forbidden by the fifth commandment. It is a sin against charity, for one cannot love his neighbor if he wishes to be avenged against him.

reverence   Deep respect given to religious persons or places.

reverend, the   The word *reverend* comes from the Latin word *reverendus,* meaning *worthy of respect.* Most priests are addressed in writing as the Reverend ——. Nuns who have the title of Mother are also addressed in writing as Reverend.

riddels   *See* **altar draperies.**

ring, use of, in the church   A bishop (or a cardinal, abbot, or Doctor of Divinity) wears a gold ring as a mark of his office. The kiss given to a bishop's ring is a sign of respect. Nuns wear a plain ring on their right hand to show their consecration to God. Most married women and some married men wear a wedding ring which has been blessed by the priest at the marriage ceremony. The ring of the fisherman which the Pope receives at his election is used as his private seal and is not worn.

rite   The way in which liturgical worship is carried out, that is, the words and actions used in performing a religious ceremony.

Ritual, the Roman   A book of forms to be used by Catholic priests for the administration of the sacraments, etc. The priest needs the Roman Ritual as well as his Missal and Breviary. In Latin this book is called the *Rituale Romanum.*

Rock   Name given to Simon by Our Lord. The name *Peter* means a *rock.* In *St. Matthew XVI 18* Our Lord said: "And I say to thee, thou art Peter, and upon this rock I will build my Church, and the gates of hell shall not prevail against it."

Rogation days   Special days of prayer set aside by the Church to ask for God's mercy and blessings. The word *rogation* means *supplication*, and the purpose of the devotions on these days is to bring God's blessings on the fruits of the earth. Rogation days are the Monday, Tuesday, and Wednesday before Ascension Thursday. On Rogation days the Litany of the Saints is chanted in procession.

Roman Catholic, a A member of the Roman Catholic Church, which has its center in Rome.

Roman collar Stiff collar worn around the neck and fastened at the back. It must be worn by a priest when he is in public. Some Protestant ministers also wear this kind of collar.

Roman Rite The manner of worship in the Latin or Roman Catholic Church. In the Western Church the Roman Rite, which is the most widely used of all rites, predominates.

Roman ritual *See* **ritual, Roman.**

Romans The book of the New Testament of the Bible called the Epistle of St. Paul the Apostle to the Romans. It is the first Epistle in the New Testament and one of the most important.

Rome The capital of Italy and the seat of the Roman Catholic Church. St. Peter, the first Pope of the Church, established his seat at Rome and was martyred and buried there. Except for the Avignon Popes, the Popes have always governed the Church from Rome. The Vatican State is located at Rome. *See* **Vatican.**

Rosary A chain of beads for saying prayers. A Rosary is a sacramental, a blessed object of devotion. To say the Rosary is to recite the prayers on the beads. The prayers of the Rosary honor the Blessed Virgin Mary, renew the main doctrines of the Catholic faith, and carry men's petitions to God. The Apostles' Creed is said on the Crucifix. On the first big bead the *Our Father* is recited and, on the three small beads following, three *Hail Marys* are said, followed by a *Glory Be to the Father*. Coming to the first decade, one recalls the mystery for the decade and recites the *Our Father*. On each group of ten beads (decade), ten *Hail Marys* are recited. Each decade is preceded by the *Our Father* and is followed by a *Glory Be to the Father*. There are five decades to the Rosary, each decade associated with a mystery of faith, which is meditated upon while the prayers are being said. Since there are fifteen mysteries in all (Joyful, Sorrowful, and Glorious), a complete Rosary would consist of fifteen decades. Usually just five mysteries are said.

It is said that early in the thirteenth century Our Lady appeared to St. Dominic, who founded the Dominican Order (the Order of Preachers), put a Rosary in his hand, and told him to go out and preach.

The word *rosary* comes from the Latin word *rosarium*, meaning a rose garden. The Feast of the Most Holy Rosary is celebrated on October 7.

rubrics   Directions given in liturgical books for celebrating Mass, reciting the Divine Office, and administering the sacraments. The word *rubrics* comes from the Latin word *ruber*, meaning *red*, and the rubrics are usually printed in red, while the prayers are printed in black.

rule, religious   The regulations followed by a particular religious order or congregation. The four main rules were once considered to be those of St. Basil, St. Augustine, St. Benedict, and St. Francis. The Society of Jesus (the Jesuits), however, has its own rule; so have the Carmelites, the Carthusians, and most modern congregations.

Ruth   A book of the Old Testament of the Bible, telling the story of Ruth, the Moabite. Ruth came to Bethlehem, after the death of her husband, with her mother-in-law, Noemi. Because of her unselfishness she refused to leave her mother-in-law and go back to her own people in Moab, although Noemi urged her to go. In Bethlehem, Boaz, a wealthy Jew and kinsman of Noemi, looked with favor on Ruth's kindness and married her. In this way Ruth the Moabite became an Israelite and one of the chosen people. Ruth and Boaz were ancestors of David and therefore ancestors of Jesus Christ.

S

Sabbath Saturday. The word *sabbath* means *rest* in Hebrew. For the Jews it was the seventh day of the week, and the day on which they rested from work and worshiped God. They chose the seventh day of the week as their day of religious observance because God finished His work of creation and rested on the seventh day. Because Our Lord rose from the dead on Sunday, Christians keep Sunday, the first day of the week, as the Lord's day, instead of Saturday.

Sabellianism A heresy which flourished in the second century and which denied that there are three persons in God.

sacrament An outward sign instituted by Jesus Christ Himself to give grace. One cannot see the grace which the sacraments give, for grace is invisible, but one can see the visible signs of the sacraments. An outward sign is a sign which can be seen, heard, or felt. The outward sign of the sacrament is some external thing or action called the *matter* (or material) of the sacrament, which is apparent to the senses. The form of the sacrament consists of the words said when the sacrament is administered. The matter and the form make up the sign of the sacrament and must be joined in some way. For example, in the Sacrament of Baptism, the words must be said while the water is being poured on the head.

The minister of the sacrament is the one who administers the sacrament. It was the will of Christ that the sacraments should be administered by men acting in His name, first His Apostles and then the bishops and priests who came after them. Those who administer the sacraments must perform the ceremony correctly and have the intention of doing it as the Church expects them to do it.

sacramentals Holy things or actions which the Church has given to the faithful for their spiritual benefit. They are called sacramentals because they have some outward resemblance to the sacraments and obtain favor from God. They must not be confused with the sacraments which were given by Christ Himself. Sacramentals obtain favor from God through the prayers of the Church offered for those who use them.

The three chief kinds of sacramentals are blessings given by priests and bishops, exorcisms against evil spirits, and blessed objects of devotion. The blessings of priests and bishops include the blessings of churches, of people, of holy water, of candles, and of palms. Some of the blessed objects of devotion most used by Catholics are holy water, candles, ashes, palms, crucifixes, medals, rosaries, scapulars and images of Our Lord, the Blessed Virgin, and the saints. Other sacramentals are the prayers of the Church and alms given in the name of the Church.

sacraments, the seven Baptism, Confirmation, Holy Eucharist, Penance, Extreme Unction, Holy Orders, and Matrimony are the seven sacraments. God gave the Church these seven sacraments to take care of the spiritual needs in the lives of men.

Everyone is born with original sin on his soul, and Baptism gives him a new spiritual life of the soul which makes him a child of God. Confirmation strengthens this life and gives the gifts of the Holy Ghost more fully. Holy Eucharist gives men food for their souls which cannot exist without nourishment, any more than their bodies can exist without food. Penance brings back into souls darkened by sin the light of grace which is lost through sins committed after Baptism. Extreme Unction comforts and strengthens the souls (and sometimes the bodies) of the sick and dying. Holy Orders and Matrimony give special graces for these particular states of life. Those receiving the Sacrament of Holy Orders also receive certain spiritual powers.

All of these seven sacraments were instituted by Jesus Christ Himself, during His work on earth and after His Resurrection, and they give grace to those who receive them with the right dispositions. The right dispositions mean those habits of mind which one must have in order to receive the sacraments worthily.

Baptism, Confirmation, and Holy Orders can be received only once, because they imprint on the soul a spiritual mark called a character, which lasts forever. This character gives the one who receives it a special place in God's service. Baptism makes one an adopted child of God. Confirmation makes him a soldier in the army of Jesus Christ. Holy Orders consecrates those who receive it to the special work of God's priests.

Confirmation, Holy Eucharist, Extreme Unction, Holy Orders, and Matrimony are called sacraments of the living, because those who receive these sacraments already have sanctifying grace. These sacraments give more grace to souls which are already alive with the life of grace. One cannot receive the sacraments of the living when one is guilty of mortal sin, because mortal sin shuts out grace from the soul.

Baptism and Penance are called sacraments of the dead because their chief purpose is to give the supernatural life of sanctifying grace to souls spiritually dead through sin. Before Baptism everyone has original sin on his soul, and if he is guilty of mortal sin after Baptism he loses sanctifying grace, until he gains it back through the Sacrament of Penance.

Each of the sacraments also gives a special grace, called sacramental grace, which helps one carry out the particular purpose of the sacrament.

sacred art *See* art, liturgical.

Sacred College *See* College of Cardinals, Sacred.

Sacred Heart The human heart of Jesus, a symbol of His love for God and for men. When one worships the Sacred Heart of Jesus, one is worshiping His human heart which is united to His divinity. St. John Eudes in the seventeenth century had a special devotion to the Sacred Heart. In the same century St. Margaret Mary Alacoque, a Visitation nun, had a number of visions, in one of which Our Lord spoke of the coldness of men and asked that a feast of His Sacred Heart be established. The Feast of the Sacred Heart is celebrated the third Friday after Pentecost. The first Friday of each month is also in honor of the Sacred Heart. *See* Fridays, to make the nine.

sacrifice Offering of a victim to God and its destruction in some way to show that God is the Supreme Lord of all things. In the Old Law or Jewish religion, sacrifices of food and animals were made to God. The food or the animals were destroyed so that man could no longer use them. These sacrifices of the Old Law were types of the Sacrifice of the Cross. *See* type and Sacrifice of the Cross, the.

Sacrifice of the Cross, the   Christ's free offering of Himself on the
Cross. This was the greatest sacrifice ever offered to God, the
sacrifice by which the whole human race was saved. All grace and
mercy come to men through the Sacrifice of the Cross.

Sacrifice of the Mass   *See* Mass, Sacrifice of the.

sacrilege   Irreverent treatment of sacred persons, places, or things.
Anything set apart for the service of God is sacred. Violently mis-
treating a person consecrated to God, such as a priest or a nun,
is a personal sacrilege. Violating a church or a chapel by committing crimes in such places is called a local sacrilege. Misusing
sacred things, such as the sacraments or blessed or consecrated
objects, is called a real sacrilege.

sacristan   A person in charge of the sacred vessels, vestments, etc.,
of a church. Sacristans may be priests, nuns, or laymen. In
cathedrals the sacristan is often a priest; in convents usually a
nun. Ordinarily, laymen act as sacristans.

sacristy   Room next to the sanctuary where the vestments and
sacred vessels are kept. Here the priest prepares for Mass or
other church services.

saint, a   One whose sanctity and heroic virtues have been confirmed by the Church in the process of beatification and
canonization. A saint is declared officially by the Church to be
in Heaven and is publicly venerated. *See* **canonization**. Besides
the canonized saints, numerous other saints remain undiscovered.
The Feast of All Saints, November 1, honors these unknown
saints as well as the canonized saints.

Saint Andrew's Cross   The x-shaped cross upon which St. Andrew
the Apostle is said to have been put to death.

Saint John Lateran   The cathedral church of the Pope, Bishop of
Rome. The Palace of the Lateran, which was the home of the
Popes for ten centuries, is now used as a pontifical museum.

Saint Martin's Summer   *See* **Martinmas**.

Saint Mary Major   The principal church of Our Lady at Rome.
Its original name was Basilica Liberiana because it was built
when St. Liberius was Pope. Another name for Saint Mary Major
is Our Lady of the Snows. There is a late-medieval legend that
Our Lady showed a wealthy Roman where she wanted a church
to be built in her honor by letting snow fall on the spot in the

middle of summer. The Feast of Our Lady of the Snows is August 5. Saint Mary Major is also known as St. Mary of the Crib, because the crib from Bethlehem is said to be preserved there.

Saint Peter's The church in Rome next to the Vatican Palace. It is often thought of as the chief church of the world, but it is not the Pope's Cathedral. *See* **Saint John Lateran.** It is the largest church in the world and contains the tomb of St. Peter. Canonizations, the opening and closing of jubilee years, and other important functions take place at St. Peter's.

Saint Vincent de Paul Society, the An association of laymen which exists to help the poor. It was founded by a number of Catholic students in France in 1833, and St. Vincent de Paul was chosen as its patron.

Saints Peter and Paul, the Feast of Holyday of obligation in certain countries, though not in the United States. The Feast of the Holy Apostles Peter and Paul is June 29. Both St. Peter and St. Paul were martyred. St. Peter was crucified, and St. Paul was beheaded three years after the martyrdom of St. Peter. St. Peter and St. Paul are the first saints named, after Our Lady, in the Canon of the Mass.

Because the Basilica of St. Peter and that of St. Paul in Rome are not close enough for a double celebration on this feast day, the celebration of the feast of St. Paul takes place June 30, a feast known as the commemoration of St. Paul.

sale of indulgences and Masses *See* **simony.**

salt, blessed Salt which has been blessed and which is used in the sacrament of Baptism and also in the blessing of holy water. The priest puts salt into the mouth of the person being baptized as a sign that he is made free from the corruption of sin. The priest says: "Receive the salt of wisdom."

In blessing holy water, the priest exorcises both the salt and the water (drives the evil spirits out of them) and then mingles them in the name of the Father and of the Son and of the Holy Ghost.

salvation The act of being saved. The salvation of the soul is the freeing of the soul from sin and its attainment of Heaven.

Salve Regina Latin name for the prayer, *Hail, Holy Queen.*

Samaria The smallest of the three provinces of Palestine at the time of Jesus Christ.

Samaritans, the The people who lived in Samaria at the time of Jesus Christ. They were looked down upon by the Jews because some of them had married pagans.

Samson One of the twelve Judges of Israel, sent by God to help the people fight their wars when they repented of their sins. Samson was one of the most unusual of the judges. When only a young man, he tore a lion to pieces, though he had no weapon. He was able to defeat the Philistines, but he was betrayed by a woman to whom he had confided the secret of his strength. Taken a prisoner and blinded by the Philistines, he was brought to their temple to be mocked at by the people. He called upon God to give him back his strength in return for the loss of his eyes. With the help of God he was able to pull down the temple of the Philistines, and he died beneath the temple with his enemies.

Samuel The last of the Judges. The books, *Samuel I* and *Samuel II* of the Old Testament (the first two Books of Kings), tell of his deeds. Samuel's mother, Anna, had long wanted a child, and she promised God that if He gave her a son she would give him to the Lord all the days of his life. When Samuel was born, Anna consecrated him to God as she had promised, and he served the Lord under the high priest, Heli. Samuel became a judge after Heli's death, and when he became old he appointed his sons as judges over Israel. The Israelites, however, wanted a king, and Samuel anointed Saul the first king of Israel.

sanctify To make holy.

sanctifying grace *See* grace.

sanctity Possession of sanctifying grace. A dedication of one's self and one's actions to God.

sanctuary, the That part of the church where the main altar stands. It is separated from the rest of the church by the altar rail. The sanctuary is generally somewhat higher than the rest of the church, so that the people may see what is going on at the altar.

sanctuary lamp Lamp hanging in the sanctuary and burning day and night before the Blessed Sacrament. One such lamp must be

kept always burning, but others may be lighted, any number so
long as it is an odd number (one, three, five, etc.).

Sanctus, the   The prayer said in the Mass at the end of the Preface.
The bell is rung three times, the people kneel, and the priest says:
"Holy, holy, holy, Lord God of Hosts. Heaven and earth are full
of Thy glory. Hosanna in the highest. Blessed is He that cometh
in the name of the Lord. Hosanna in the highest." The Sanctus
is a prayer of joy, a cry of welcome to Our Lord who at the
moment of consecration will be really present under the appearances of bread and wine.

Sanctus bell   Bell rung at the most solemn parts of the Mass.
It is first rung at the *Sanctus* (Holy, holy, holy, Lord God of
Hosts) which comes at the end of the Preface. It is rung again
at the *Hanc igitur* to indicate that the consecration is near. It is
rung during the *consecration,* at the *elevation of the Host,* and
the *elevation of the chalice.* In some places it is rung at the
Domine non sum dignus (Lord I am not worthy) just before
Communion.

sandals, episcopal   Embroidered slippers worn by cardinals and
bishops in celebrating a High Mass.

Satan   The chief fallen angel, or the devil. *See* **devil, the.**

satisfaction for sin   Making up to God for sins committed against
Him. The penitent satisfies in part for his sins when he says his
Penance after Confession. Jesus Christ Himself, by His suffering
and death, made infinite satisfaction for the sins of men. This is
called vicarious satisfaction.

Saturday   *See* **Sabbath.**

Saturday, First   *See* **First Saturday.**

Saul   First King of Israel, and a descendant of the tribe of Ben-
jamin. Samuel anointed Saul king, but Saul disobeyed God, and
so his sons did not become kings after him.

Savior   One who saves. Jesus Christ is the Savior of all men
because He died to save all men.

scandal   Any word, act, or omission which causes others to sin.
Scandal is a sin against charity, because by scandal one harms
his neighbor.

scapular   (1) A garment worn by members of some religious orders.
It is made of two pieces of cloth and is put on over the head,

with one part in front and one in back. *See* **habit, religious.**
(2) Badge of a religious confraternity. *See* **confraternity.** There
are a number of such scapulars which are similar in appearance.
The scapular consists of two small pieces of cloth joined by
strings and worn back and front. The brown scapular, which is
the scapular most often worn by the laity, is the badge of the
Confraternity of Our Lady of Mount Carmel. Tradition tells us
that Our Lady appeared to St. Simon Stock, Prior General of
Carmel, on July 16, 1251, and put a brown scapular into his
hands. She promised him that whoever died piously wearing this
scapular would not suffer eternal flames.

scapular medal   Medal which may be worn instead of the cloth
scapular by anyone enrolled in the scapular. The scapular medal
has on one side the image of Our Lord, showing His Sacred
Heart, on the other an image of Our Lady.

scapulars, the five   The five principal scapulars worn by the laity.
They are the scapulars of Our Lady of Mount Carmel, the
Holy Trinity, Our Lady of the Seven Dolors, the Passion, the
Immaculate Conception.

schism   Separation from the unity of the Church by refusing to
recognize the authority of the Pope. The word *schism* comes from
the Greek and means a *tearing away.* Schism is to be distinguished
from heresy. Schism is the tearing away from the authority of the
Pope and communion with the Church; heresy is the refusal of
a baptized person to accept one or more truths of the Catholic
faith. Schism easily leads to heresy. *See* **heresy.**

scholasticism   In its historical meaning the term *scholasticism*
refers to the teaching of the medieval schoolmen, that is, the
teachers of theology and philosophy in medieval universities. In
the modern world scholasticism is the common name of the
doctrines of those Catholic philosophers who consider themselves
the followers of the medieval schoolmen.

Several schools of thought have developed within scholasticism.
Augustinianism was developed in the thirteenth century, mainly
by St. Bonaventure and his disciples, in order to follow the teaching of St. Augustine against the growing influence of Aristotle.
Thomism, in general, refers to the teaching of the Dominican
theologian, St. Thomas Aquinas (1225-1274) in theology and

philosophy. Thomism is commonly extended to include the teachings of St. Thomas' important interpreters. In its strict meaning, however, Thomism includes such doctrines as can be found in the writings of St. Thomas Aquinas himself. *Scotism* is the teaching of the Franciscan theologian, John Duns Scotus (1266-1308) or of his school. *Suarezianism* is the teaching of the Jesuit theologian, Francis Suarez (1548-1617).

Scotism *See* **scholasticism.**

Scourging at the Pillar, the One of the chief sufferings of Jesus Christ. Jesus was tied to the pillar and beaten until He was disfigured with wounds. The Scourging at the Pillar is the second Sorrowful Mystery of the Rosary. Pilate ordered Jesus to be scourged because he hoped thus to save Him from undeserved death. He thought that by scourging Jesus he would satisfy the anger of the people.

Scriptures, the The Holy Bible, that is, the books of the Old and New Testaments.

scruples Worries over imaginary sins. A person has scruples when he examines his conscience to the point that he finds sin when it does not exist or imagines venial sins to be mortal sins.

seal of Confession Absolute secrecy which must be observed by the confessor concerning the sins told to him by the penitent in sacramental Confession, even to the extent of giving his life to preserve the secret.

Secret Prayer or prayers said in silence by the priest at Mass after the Offertory and before the Preface. The Secret is the last prayer of the Offertory of the Mass. It is said in such a low voice that only the priest himself can hear it. It was formerly called "the prayer over the oblation," and was the only Offertory prayer in the old Roman Rite. The name *secret* probably comes from the Latin word *secernere,* to *set apart,* and indicates that this is a prayer over the offerings which are *set apart.* The Secret varies according to the Proper of the day.

secular Of the world. The word *secular* comes from the Latin word *world.* As used by Catholics, it may mean a secular priest, one who does not belong to any particular religious order, or it may mean a lay person, one who is not a priest or nun.

secular clergy Priests who do not belong to any particular religious order but live independently in the world. The work of the secular clergy is usually in parishes as parish priests. They are sometimes said, with some reason, to belong to "the Order of St. Peter."

sedilia   A bench at the side of the sanctuary used by the priest and ministers during any part of the Mass or other ceremonies at which they sit down.

self-existence (of God)   Independent existence of God who needs no other being to create Him or to keep Him in existence.

seminary   A school for training young men for the priesthood.

Septuagesima   The third Sunday before Ash Wednesday. The name *Septuagesima* is also applied to that period of the cycle of Easter which comes just before Lent. It begins on Septuagesima Sunday and extends up to Ash Wednesday. This period is a preparation for the Lenten season. The joy of the Christmas cycle is put away before the Penance of Lent is begun. Vestments are violet and the Gloria and the Alleluia are not sung.

sepulchrum (or sepulcher)   The opening in the altar stone in which the relics of martyrs are placed.

sequence   A hymn sometimes said or sung between the Gradual and the Gospel of the Mass. Not every Mass has a sequence. The five in the Roman Missal are: Easter, *Forth to the Paschal Victim*, said from Easter Sunday to and including the Saturday before Low Sunday; Pentecost, *Come, Holy Ghost;* Corpus Christi, *Sion, lift thy voice and sing;* the Seven Sorrows of Our Lady (September 15 and the Friday in Passion Week), the *Stabat Mater;* and Requiem Masses, the *Dies Irae.* This last sequence is not said at all Requiem Masses.

sermon   A discourse preached for religious instruction. The sermon at Sunday Mass usually follows the Gospel and is often an instruction on the Gospel.

Sermon on the Mount   A sermon given by Jesus Christ to a great many people including His Apostles, during the first year of His public teaching. On the mountain side behind the town of Capharnaum Jesus spoke to the people in simple words. He began by giving them the eight Beatitudes, and held up to them an ideal of perfection. "You therefore are to be perfect, even as your heavenly Father is perfect," He said to them. *Matthew V 48.* Jesus told the people that He had not come to destroy the Old

Law but to fulfill it. He taught them the Lord's Prayer and gave them the Golden Rule: "Therefore all that you wish men to do to you even so do you also to them." *Matthew VII 12.*

Love was at the very heart of this powerful sermon, love for the poor and rich alike, love for His chosen disciples and for the crowds that had followed Him. He gave Himself to all mankind in His sermon, and the people who heard Him gave themselves to Him. "And it came to pass when Jesus had finished these words, that the crowds were astonished at His teaching; for He was teaching them as one having authority, and not as their Scribes and Pharisees." *Matthew VII 28–29.* The Sermon on the Mount may be found in the New Testament, *Matthew V, VI, VII.*

server One who helps the priest at Mass. The server answers the prayers, helps the priest at the Offertory, the Lavabo and the Ablutions, moves the Missal, and rings the bell. He is sometimes called the altar boy.

servile work Work of the body rather than of the mind. It is called servile work because it was once the work of slaves rather than free men. By the third commandment we are forbidden to do unnecessary servile work on Sundays and holydays of obligation.

Servites *See* religious orders and congregations of men.

Seven Dolors *See* Sorrows of Our Lady, the Seven.

seven gifts of the Holy Ghost *See* gifts of the Holy Ghost, the seven.

seven last words, the The words spoken by Our Lord from the Cross. (1) "Father, forgive them, for they do not know what they are doing." *Luke XXIII 34.* In His first words from the Cross Our Lord asked His Father to forgive those who were crucifying him. (2) "Amen I say to thee, this day thou shalt be with me in paradise." *Luke XXIII 43.* Our Lord spoke these words to the Good Thief who repented his sins and asked Jesus to remember him when He came into His kingdom. (3) "Woman, behold thy son . . . Behold thy mother." *John XIX 26, 27.* With these words, the first of which were spoken to His mother, the latter to John the Apostle, Our Lord gave His Blessed Mother to all mankind. (4) "My God, my God, why hast thou forsaken me?" *Mark XV 34.* Our Lord, who was God Himself, could have ended His own suffering at any moment, but He wanted to give Himself entirely

to the will of His Father. (5) "I thirst." *John XIX 28.* When Our
Lord said, "I thirst," a soldier dipped a sponge in vinegar and
held it up for Him to drink. It was more than physical thirst which
tormented Jesus Christ on the Cross. He thirsted for the love of
the people He had come to save. (6) "It is consummated!" *John
XIX 30.* Our Lord was almost at the end of His suffering when He
spoke these words. The work of redemption was finished. (7)
"Father, into thy hands I commend my spirit." *Luke XXIII 46.*
With these words Our Lord died on the Cross.

Sexagesima The second Sunday before Ash Wednesday.

Sext Hour of the Divine Office to be said at the sixth hour. It
take its name from the Latin word *sexta (sixth). See* canonical
hours.

shrine A place of special religious devotion, often one to which
pilgrimages are made. Small shrines may be sacred images to
which special devotion is given, a shrine within a church or a
chapel, or a home, or a shrine built outdoors and protected from
weather. The more famous shrines are the holy places in Palestine,
shrines of the Blessed Virgin Mary, and shrines of angels and
saints. *See* **Shrines of Our Lady.**

Shrines of Our Lady Places of special devotion to Our Lady. Many
of these shrines were built because of an appearance or appearances of Our Lady to certain persons in the world. Two of the
ancient shrines of Our Lady are Our Lady of Paris (Notre Dame
de Paris) in France, and the Holy House of Nazareth in Italy.
Two of the most famous shrines of modern Europe are those of
Our Lady of Lourdes at Lourdes, France, and Our Lady of
Fatima at Fatima, Portugal. In Central America there is the
famous shrine to Our Lady of Guadalupe at Guadalupe, Mexico.
Some well-known shrines in North America are: Our Lady of
La Leche (the first Catholic mission in the United States) at St.
Augustine, Florida; Our Lady of Perpetual Help at Boston,
Massachusetts; Our Lady of the Cape at Cap de la Madeleine,
Canada; and St. Anne de Beaupré at Quebec, Canada. *See*
Appendix, St. Anne, July 26.

Shrovetide The Monday and Tuesday before Ash Wednesday. The
word *shrove* comes from the Old English word meaning to *shrive*
or *to make a confession.* Before Lent began on Ash Wednesday

people went to confession and also engaged in much merry-making. Shrovetide is sometimes known as Carnival.

Shrove Tuesday   The Tuesday before Ash Wednesday and the last day of Shrovetide. Shrove Tuesday is sometimes called Pancake Tuesday because the people in England were accustomed to eat pancakes on this day.

Sign of the Cross   *See* **Cross, Sign of the.**

sign, outward   *See* **sacrament.**

simar   *See* **zimarra.**

simony   Buying or selling spiritual things such as Masses, blessings, indulgences, etc. An offering made to a priest who offers the Sacrifice of the Mass for a special intention is not considered, in any way, as the price of a Mass but as a contribution to the support of the priest. *See* **stipend.** A Rosary to which an indulgence has been attached loses its indulgence if it is sold.

The name *simony* comes from a certain Simon who offered money to Peter if he would give him the power to give the Holy Ghost through the laying on of hands. Peter answered him: "Thy money go to destruction with thee, because thou hast thought that the gift of God could be purchased with money." *Acts VIII 20.*

sin   An offense against God. Original sin is the sin inherited from Adam and is the sin with which each one of us is born. Because of original sin men inherit all the punishments of Adam: death, suffering, ignorance, and a strong inclination to evil. The Blessed Virgin Mary was the only human person who was kept free from original sin from the moment of her conception. This freedom from sin was given to her by a special privilege from God. Original sin in man is wiped out through Baptism, which gives sanctifying grace.

Original sin comes to a man as a result of Adam's sin, but actual sin is sin which the man himself commits. Actual sin is any willful thought, desire, word, action, or omission forbidden by the law of God. Some of the actual sins which men commit are mortal sins, while others are venial. Mortal sin is the worst kind of sin, because it causes the death of the soul. It takes from the sinner sanctifying grace, which he received with his Baptism and which gave him a new supernatural life of the soul. Mortal sin makes the soul an enemy of God and deserving of eternal punishment.

A sin, in order to be mortal, must be a serious sin, one that is seriously wrong or considered seriously wrong. The sinner must know it is seriously wrong and realize at the time he commits the sin that it is a sin. A sin, to be mortal, must be a deliberate sin. The sinner must freely choose to do the evil. If he is forced into doing it, it is no sin for him.

A venial sin is a lesser sin, a sin that is not so serious as a mortal sin. It is a sickness of the soul rather than the death of the soul. It is a less serious offense against the law of God. Sometimes, however, a serious sin may be venial for the sinner, because he does not realize he is committing a serious sin or does not give the full consent of his will to it. Venial sin does not deprive the soul of God's friendship, and grace is still left in the soul. Venial sin weakens God's grace in the soul, however, and often leads to mortal sin. A venial sin can be pardoned without Confession by an act of contrition.

The sacrament of Baptism takes away all sins—original sin and actual sin (both mortal and venial)—if there are any actual sins. After Baptism, sin is taken away through the Sacrament of Penance or an act of perfect contrition, with the intention of going to Confession as soon as possible. The Sacrament of Extreme Unction takes away venial sin and also mortal sin if the sick person is unconscious but has made an act of imperfect contrition.

Sinai, Mount   The place where the Covenant of the Old Testament was established. Moses went up on Mount Sinai, where the Lord gave him two stone tablets on which were written the ten commandments. When Moses came down from the mountain he found that the Israelites had made a golden calf and were sacrificing to it. In anger Moses threw down the tablets containing the ten commandments and broke them. Moses returned to the Lord on the mountain and prayed for his people. The Lord heard his prayers and made him two more tablets of stone, on which He wrote for him again the ten commandments.

sister   A woman who consecrates her life to God by vows of poverty, chastity, and obedience. *See* **nun.**

Sistine Chapel The principal chapel of the Vatican Palace and the chapel used for papal elections.

slander *See* **calumny.**

sloth *See* **capital sins.**

sodality A pious association of laymen or women sometimes known as a confraternity. *See* **confraternity.** The Blessed Virgin Mary Sodality is sometimes spoken of as *The Sodality.*

soldier of Christ One who is willing to fight for his Catholic faith. A person who receives the Sacrament of Confirmation becomes a soldier of Jesus Christ. *See* **Confirmation.**

Solemn Mass A Mass sung with all its ceremonies, with deacon and subdeacon assisting the celebrant, and with incense and music. A Solemn Mass is sometimes called a High Mass.

solemnity A feast celebrated with as much solemn liturgical observance as possible. The Solemnity of St. Joseph, a feast formerly kept on the Wednesday after the second Sunday after Easter, has been dropped from the Church calendar and its place taken by the Feast of St. Joseph the Workman, on May 1.

solemnization (of a marriage) Performance of the marriage ceremony with Nuptial Mass and blessing.

Solomon The son of David, King of Israel. Solomon succeeded his father as King of Israel and for many years ruled Israel wisely. He built the Temple to the Lord which his father David had once dreamed of building. In the latter part of his life, Solomon turned away from the true God and built temples to idols. For this sin the Lord divided Solomon's kingdom at his death. Solomon's wisdom, however, which was apparent in the first part of his reign, has been handed down in the *Book of Proverbs,* much of which was written by him, and the *Book of Wisdom* in the Old Testament.

Son, the God and the Second Person of the Blessed Trinity, Jesus Christ.

Sophonias The book of the Old Testament of the Bible concerning the prophecy of Sophonias, a minor prophet who lived at the time of Jeremias.

sorrow for sin *See* **contrition.**

Sorrowful Mysteries, the five Those mysteries of the Rosary which call to mind the sufferings of Jesus Christ. The Sorrowful

Mysteries are: (1) the Agony of Our Lord in the Garden; (2) the Scourging at the Pillar; (3) the Crowning with Thorns; (4) the Carrying of the Cross; and (5) the Crucifixion and Death of Our Lord. The Sorrowful Mysteries are said on Tuesday and Friday.

Sorrows of Our Lady, the Seven The seven sorrows which Our Lady experienced during her life: (1) *The prophecy of Simeon.* When Mary and Joseph took Jesus to the Temple, as was the custom, to present Him to God, Simeon, a holy man, warned Mary that a sword would pierce her soul. The sword piercing her soul was to be the Crucifixion of her Divine Son. (2) *The flight into Egypt.* Mary and Joseph were forced to fly into Egypt with the Infant Jesus because Herod was threatening His life. (3) *The loss of Jesus in Jerusalem.* When Jesus was twelve years old, He went with His parents and other relatives and friends to Jerusalem. When it came time to return home, His parents, thinking that He was traveling with other members of their party, journeyed for three days before they discovered that He was lost. (4) *Our Lord's painful journey to Calvary.* Our Lady met her Divine Son on His way to Calvary (Fourth Station of the Cross) and she was overwhelmed with sorrow. (5) *The Crucifixion of Our Lord.* When Our Lady stood at the foot of the Cross and saw her Son die a cruel death, a sword pierced her heart. (6) *The removal of the body of Jesus from the Cross.* Joseph and Nicodemus, two of the disciples of Jesus, took Him down from the Cross and placed Him in the arms of His sorrowing Mother. (7) *The entombment.* Our Lady herself sorrowfully arranged the body of Jesus in the sepulcher.

There are two Feasts of the Seven Sorrows of Our Lady, the Friday in Passion Week and September 15.

soul The spiritual part of man as distinct from his body. Man is composed of body and soul, but it is the soul of man which gives unity to him as a human being. The soul is not in any particular part of the body but is whole and entire in every part. The soul of man is immortal and will never die.

souls in Purgatory Those holy souls who are being punished in Purgatory for a time, to satisfy for their sins. They are called Holy Souls because they are in God's love and grace and will enter Heaven as soon as their time of punishment is over. These souls are the members of the Church Suffering. The faithful on earth (the Church Militant) can relieve the sufferings of the souls in Purgatory by prayers and good works, by indulgences, and by having Masses offered for them. The faithful on earth may also ask these souls to pray for them. The month of November is devoted to the Poor Souls.

spirit A being that has understanding and free will but no body and will never die.

spiritual bouquet card A card containing a list of prayers, Masses, good works, etc., offered for the living or the dead.

Spiritual Exercises, the Name given to a series of meditations on religion written and arranged in logical order by St. Ignatius Loyola, the founder of the Jesuit order.

sponsor The word *sponsor* comes from the Latin word *spondere* which means *to promise*. A sponsor (in Baptism or Confirmation) makes certain promises for the person he offers to be baptized or confirmed and takes on himself a certain responsibility for the faith of that person. There is only one sponsor in Confirmation. There may be two in Baptism.

spouse Partner in marriage. St. Joseph, the spouse of Our Lady, was the husband of the Blessed Virgin Mary. Mary and Jesus needed someone to take care of them, and God the Father chose Joseph as their protector. Under the safeguard of marriage Our Lord came into the world, even though the marriage of Mary and Joseph was not an ordinary marriage. Mary remained a virgin after marriage just as she was at the time of the Annunciation.

Spy Wednesday Wednesday in Holy Week. It is probably called Spy Wednesday because on this day the betrayal of Judas Iscariot is read in the Passion. Judas was a spy against Our Lord; it was he who led the soldiers to Jesus and betrayed Him with a kiss.

Stabat Mater First words of the Latin hymn (called a sequence) said or sung for the two feasts of the Seven Sorrows of Our Lady, the Friday in Passion Week and September 15. *See* Sequence. *Stabat mater* are Latin words meaning *the mother was standing*. The hymn shows Our Lady's sorrow as she stood at the foot of the Cross.

Star of Bethlehem, the   The star seen by the Magi, the wise men who came to see the Infant Jesus at His birth. This was the star that guided the wise men to Bethlehem.

state of grace   That state of the soul in which one is free from original sin and actual mortal sin. A person who is in the state of grace possesses sanctifying grace, and the Holy Ghost is present in his soul.

station day   Name found in the Missal and handed down from the Middle Ages when, on Sundays, important feast days, and days of Lent, the Pope used to celebrate Mass in the basilicas and other churches of Rome. This was called "making the station," and the churches were called "stational churches." In the Missal, for example, the First Sunday of Advent notes the Station of St. Mary Major. Certain indulgences may be gained by visiting a stational church.

Stations of the Cross   The fourteen crosses on the walls of the church which make up the Way of the Cross in memory of the Passion of Our Lord. Pictures or images showing events in Our Lord's Passion accompany the crosses. They are usually placed in order around the church, the first seven stations on one side of the church and the last seven stations on the other side. The Stations of the Cross tell the story of what happened to Jesus from the moment Pilate condemned Him until He died and was buried. When a person "makes" the Stations of the Cross, he meditates on these scenes as he moves from one station to another.

The Stations of the Cross may be made alone, or with others, or with a priest reading the prayers and meditations. The fourteen Stations of the Cross are: (1) Pilate condemns Jesus to death; (2) Jesus takes up the heavy cross; (3) Jesus falls for the first time; (4) Jesus meets His sorrowing mother; (5) Simon is forced to help Jesus carry the cross; (6) Veronica wipes the face of Jesus; (7) Jesus falls for the second time; (8) the women of Jerusalem grieve over Jesus; (9) Jesus falls for the third time; (10) Jesus is stripped of His garments; (11) Jesus is nailed to the Cross; (12) Jesus dies on the Cross; (13) Jesus is taken down from the Cross and given into the arms of His sorrowing mother; (14) Jesus is buried.

The Stations of the Cross, begun in the Franciscan Order, are a very popular devotion in the Catholic Church. The first Stations of the Cross were in Jerusalem where pilgrimages were made to the scene of Our Lord's Passion and Death.

stigmata Miraculous wounds impressed on certain holy persons. These wounds are similar in appearance to those which Jesus Christ suffered at His Crucifixion. The wounds are painful and sometimes there is pain without any marks. St. Francis of Assisi and St. Catherine of Siena are examples of saints who had these marks.

stipend Offering given for a Mass. A person may give a stipend for a Mass to be said for some particular intention. Mass stipends are given to the priest not in payment for the spiritual benefits, but as a means of his support.

stipes The pillars or pillar on which the top of the altar (the mensa) rests. *See* **mensa.**

stock Metal container for holy oils. Each church has three such containers, one for each oil kept in the ambry. Parish priests have smaller containers for their own personal use on sick calls.

stole. A long narrow band of cloth the same color as the vestments of the day. Deacons wear it over the left shoulder and priests around the neck. It signifies the priest's authority to judge the sins of men. *See* **vestments.**

stoup (for holy water) Sometimes called a font. A basin for holy water close to the door of the church.

stripping of the altar Ceremony which takes place after the Mass of the Lord's Supper on Holy Thursday. The altar is left bare except for the Cross and candlesticks. The antiphon and psalm sung during the ceremony show that the stripping of the altar represents the stripping of Our Lord of His garments. The antiphon is: "They divide my garments among them and for my vesture they cast lots." The stripping of the altar is now repeated after the Communion on Good Friday.

Suarezianism *See* **scholasticism.**

subdeacon A member of the clergy in the third major order just below the deacon. His duties are to prepare the sacred vessels for Mass, sing the Epistle, and pour the water into the chalice at the Offertory during a High Mass.

substance   The word *substance* comes from the Latin *substantia* and means *that which underlies* or is the subject of accidents. A substance such as a dog, a tree, or a stone is said *to be,* while an accident, a color, or a shape, is said *to be in,* as black is in a kitten or hardness is in a stone.

sufferings of Christ, the chief   Christ suffered in His human nature, but His sufferings were of infinite value because He was both God and man. The chief sufferings of Jesus Christ were His agony of soul, His bloody sweat, His cruel scourging, His crowning with thorns, His Crucifixion, and His death on the Cross. The Sorrowful Mysteries of the Rosary and the Stations of the Cross commemorate these sufferings.

Sunday   The Lord's Day. On this day a Catholic must assist at Mass and refrain from unnecessary servile work. Sunday is never a fast day. *See* **Lord's Day, the.**

Sung Mass   A Mass which is sung, but without deacon and subdeacon as in a High Mass.

superior, a   One who has authority over others because of his ecclesiastical rank. The head of a monastery or convent is usually called a superior. Sometimes the head of a religious order is called a superior general. *See* **general.**

supernatural   Something which is above nature.

superstition   Any act that gives false honor to God or gives to a creature honor that belongs to God alone. It is superstitious to believe dreams or fortunetellers, to visit spiritists in order to get in touch with people who are dead, to use spells or charms, to believe in omens.

Supplices te rogamus (We most humbly beseech thee)   First words of the third prayer after the consecration at Mass. It is a prayer to God Almighty that the offerings be carried by God's holy angel to the altar of Heaven.

Supra quae (Upon which)   First words of the second prayer after the consecration at Mass. In this prayer the priest asks God to look with favor upon these offerings as He accepted the gifts of Abel, of Abraham, and of Melchisedech.

Supreme Being, the   The highest and most perfect Being, God.

surplice   A loose white garment with wide sleeves. It is worn over the cassock by priests in choir or procession or when administering the sacraments. It may also be worn by laymen or boys serving Mass. *See* **vestments.**

Swiss Guards Papal guards responsible for the safety of the Vatican Palace and City and the Pope. They guard the gates of the Palace and City and the apartments of the Pope and attend all papal functions. The parade uniform of the Swiss Guards is very colorful—of yellow, blue, and red stripes.

symbol Something material which is used to represent something that is not material. From the beginning the Christians used symbols to represent their religion. One of the earliest symbols of Christianity is that of the fish and bread, representing Our Lord and the Blessed Sacrament and recalling the miracle in which He fed the multitudes with only a few little fishes and a few loaves of bread.

The Cross is the most widespread symbol of Christianity, because Jesus Christ died on the Cross to redeem the world. Symbols of the Holy Ghost are the dove, tongues of fire, air or wind, and a cloud.

synagogue A place of public worship for the Jewish people. Jesus Christ preached in the synagogue at Bethlehem. The Temple of sacrifice was at Jerusalem.

synoptic Gospels Gospels taking a common view. The first three Gospels, St. Matthew, St. Mark, and St. Luke, are called synoptic Gospels because they tell the story of Our Lord's life in much the same way, relating the events in much the same order, and giving a similar viewpoint.

T

tabernacle   The receptacle, placed at the center of the main altar, in which the Blessed Sacrament is kept. The inside of the tabernacle is lined with silk, and there is a corporal folded on the floor. The tabernacle is kept locked, and the key is in charge of the priest.

The word *tabernacle* comes from the Latin word *tabernaculum*, meaning *tent*. A tentlike covering, called a tabernacle, was used by the Jews of the Old Testament to cover the Ark of the Covenant. *See* **Ark of the Covenant.** Moses was commanded by God to build this tabernacle, and he was told exactly how to build it. The tabernacle was divided into two parts, the Holy of Holies and the Sanctuary. It was within the Holy of Holies that the Ark of the Covenant was placed.

tabernacle veil   The piece of cloth covering the top and sides of the tabernacle. It is divided in front so that the door of the tabernacle may be opened. It is usually of the same color as the priest's vestments for the day, but it may not be black. Purple is used for the tabernacle veil at Masses for the Dead.

taking God's name in vain   Using the name of God or the holy name of Jesus Christ without reverence, as in anger or surprise. The second commandment of God forbids taking God's name in vain.

Tantum ergo   The first words of a hymn sung at Benediction of the Blessed Sacrament. It contains the last two verses of the hymn *Pange lingua* which St. Thomas Aquinas composed for the Feast of Corpus Christi.

Te Deum   Hymn sung at Matins on all feast days and some other times. It is also sung as a hymn of thanksgiving on special occasions. It begins *Te Deum laudamus* (*We praise You, O God*).

Temple, the   A place of worship and sacrifice for the Jewish people under the Old Law. The sacrifice of the Old Law was offered in the Temple at Jerusalem. The Jews had many synagogues, but there was only one Temple, the one at Jerusalem.

temporal punishment Punishment for a time. After a penitent's sins have been forgiven, punishment can be paid in this world by good works or, if it is not sufficiently paid in this world, it will be paid in Purgatory. The Church has the power to remit temporal punishment due to sins already forgiven by indulgences. *See* **indulgence.**

temptation Anything that makes sin attractive to a person. This may be something outside him or a leaning toward sin within him. Temptation in itself is not a sin, for Our Lord allowed Himself to be tempted by the devil in the desert.

Tenebrae A service formerly held on Wednesday, Thursday, and Friday evenings of Holy Week. It is now permitted only on Wednesday evening in the church where the bishop celebrates the Mass of the Chrism on Holy Thursday morning. *See* **Chrism, Mass of the.** The word *tenebrae* is a Latin word which means *darkness.* The service is a symbol of the darkness of the last days of Holy Week. During Tenebrae service, the lights are gradually put out in the church until there is complete darkness. The last candle is hidden and not put out, to show that Jesus Christ will triumph over darkness. The clapping at the end of the service is a symbol of the confusion following Christ's death.

Terce The hour of the Divine Office said at the third hour. Its name comes from the Latin word *tertia* (*third*). *See* **canonical hours.**

tertiary A member of a third order. *See* **Third Order.**

testament Another word for covenant. *See* **Covenant.** The Holy Bible is divided into the Old and the New Testaments. The Old Testament deals with the covenant (agreement) which God made with His chosen people, and the New Testament deals with the new covenant which Jesus Christ made with man.

theft The wrongful taking of another's property. The seventh commandment of God forbids theft.

theological Pertaining to God. The word *theological* comes from the Greek word *theos* meaning *God.*

theological virtues *See* **virtues, theological.**

theology The word *theology* comes from the Greek and means *the study of God.* Theology differs from philosophy because philosophy depends on reason, while theology depends on revelation and the authority of God Himself. It is Catholic teaching that theology and philosophy, correctly developed, will never be opposed to one another. *See* **philosophy.**

Thessalonians I, II Books of the New Testament of the Bible. They are the Epistles of St. Paul the Apostle to the church at Thessalonica, which was the capital of Macedonia.

Third Order A middle order or rule, originated by St. Francis of Assisi, between the world and the cloister.

The name Third Order, by itself, usually refers to the *Third Order Secular,* a religious rule for people living in the world. Members of a third order secular are not bound by any vow, but they do have a rule, an office, and a habit which is not worn in public without permission. The rule does not bind under pain of sin. Among the best-known Third Orders Secular in the Church are the following: St. Francis, St. Augustine, Our Lady of Mt. Carmel, and St. Dominic. Members of a third order secular are called tertiaries or secular tertiaries.

The *Third Order Regular* is made up of those members of a third order who leave the world and live in a religious community. They are bound by simple vows and are known as regular tertiaries.

Thomism *See* **scholasticism.**

Three Hours, the Popular devotion observed on Good Friday in memory of the three hours Jesus Christ hung on the Cross. This service is sometimes called by its Italian name, *Tre Ore.* While the new order for Holy Week does not abolish this devotion, it must be brought into harmony with the liturgy.

throne (1) The seat of a bishop. *See* **cathedra.** (2) A small platform on which the Monstrance is placed at Benediction or Exposition of the Blessed Sacrament.

thurible *See* **censer.**

thurifer The acolyte who carries the thurible (censer) when incense is used.

tiara Headpiece worn by the Pope at his coronation and on some other occasions. The tiara has three gold crowns and is decorated with precious stones. The meaning of the triple crown is that the Pope is the Bishop of Rome, Vicar of Christ, and temporal sovereign of the Vatican State.

Time after Epiphany That part of the cycle of Christmas from January 6 to Septuagesima Sunday. The Time after Epiphany is usually five Sundays, but when Easter comes early there are fewer, sometimes only one. The Sundays which are left out are included in the Time after Pentecost. *See* **Time after Pentecost**. Green is the liturgical color for the Time after Epiphany.

Time after Pentecost The third and last cycle of the ecclesiastical year. It begins on the Sunday after Pentecost (Trinity Sunday) and continues to Advent. When Easter, which is a movable feast, comes early, Sundays from the Time after Epiphany are used to fill in the gap between the twenty-third and the last Sunday after Pentecost. Green is the liturgical color for the Time after Pentecost.

Timothy I, II Books of the New Testament of the Bible. They are the Epistles of St. Paul the Apostle to St. Timothy, Bishop of Ephesus. These, with the Epistle of St. Titus, are called Pastoral Epistles because they are addressed to the head or pastor of a church. St. Timothy had been a missionary companion of St. Paul.

Tobias The book of the Old Testament of the Bible concerning the history of the family of Tobias. The elder Tobias, though captured by the Assyrians, did not give up his own faith in God. He continued to perform works of mercy. He and his family were blessed by God, who sent the Angel Raphael to cure him of blindness and to guide his son, the young Tobias, on a long journey.

tongues of fire Symbols of the Holy Ghost. When the Holy Ghost came down upon the Apostles on Pentecost, flames shaped like tongues rested upon each one present.

tonsure The shaving or clipping of part of the hair from the head of a cleric. In this ceremony hair is cut from the cleric's head in the form of a cross to show that he has dedicated himself to God's service.

Titus A book of the New Testament of the Bible. It is the Epistle of St. Paul the Apostle to Titus, who was Bishop of Crete.

tract Verses of Scripture which follow the Gradual instead of the Alleluia at Mass from Septuagesima till Holy Saturday (the Lenten season), on Ember days, some vigils, and at Requiem Masses. These verses are often taken from the Psalms.

Tradition, Divine   Revealed teaching handed down from Jesus Christ through the Apostles, but not written down. Many of these truths were later written by the Fathers of the Church.

Transfiguration   The miraculous change in the body of Jesus Christ when He showed His divinity to Peter, James, and John on the mountain of Tabor in Galilee. His countenance was changed and His clothing was radiant white. This was caused by the Divine Light shining through His body. The Feast of the Transfiguration is August 6.

transubstantiation   The change of the entire substance of the bread and wine into the substance of the body and blood of Jesus Christ at the words of consecration during the Sacrifice of the Mass.

treasury of merits   The store of merits of Jesus Christ, which was more than what was needed for the salvation of men, and the merits which Our Lady and the saints gained during their lifetime but did not use. All these merits form a treasury from which the Church grants indulgences.

Trent, the Council of   Famous council of the Church held at Trent, Italy, 1545-1563. Its purpose was to consider the problem of Protestantism and to reform the Church from within.

Tre Ore   *See* **Three Hours, the.**

Triduum   Three days of prayer before a great feast or for some other special occasion. The last three days of Holy Week are called *Triduum Sacrum* (*The Sacred Triduum*). *Triduum* is the Latin word meaning *a space of three days*.

Trinity, the Blessed   *See* **Blessed Trinity, the.**

Trinity Sunday   Feast of the Most Holy Trinity. It is the first Sunday after Pentecost, which it replaces in the liturgy, and eight weeks after Easter.

tunic   (1) The official garment of a subdeacon. It is worn under the dalmatic by a cardinal, bishop, or abbot at a Pontifical Mass. The tunic is shorter than the dalmatic and has narrower sleeves. *See* **vestments.** (2) A loose garment worn under the religious habits of men and many religious habits of women.

Twelfth-night   The eve of the twelfth day after Christmas. The twelfth day after Christmas is the Epiphany, so Twelfth-night is the eve of the Epiphany. *See* **Epiphany, the Feast of.**

type   Some person or event in the Old Testament which seems to give an indication of what will be found in the New Testament. The word *type* originally meant *form* or *figure* and is used in this way in the Old and New Testament.

Abel is a type or figure of Jesus Christ, and Cain, who killed him, is a figure of Judas who betrayed Jesus. The ark in which Noe saved his family from the Great Flood is a figure of the Catholic Church, while Noe himself is another figure of Jesus Christ. The sacrifice of bread and wine by Melchisedech, King of Salem, is a type or figure of the Sacrifice of the Mass. The Old Testament is full of such types or figures which point to the New Testament.

U

Unction *See* **Extreme Unction, the Sacrament of.**

Unde et memores (Wherefore calling to mind). The first words of the prayer which follows the consecration in the Mass. In this prayer, the Passion, Resurrection, and Ascension of Our Lord are recalled. The people join with the priest in offering the Holy Victim. The priest makes five crosses over the body and blood of Jesus Christ, who is offering Himself to the Heavenly Father.

union, hypostatic The union of the human and divine nature in the Second Person of the Blessed Trinity, Jesus Christ.

unity (of the Catholic Church) One of the four marks of the Church. *See* **marks of the Church.**

unity (of God) The oneness of God. The three Persons of the Blessed Trinity have one and the same divine nature.

unleavened bread Bread made without yeast. In the Western Church unleavened bread is used to make the hosts which are consecrated at Mass.

use of reason *See* **age of reason.**

V

Vatican, the   The official residence of the Pope at Rome. It is built on the Vatican Hill.

Vatican City   That part of Rome belonging to the Holy See. It is an independent state within the city of Rome about a square mile in area and with a population of about 1,000, most of whom are ecclesiastics. The Pope is the head of Vatican City, and its government is in his hands.

veil   A covering over head and shoulders used as part of the habit of most nuns. *See* humeral veil. *See* chalice veil.

veneration   That respect and honor given to the saints. The veneration which is given to Our Lady and the saints is different from the worship given to God alone. God is adored, and the saints are venerated.

venial sin   *See* sin.

Veronica's veil   The veil which a woman who pitied Our Lord on His way to Calvary gave to Him that He might wipe the perspiration from His face. It is not certain that the woman's name was Veronica. According to tradition, the imprint of His face was made on this veil. Veronica's veil is one of the greater relics in St. Peter's at Rome.

verse   (1) A Biblical verse is a short division of a chapter of the Bible. (2) A *verse* or versicle in the liturgy is a short prayer followed by a response. It is indicated by this sign, ℣.

Vespers   Evening hour of the Divine Office. *See* canonical hours. Evening services in the Church are commonly called Vespers.

vessels, sacred   Various containers used in church services. These are blessed or consecrated and are usually made of gold or silver. The chalice, paten, ciborium, pyx, capsula, lunette, and monstrance are sacred vessels.

vestments   The special clothes worn by a priest when he says Mass or engages in other acts of worship. As he puts on each garment in the sacristy, the priest says a prayer in Latin which shows the symbolical meaning of each vestment. A bishop, when celebrating a Pontifical Mass, takes his vestments from the altar. The vestments for Mass, in the order that the priest puts them on, are the amice, the alb, the cincture, the maniple, the stole, and the chasuble. *See* **amice, alb, cincture, maniple, stole,** and **chasuble.** Most of the vestments are marked with the Cross. The five approved colors of vestments are white, red, green, violet, and black. Rose-colored vestments are allowed on Gaudete Sunday and Laetare Sunday. Other vestments used in church services are the surplice, cope, dalmatic, and tunic. *See* **surplice, cope, dalmatic** and **tunic.**

viaticum   Communion given to those who are in danger of death. Fasting is not necessary to receive viaticum, and it may be received at any hour and more than once during an illness. It is given at the same time as Extreme Unction. The word *viaticum* means *provision for a journey,* and it is the food which prepares a person for his journey out of this world.

Vicar of Christ   The Pope who is the Vicar of Christ on earth and the visible head of the Church.

vice   A bad habit which leads men into sin. A vice is the opposite of a virtue.

victim   That which is offered in a sacrifice. In the Sacrifice of the Mass, Jesus Christ is the victim, just as He was the victim in the Sacrifice of the Cross.

Vidi Aquam   Antiphon sung instead of the Asperges before High Mass during Eastertide. The Latin words *vidi aquam* mean *I saw water.* The antiphon continues: "I saw water flowing from the right side of the temple, alleluia; and all to whom that water came were saved, and they shall say: alleluia, alleluia."

vigil   The day and evening before certain feast days. Vigils, or eves, have a special Office in preparation for the feast day. The vigils of Christmas and Pentecost are called privileged vigils and do not give place to any feasts. The other vigils observed are those of the Feasts of the Ascension, Assumption, St. John the Baptist, Sts. Peter and Paul, and St. Lawrence. The word *vigil* comes from the Latin word *vigilia* meaning *a watching.* Originally a vigil was a watch kept the night before the feast. *See* **wake.**

vigil lights   Small candles placed in glass cups and burned before a shrine or image.

Virgin Birth Jesus Christ's birth of Mary who was a virgin. Christ had no human father, and He was conceived by the Holy Ghost in the womb of His virgin mother. Mary was a virgin before the birth of her Divine Son, at the time of His birth, and after His birth. The brothers and sisters of Christ mentioned in the Gospels are merely relatives.

virtue A habit which inclines a person to do good and to avoid evil. Virtues are natural or supernatural. Natural virtues are habits which are acquired by doing good things many times. Natural virtues—that is, good natural habits—are good to have, but they do not necessarily deserve a reward in Heaven. When a newly baptized person receives sanctifying grace for the first time, he receives the infused virtues: faith, hope, charity, and the moral virtues. *See* **virtues, moral.** These virtues are called infused virtues because they are not acquired as the result of constant practice but are produced in the soul by God. These virtues help him to act in a supernatural manner and give him a special inclination to do good. With sanctifying grace the newly baptized person receives the seven gifts of the Holy Ghost, which are also habits of the soul. *See* **gifts of the Holy Ghost, the seven.**

virtues, cardinal Name for the four chief moral virtues: prudence, justice, fortitude, and temperance.

virtues, moral Habits infused into the soul by God when sanctifying grace is received for the first time. These habits put a person in the proper disposition to lead a moral or good life. They help him treat persons and things the way God wants him to treat them. The chief moral virtues are prudence, justice, fortitude, and temperance. These four virtues are sometimes called cardinal virtues. The word *cardinal* comes from the Latin word *cardo* meaning *hinge.* The four chief moral virtues are called cardinal virtues because the Christian life is "hinged" on them.

Prudence helps a person make up his mind as to what he must or must not do. Justice makes him fair in his dealings with his neighbor. Fortitude, which is really moral courage, encourages him to do what is right in spite of difficulties. Temperance helps him control his likes and dislikes in the things which please the senses.

Some of the other moral virtues are patriotism, obedience,

veracity (truthfulness), liberality, patience, humility, and purity.

virtues, theological Faith, hope and charity, the three virtues most closely related to God. These three virtues, belief in God, hope in God, and love of God, have God as their immediate object. The theological virtues are supernatural virtues because they are above nature and because they help man attain his supernatural end, which is happiness with God in Heaven.

Visible Church, the The Church, as founded by Jesus Christ, on the Apostles. It was and is a visible society ruled by the Pope with the bishops under him. *See* **soul of the Church.**

vision A supernatural appearance of God, the angels, the saints, or the devil. *See* **apparition.**

visit (of a bishop) The visit of duty which a bishop in charge of a diocese must pay to Rome every five years. A bishop is required to visit the tombs of the Apostles Peter and Paul and to report on the state of his diocese to the Pope. This visit is called a visitation *ad limina Apostolorum (to the threshold of the Apostles).*

visit to the Blessed Sacrament A visit to church or chapel to pray before the Blessed Sacrament.

Visitation, the (1) The visit which Our Lady paid to her cousin Elizabeth just after the Annunciation, when the Angel Gabriel made known to her that she was to become the mother of God. Elizabeth was filled with the Holy Ghost when she saw Mary and cried out: "Blessed art thou amongst women, and blessed is the fruit of thy womb." Mary answered with the Magnificat. *See* **Magnificat.** Mary stayed with her cousin Elizabeth until after the birth of John the Baptist. The second Joyful Mystery of the Rosary is in memory of the Visitation. (2) A canonical inspection of a religious house made by a bishop or by a major superior of a community or order.

vocation God's call to the soul. The word vocation does not necessarily mean a religious vocation. Some people are called to serve God in the religious life, but others are called to serve God in various ways in the world. A person may have the vocation to be a lawyer, a doctor, or a housewife and mother. Vocation to religious life, however, means that call by which a person is invited to serve God in a special state—as a priest or religious.

Votive Mass A Mass which is not the same as that of the office or feast of the day. A Votive Mass is usually said for a particular intention of the priest or at the wish (*votum*) of someone requesting the Mass. There are Votive Masses of the Trinity, the Angels, Sts. Peter and Paul, the Holy Ghost, Masses for the Dead, and for various special occasions. The word *votive* comes from the Latin word *votum* meaning *wish*.

vow A deliberate promise freely made to God by which a person places himself under the obligation of doing something especially pleasing to God. In making a vow a person must have the intention of binding himself under pain of sin. Vows are public or private, and they may be solemn or simple. Public vows are made before a Church authority and are accepted in the name of the Church, while private vows are made directly to God.

vows, religious The three vows of poverty, chastity, and obedience by which a religious binds himself. These are the evangelical counsels recommended by Our Lord Himself. By the vow of poverty, the religious gives up all personal property. (Religious orders differ in their understanding of this vow.) By the vow of chastity, the religious promises to keep away from the desires of the flesh. By the vow of obedience, the religious submits himself to the authority of his superiors.

Vulgate The Latin translation of the Bible commonly used in the Catholic Church. The word *vulgate* means *common* and the Vulgate edition is the common edition. The Vulgate version of the Bible was translated by St. Jerome in the fourth century. An earlier translation is known; it is called the *Itala* version.

W

wafer bread *See* **Host.**

wake The watch or vigil over the dead body of a person the night before his burial.

walls of Jerico *See* **Jerico.**

Washing of the Feet, the Ceremony at the Solemn Evening Mass of Holy Thursday. This ceremony is called *Mandatum* from the first word of the first antiphon sung during the ceremony, "Mandatum novum," etc. "A new Commandment I give you, that you love one another: that as I have loved you, you also love one another." *John XIII 34.*

While the Washing of the Feet formerly took place only in the cathedral church of the diocese and in the chapels of some religious orders, it is now, in the new order for Holy Week, allowed in all Catholic parishes. The Washing of the Feet takes place in the sanctuary, and prayers and antiphons are sung during the ceremony. The celebrant, assisted by deacon and subdeacon, washes the right foot of each of twelve men and dries it with a towel.

The ceremony of the Washing of the Feet is in memory of Jesus Christ's washing the feet of the Apostles after He had eaten with them at the Last Supper. It is a symbol of brotherly charity.

washing (of hands) *See* **Lavabo.**

watcher One who watches over the Blessed Sacrament when it is publicly exposed.

water, the use of Water is frequently used in church ceremonies. At the Offertory of the Mass a few drops of water, representing humanity, are added to the wine to be consecrated. Washing with water is a symbol of purification. Water is used at the Lavabo and at the Ablution of the Mass. Water is the matter of the Sacrament of Baptism, that is, the outward sign of the sacrament. *See* **holy water.**

223

wax The beeswax used in making church candles. Candles used in church services should be made principally of beeswax. Because of its purity, the beeswax came to be regarded as a symbol of Christ's flesh.

way of the Cross, the *See* Stations of the Cross.

Whitsunday Another name given to the Feast of Pentecost in England. Whitsunday means *White Sunday* and probably refers to the white garment used in baptism.

will The spiritual power of the human soul by which man seeks that which is or seems to be good. The will is also called a *rational appetite*, because it is the tendency of the human soul which is endowed with reason. Catholic theologians and philosophers distinguish between the will as *tending to* its end, the good, and *choosing* the means to the end. What is commonly called *free will* is the will *choosing* some means to a given end. The will is said to be free, or to have freedom of choice, because it has the power of choosing between two or more things or courses of action.

wimple A starched piece of linen worn about the head and under the chin of a nun.

wine, altar Wine used in the Sacrifice of the Mass. It must be pure grape juice which has been naturally fermented.

wisdom One of the seven gifts of the Holy Ghost. Because of the gift of wisdom the soul sees in God the infinitely good. The Holy Ghost is sometimes spoken of as the Spirit of Wisdom.

Wisdom (Book of) A book of the Old Testament of the Bible written by an unknown author around 100 B.C.

Wise Men, the three *See* Magi, the.

Word, the The Second Person of the Blessed Trinity, Jesus Christ. The prologue to the Gospel of St. John begins with the Word. St. John uses the term *Word* to show the eternal existence of Jesus Christ with the Father. The Word existed before all time and before anything was created. The Word is God, and yet the Word is distinct from God the Father, just as words spoken are distinct from the speaker. The Last Gospel at Mass relates: "And the Word was made flesh and dwelt among us." Jesus Christ, the Living Word, was made flesh and came into the world to save men from their sins.

worldliness Excessive love of the things of this world and the neglect of one's spiritual needs.

worship, divine The adoration given to God by man. This may be private or public worship. For public worship, *see* liturgy.

Y

year, the ecclesiastical The yearly cycle of sacred seasons and feasts. The ecclesiastical or liturgical year celebrates the life of Jesus Christ from the period of waiting before His birth to His Passion, Death, Resurrection, and Ascension. It closes with an account of the early life of the Church.

The ecclesiastical year begins on the first Sunday of Advent and ends on the Saturday after the twenty-fourth Sunday after Pentecost. Its temporal cycle (cycle of time) is divided into the Christmas cycle (from the first Sunday of Advent to Septuagesima), the Easter cycle (from Septuagesima to the Saturday after Pentecost), and the Time after Pentecost (from the Feast of the Most Holy Trinity to the first Sunday of Advent).

The Christmas cycle has its period of preparation, Advent; its period of celebration, Christmastide; and its period of thanksgiving, the Time after Epiphany. The Easter cycle also has its period of preparation, Lent, and its period of celebration, Eastertide. The Time after Pentecost, which is the third division of the ecclesiastical year, might be considered the period of thanksgiving for the Easter cycle.

Besides the temporal cycle, based on the life of Our Lord, into which the ecclesiastical year is divided, there is also the cycle of the saints. This cycle begins on November 29 (about the beginning of Advent) and does not follow the temporal cycle exactly. It is made up of feasts of the Blessed Virgin, the angels, and the saints.

A Sunday Missal has only the Masses of the temporal cycle, that is, the Proper of the time. *See* **Proper of the Mass.** A daily Missal also includes the Proper of the Saints.

Year, the Marian *See* **Marian Year, the.**

Z

Zacharias A book of the Old Testament of the Bible. Zacharias, a minor prophet, is said to have written at least the first part of this book, about the year 500 B.C. Zacharias prophesied Jesus' entrance into Jerusalem, which was fulfilled on Palm Sunday.

Zachary The father of John the Baptist. *See* **John the Baptist.**

zimarra (or simar) Cassock worn informally by a bishop when at home. It is black edged with purple and has a purple cape, sash, and buttons.

zuchetto Skullcap worn by a bishop and other prelates.

Appendix

SAINTS

The names of some 20,000 saints are mentioned in missals, histories of the martyrs, and lives of the saints. A list of patron saints alone runs into the hundreds. There are so many popular saints, so many well-loved and even favorite saints that it is difficult to choose which ones to mention. As the saints who were Apostles have already been considered under the entry, **Apostles,** I have not included their names in this list of saints. John the Baptist (St.) and St. Joseph also have separate entries in the dictionary. Here are just a few saints, some of the better known ones, set down as they are in the calendar of the Church, in the month to which each belongs.

JANUARY

St. Agnes (third century). Feast day, January 21. This young saint was a martyr at twelve years of age. She lived in Rome in the third century when Christians were persecuted if they did not worship the gods of the emperor. She refused to offer sacrifice to the false gods, and she also refused to marry since she had consecrated herself to Jesus Christ. In the midst of torture Agnes appeared happy, and she laid her head on the block rather than lose her religion and her innocence. The name of Agnes is inscribed in the Canon of the Mass. Her name comes from the Latin word *agnus,* meaning lamb. Once a year on her feast day, two lambs are blessed on the altar of the basilica of St. Agnes built over her tomb. The Pope blesses these lambs again at the Vatican and gives them to the nuns to care for until Good Friday. The pallium is woven from the wool of these lambs. *See* **pallium.** St. Agnes is the patron saint of the Children of Mary.

St. Francis de Sales (died, 1622). Feast day, January 29. Although Francis was born of wealthy parents and could have had a career as a statesman, he preferred to become a priest. He was made Bishop of Geneva in 1603 and was offered a famous French bishopric, which he refused. He said he was married and could not leave a poor wife (his bishopric of Geneva) for a rich one. With St. Jane Frances de Chantal he founded the Order of the Visitation (Visitation Nuns) in 1610. Francis de Sales was a talented writer and correspondent, and he is known as the patron saint of writers and journalists.

St. John Bosco (1815–1886). Feast day, January 31. John Bosco spent his life helping young boys and girls, especially those of the poorer classes. He became a priest and began his work in Turin, Italy. John Bosco was very devoted to his saintly mother, and when she died he asked Our Lady to become his mother and help him look after his big family of abandoned children. In 1872 he founded the Congregation of the Salesian Fathers which he named after St. Francis de Sales.

FEBRUARY

St. Brigid (453–523). Feast day, February 1. St. Brigid is one of the patron saints of Ireland. As a young girl she was so beautiful that she prayed that she might be ugly so that she would not be sought by any young men who might want to marry her. Her one desire was to give herself to Jesus Christ. St. Brigid is said to have made her religious vows before the nephew of St. Patrick. She founded the first convent in Ireland and became its superior. Visiting the different parts of Ireland at the request of the bishops, she founded other convents, including one at the spot where the city of Kildare now stands. Here she died at the age of seventy, after fifty years spent in the religious life.

St. Blaise (died about 316). Feast day, February 3. St. Blaise had been a physician before he became a priest, and his whole life was devoted to curing the bodily and spiritual ills of men. He also took care of sick animals and is considered as their protector. Although he was appointed Bishop of Sebaste in Armenia, he retired to a cave on Mount Argeus to pray and do penance. Here the sick came to him, animals as well as men, and he brought about many cures. At the time of St. Blaise, Christians were being persecuted in Armenia, and he was thrown into prison and finally beheaded. Even while he was in prison, the sick came to him for help. He brought about the cure of a child who had swallowed a fishbone and was choking to death. Because of this miracle St. Blaise is called upon for help in throat diseases. *See* **Blaise, St., Blessing of.**

St. Valentine (died about 270). Feast day, February 14. There was more than one St. Valentine. One was a priest at Rome at the time of Claudius II. He refused to give up his faith and worship the false gods. This St. Valentine was beheaded on February 14, about the year 270. Another St. Valentine, whose feast day also falls on February 14, is said to have been a bishop of Terni in Umbria. He was noted for his miracles, and he converted a number of pagans to Christianity. He also was beheaded for his faith. Neither St. Valentine has anything to do with the custom of sending valentines on the fourteenth of February. A springtime festival kept by the Romans happened to fall on the feast day of St. Valentine, and the messages sent on this day gradually became known as valentines. Probably because of the day of this feast, St. Valentine is known as the patron saint of engaged couples and of greetings.

MARCH

St. Thomas Aquinas (1225–1274). Feast day, March 7. St. Thomas Aquinas is the patron saint of Catholic schools. A man of unusual wisdom and learning, he was also a man of great holiness and is called the Angelical Doctor. He was born of a wealthy, noble family, but he decided to become a Dominican monk in spite of family opposition. He studied under Albert the Great (St. Albert) in Cologne and became a famous teacher himself. Among his best known writings is the *Summa Theologiae* (*Theological Summary*).

St. Gregory the Great (died about 604). Feast day, March 12. Gregory was born of a wealthy Roman family and when still a young man became governor of Rome. Deciding to leave the world in order to become a monk, Gregory gave his vast fortune away and founded a monastery. He was called by the Pope from his life of seclusion to an active life as one of the seven deacons of Rome. He served as secretary of Pope Pelagius II and succeeded him as Pope in 590 as Pope Gregory I. St. Gregory the Great is known above all for his contributions to the Liturgy of the Mass and the Office. The Gregorian chant is named after him. He is the patron saint of singers and scholars.

St. Patrick (died about 461). Feast day, March 17. This well-loved patron saint of Ireland was not of Irish descent nor was he born in Ireland. He was born in Scotland and was a Briton and a Roman by ancestry. As a young man he was taken into Ireland as a slave. Later, when he had regained his freedom and was in his own land, he was called by God to go into Ireland and convert the country to Christianity. Many legends are told about St. Patrick, and his feast day is universally celebrated among people of Irish descent.

APRIL

St. Bernadette (1844–1879). Feast day, April 16. This saint, so close to modern times, was born Bernadette Soubirous at Lourdes, France, on January 7, 1844. Small for her age and suffering from asthma, she was only fourteen years old when the Blessed Virgin Mary appeared to her. Bernadette had gone with her sister and a friend to gather firewood on the banks of the Gave River. The date of the first appearance of Our

Lady to Bernadette was February 11, now the Feast of Our Lady of Lourdes. Between that time and July 16 Our Lady appeared to the little girl eighteen times. The Blessed Virgin Mary talked with Bernadette, promising to make her happy, if not in this world, in the next, and asking her to pray for sinners. On one of her visits she asked that a chapel be built at the spot of her appearance. When Bernadette begged her to reveal who she was, she said on another visit (March 25) "I am the Immaculate Conception." Many people did not want to believe these stories which Bernadette told of the appearances of Our Lady, and Bernadette suffered much humiliation. Her life in the world was indeed not an easy one. Though in ill health, she became a nun and spent her life in prayer and such work as she was able to do.

St. Mark the Evangelist (first century).   Feast day, April 25. St. Mark, sometimes known as John Mark, is the author of the second Gospel. He lived in Jerusalem where his mother's house was a meeting place for Christians and was himself one of the seventy-two disciples. Mark was probably baptized by St. Peter, who calls him "my son Mark." *I Peter V 13.* He was very devoted to St. Peter who has an important place in his Gospel. It is thought that Mark was the founder of the Church in Alexandria and was martyred there. St. Mark is the patron saint of lawyers and is the patron saint of the city of Venice.

St. Catherine of Siena (1347–1380).   Feast day, April 30. St. Catherine, though the daughter of a poor tradesman, became the guide of the Church and the adviser of Popes. As a child her holiness was extraordinary, and at the age of fifteen she became a member of the Third Order of St. Dominic. She traveled through Italy and persuaded Pope Gregory XI to return from Avignon to Rome. It would seem that her life was an active one, but it was also contemplative, for she was a great mystic. Our Lord gave her the stigmata, wounds similar to those in His own feet, hands, side, and brow, and He entrusted her with many revelations. St. Catherine of Siena is one of the patron saints of Italy.

MAY

St. Monica (fourth century).   Feast day, May 4. St. Monica, the mother of St. Augustine, found her vocation in being a good wife and mother. Brought up a Christian, she was married to a pagan who was much older than herself and who treated her with cruelty. Through prayer and patience she made her marriage a peaceful if not a happy one, and her prayers were answered when her husband was baptized on his deathbed. Her son, Augustine, who had been instructed in the Christian faith, was her pride and her sorrow, for he was brilliant and successful but he had turned from his religion and was leading a sinful life. She never stopped praying for him, and when he was twenty-eight years old he gave up his life of sin and became a zealous Christian. Soon after Augustine had regained his faith, his mother died, as if her mission in life had been completed. St. Monica is the patron saint of mothers.

St. Philip of Neri (1515–1595).   Feast day, May 26. St. Philip Neri might be called the happy saint. He was born at Florence in the sixteenth century of parents who were in comfortable circumstances. Though his mother died when he was very young, he had a good stepmother, and his childhood was a happy one. As a young man he went to Rome, where he lived for a number of years studying and preaching and making many good friends. Here he founded the Congregation of the Oratory and became a priest. Philip Neri was very popular, and his friends loved to be with him. The Holy Ghost had flooded his soul with so much grace that he sometimes cried out, "Enough, Lord, enough!" He lived to be eighty years old and died on the feast of Corpus Christi.

St. Joan of Arc (died, 1431).   Feast day, May 30. Love of country and love of God were mingled in this young shepherdess who was to be known as the saintly Maid of France. St. Michael, St. Catherine, and St. Margaret spoke to Joan from the time she was thirteen years old. France was being overrun by the English and in May 1428 the voice of St. Michael told Joan to help the King of France regain his kingdom. For a time

Joan was successful and had Charles VII crowned king at
Rheims. Betrayed by her own people, she fell into the hands
of the English, who had her burned at the stake as a heretic.
She was canonized May 13, 1920 by Pope Benedict XV. St.
Joan is one of the patron saints of France and is also patron
saint of soldiers.

JUNE

St. Anthony of Padua (1195–1231). Feast day, June 13. St.
  Anthony, who is often called the wonder-worker because of
  the many miracles attributed to him, was born in Lisbon in
  1195. He was already a Canon Regular when, inspired by the
  spirit of St. Francis, he decided to become a Franciscan and
  go to preach in Africa. Illness kept him from going to Africa,
  and for a time he lived in a cave at Sao Paolo, praying and
  doing the humblest tasks. By chance his ability to preach was
  discovered by his religious brothers, and he became a famous
  preacher. He died in Padua in 1231 when he was only thirty-six
  years old. St. Anthony of Padua is often pictured with the Child
  Jesus in his arms. It is said that the Holy Child frequently
  came to this saint when he was alone. St. Anthony of Padua
  is one of the patron saints of the poor. He is often called upon
  for help in finding lost objects.

St. Basil (330–379). Feast day, June 14. St. Basil, known as St.
  Basil the Great, belonged to a family of saints. His grandfather
  had been martyred, and his mother, sister, and two of his
  brothers are known as saints. One of his brothers is St. Gregory
  of Nyssa whose feast day is March 9. St. Basil was born at
  Caesarea in Cappadocia and studied at Athens, where he and
  St. Gregory Nazianzen became close friends. He might have
  had a career in the world as an orator, but he gave up his
  successful life to become a monk. This period of retirement
  from the world was not long, for he was called from his
  hermit's life by the Bishop of Caesarea to help fight the heresy
  of Arianism which denied the divinity of Jesus Christ. St. Basil

became Bishop of Caesarea, and from then on his life was a constant struggle to oppose Arianism and keep unity in the Church. *See* **Arianism.** St. Basil established the Rule of St. Basil which is still followed by the monks of the Eastern Church.

St. Aloysius Gonzaga (1568–1591). Feast day, June 21. This saint, who died when he was only 23 years old, was named a patron saint of youth by Pope Pius XI in 1926. A prince of a noble family, as a child he was torn between his mother who wanted him to be a saint and his father who wanted him to be a soldier. At nine years of age he made a vow of perpetual chastity, and it is said that he never committed a mortal sin in his life. Aloysius' father finally consented to let him enter the Jesuit novitiate. When he was studying at Rome in his last year of theology, a fever epidemic broke out and he immediately volunteered to care for the sick. He himself caught the fever and died of its effects a few months later. Purity and penance were the keynotes of the short, holy life of this young man, whom God had made "a little less than the angels." (*Psalms VIII 6,* from the Introit of the Mass for the Feast of St. Aloysius Gonzaga, June 21).

JULY

St. Vincent de Paul (died, 1660). Feast day, July 19. Vincent de Paul came from a French peasant family. As a boy he tended sheep, and his father sold two oxen to pay for his son's studies for the priesthood. As a young priest, he was captured by Turkish pirates who took him to Africa. He escaped and returned to France, where he was in the favor of the king who would have given him many benefits if he had wanted them. However, Vincent de Paul gave up all his honors and devoted himself to the poor and needy. He became chaplain of galley slaves in 1619 and brought new hope to the prisoners. In 1625 he founded the Congregation of the Lazarists and in 1634 the Congregation of the Sisters of Charity. On the streets of Paris Monsieur Vincent, as he was known, saved abandoned children, helped the sick, and relieved the suffering of the poor. The St. Vincent de Paul Society is named after him. He is known as the patron saint of charitable societies.

St. Anne (first century).   Feast day, July 26. St. Anne was the mother of the Blessed Virgin Mary. Our Lord's grandmother is known only through tradition. She and her husband, St. Joachim, lived in Nazareth and were of the royal family of David. They were very old before Mary, the immaculate Mother of God, was born to them, and they were overjoyed to have a child at last. It is said that when Mary was three years old they took her to the Temple at Jerusalem and dedicated her to God. St. Anne is a very popular saint. She is the patron saint of lacemakers, seamstresses, housekeepers, and broommakers. Along with St. Anthony of Padua she is called upon for help in finding lost objects. She is one of the patron saints of Canada. The shrine of St. Anne de Beaupré in Quebec is visited by thousands of pilgrims every year, and many miracles have been worked at this shrine. The original chapel was built in 1658 by Breton sailors who had been saved from shipwreck through the intercession of St. Anne.

St. Ignatius Loyola (died 1556).   Feast day, July 31. This soldier saint who founded the Jesuit Order was born of a noble family in the city of Loyola in Spain. In his youth he was a courtier and a soldier of the king. Wounded in a battle against the French, he was expected to die and had received the last sacraments when he suddenly became much better. During his convalescence he read the lives of Jesus Christ and the saints and was so moved by these books that, as soon as he was well, he took a vow of chastity and renounced his soldier's life by leaving his sword at the feet of the Virgin in the Benedictine Abbey at Montserrat. For a time he lived in a cave as a hermit and here he wrote his famous *Spiritual Exercises. See* **Spiritual Exercises, the.** He began his studies to become a priest, and when he was at the University of Paris he met a number of other young men with whom he began the Society of Jesus. St. Ignatius Loyola is the patron saint of retreats.

AUGUST

St. Dominic (1170–1221).   Feast day, August 4. St. Dominic was
born in a castle in Old Castile, Spain, and as a young man
became a priest. He went with his bishop to France, where
he was soon engaged in the almost hopeless struggle of fighting
heresy. It was at this time, tradition tells us, that Our Lady
appeared to Dominic, put a Rosary in his hands, and told
him to go out and preach. St. Dominic founded the Order of
the Friars Preachers (the Dominican Order), the Dominican
Sisters and the Third Order of Dominicans. It is said that
Dominic's mother, Juana of Aza, who has been beatified, once
saw her son in a vision as a little dog with a torch in his mouth.
This was understood to mean that her son was to rekindle the
flame of faith in the Catholic Church. St. Dominic is the patron
saint of astronomers.

St. Clare (died 1253).   Feast day, August 12. St. Clare of Assisi
ran away from a palace to become the poorest of nuns. Stirred
by the ideals of St. Francis, Clare and a companion fled to
Francis at the Church of the Portiuncula, on Palm Sunday
night, 1212. Francis cut off their hair, gave them coarse brown
wool garments, and made them nuns of the second order of
St. Francis. This order is known as the Poor Clares. The first
home of the new religious order was a poor house outside of
Assisi, and here Clare was joined by her mother and other
women of Assisi who wished to devote their lives to God. Like
St. Francis, Clare was a happy saint, joyful in spirit, charmed
with the beauties of God's world, practicing poverty with a
happy heart. St. Clare is the patron saint of embroidery workers
and of washerwomen.

St. Augustine (354–430).   Feast day, August 28. This famous
Doctor of the Church was born in North Africa of a pagan
father and a saintly mother, *See* Saints, **St. Monica,** May 4.
Though his mother had had him instructed in the Christian
faith, he fell away from his religion and was living a sinful
life. His mother, St. Monica, never stopped praying for him,
and it was her prayers and tears, along with the grace of God,

that brought him back to his faith in 386. After his conversion, St. Augustine became a priest and later Bishop of Hippo. St. Augustine is one of the great Doctors of the Church. Among his most-read works are the *Confessions* and the *City of God*. St. Augustine is one of the patron saints of printers and of theologians.

SEPTEMBER

St. Januarius (died 305).   Feast day, September 19. This early Christian martyr, Bishop of Beneventum, was beheaded with his companions during the persecutions of Diocletian, Roman emperor from 245 to 313. The miracle of the blood of St. Januarius is known everywhere. His head and body were taken to Naples, and with these was buried some of his blood which was kept in two glass phials. When this blood, which is congealed, is brought near the martyr's head, it melts and flows as if it were the blood of a living person. Three times a year, September 19 (his feast day), December 16, and the first Sunday in May this miracle takes place.

St. Wenceslaus (died 929).   Feast day, September 28. This saint is the good King Wenceslaus of the popular Christmas carol. His life was not a happy one. He was opposed by his mother when he tried to practice the Christian religion, and his own brother plotted to kill him. Son of the Christian Duke of Bohemia, he was only thirteen when his father died. His mother, who was to rule for him until he came of age, persecuted the Christians and tried to force Wenceslaus to become a pagan. He was obliged to receive the sacraments secretly at night. The people of Bohemia were divided in their religious beliefs, and some of them supported Wenceslaus so that he was able to claim part of the country as his kingdom. He ruled his people well, welcomed Christian missionaries into the country, and was noted for his charity. The young king's brother had Wenceslaus assassinated when he was about 22 years old. St. Wenceslaus is one of the patron saints of Bohemia.

St. Jerome (died 419). Feast day, September 30. St. Jerome, a Doctor of the Church, is best known for his Latin translation of the Bible known as the Vulgate. *See* **Vulgate.** St. Jerome was born in Dalmatia of a rich Christian family, but he was baptized and educated at Rome. He was an excellent student and had an almost immoderate passion for books. Having decided to become a monk, he spent a number of years of prayer and penance in the Syrian desert. He received Holy Orders at Antioch, studied in Constantinople under Gregory of Nazianzen, and was called back to Rome in 382 by Pope Damasus. The last years of his life were spent in a monastery at Bethlehem built for him and his companions by St. Paula, a Roman lady whose spiritual director he had been. Here he wrote and translated many books. St. Jerome's body lies in the Church of St. Mary Major at Rome. He is the patron saint of librarians.

OCTOBER

St. Thérèse of the Child Jesus (1873-1897). Feast day, October 3. The "Little Flower," as St. Thérèse of the Child Jesus is known, was born in Alençon, France, on January 2, 1873. The youngest of nine children, of whom only five lived, Mary Frances Teresa Martin seemed to be from babyhood dedicated to God and the Blessed Virgin. Our Lady's statue smiled down on her during a severe childhood illness. The Martins were a deeply religious family. Both Louis Martin and his wife, Zélie Guérin, had, when they were young, unsuccessfully sought religious vocations for themselves. Their five daughters were all to become nuns. When little Thérèse was four years old she lost her mother, but she found a second mother in her older sister, Pauline. When Pauline entered Carmel five years later and became Sister Agnes of Jesus, Thérèse's one desire was to follow her sister. This she did when she was only fifteen, against the opposition of her uncle and the prioress of Carmel.

Thérèse's way of sanctity was the "little way," as she calls it in her autobiography. Her life in the convent at Lisieux was uneventful. She worked in the laundry, the refectory, the sacristy. Later she became assistant to the novice mistress. At the command of her superior she began her autobiography, *The Story of a Soul*. Though her life may have been uneventful, her sufferings were intense. She grieved over the blindness and death of her father soon after she entered Carmel. She suffered much from criticism and humiliations. The illness which took her life when she was only twenty-four was long and painful. She had written not long before her death that she would spend her Heaven in doing good upon earth. Many miracles were worked through her intercession after her death. St. Thérèse of the Child Jesus was beatified in 1923 and canonized two years later (1925). She was proclaimed patron saint of the Catholic Missions by Pope Pius XI in 1923. She is also a patron saint of aviators and one of the patron saints of France.

St. Francis of Assisi (died 1226). Feast day, October 4. A rich man's son who loved poverty and became a beggar, St. Francis is one of the best known of the saints. He was the founder of the Franciscan Order (Order of Friars Minor), The Franciscan Poor Clare Nuns (Order of St. Clare), which he founded with St. Clare in 1212, and the Third Order Secular of St. Francis. In his life, St. Francis tried to imitate Our Lord in all things, by preaching to the people, by fasting, by meditation. He received the stigmata, the print of the five bleeding wounds of Jesus Christ, on his hands, feet, and side. St. Francis loved all created things for love of God. He sang songs to the sun, gave sermons to the birds, and talked with the wolves. He welcomed death at Portiuncula, the chapel of St. Mary of the Angels which the Benedictines had given to him at the beginning of his work. *See* **Portiuncula**. St. Francis of Assisi is the patron saint of Catholic Action.

St. Teresa of Avila (1515–1582). Feast day, October 15. This sixteenth-century saint, for whom St. Thérèse of the Child Jesus was named, ran away from her home in Avila, Spain, when she was seven years old. She wanted the Moors to cut off her head so that she could see God. Like the nineteenth-century Teresa, she was one of nine children and lost her mother at an early age. *See* **St. Thérèse of the Child Jesus, October 3.** She became a Carmelite nun when she was eighteen years old, and in 1562 she began the reform of the Order. With the help of St. John of the Cross she was able to reform most of the convents and to found many new ones. In her youth and even after she had become a nun, Teresa enjoyed talking to people, but she finally realized that she could not enjoy both conversation and contemplation. She is one of the great mystics of the Church, and several Popes have considered her writings of equal value to those of a Doctor of the Church. St. Teresa lived to be sixty-seven years old and was active to the end of her life.

NOVEMBER

St. Charles Borromeo (died 1584). Feast day, November 4. Named a cardinal when he was only twenty-two and Archbishop of Milan at twenty-three, Charles Borromeo had a great deal of influence at the Roman court and had an important part in the Council of Trent. *See* **Trent, Council of.** As Archbishop of Milan he founded schools, seminaries, and (with Don G. M. Martinelli) the Oblates of St. Charles. In his own private life he fasted on bread and water, meditated for hours, and examined his faults with such care that he even ordered two priests to point them out to him. He died caring for the poor during the great plague at Milan. St. Charles Borromeo is the patron saint of seminarians.

St. Elizabeth of Hungary (1207–1231). Feast day, November 19. Daughter of the King of Hungary, the little Princess Elizabeth was engaged when she was only four years old to the eleven-year-old Duke of Thuringia, Louis IV. Their early marriage was a happy one in spite of the persecutions to which her husband's mother subjected her. As queen, Elizabeth cared for the poor at her palace, and built hospitals to relieve their sufferings. It is said that once, as she was carrying provisions in her cloak to the poor, she met her husband returning from hunting. Displeased to see her bent with her burden, Louis pulled open her cloak to see what she was carrying. What was his

surprise to see red and white roses fall to the ground! Her
husband, knowing she was a saint, kept one of the roses all
the rest of his short life. When Louis IV was killed in the
Crusades, Elizabeth, with her four children, was driven from
the court. She became a member of the Third Order of St.
Francis in 1227 and died when she was only twenty-four.
St. Elizabeth of Hungary is one of the patron saints of bakers
and of members of the Third Order.

St. Cecilia (period unknown).   Feast day, November 22. Little is
known of this young saint who is called the patron saint of
musicians. Legend tells us that as a child she vowed to remain
a virgin. When forced to marry a young pagan, Valerian, she
told him of the angel who guarded her virginity. Valerian was
moved by her story and wanted to see the angel. He and his
brother Tiburtius were baptized, saw the angel, and were
martyred for their faith. It is said that soon after their death,
Cecilia was arrested and sentence placed upon her. Unable
to kill her by suffocation, her executioners finally had her
beheaded. The name of St. Cecilia is mentioned in the Canon
of the Mass. She is known as the patron saint of musicians
probably because of a legend concerning her marriage. The
story is that while her wedding music was being played she
was singing a hymn of love to Jesus in her heart. There is no
reason to believe that St. Cecilia herself had any musical
talent.

DECEMBER

St. Francis Xavier (1506–1552).   Feast day, December 3. Francis
Xavier was Professor of Philosophy at the University of Paris
when he met St. Ignatius, fell under the spell of his zeal, and
became a member of the newly formed Society of Jesus.
Francis Xavier, who is patron saint of the Propagation of the
Faith, became one of the most amazing missionaries the world
has ever known. In India and in Japan he preached to one
kingdom after another, worked many miracles, converted

thousands of souls. He was on his way to China where he hoped to continue his missionary work when he fell ill and died. The Gospel for his feast day is taken from *Mark XVI 15–18*. In this Gospel Jesus Christ said to His disciples, "Go into the whole world, and preach the gospel to every creature." *Mark XVI 15*.

St. Nicholas (died 324). Feast day, December 6. St. Nicholas is known as the patron saint of children. Legend tells us that he was born in Asia Minor at Lycia where his uncle was Archbishop of Myra, a position he himself was later to hold. His kindness, his childlike ways, and his holiness endeared him to all who knew him. It is said that so great was his charity that he once threw a purse filled with gold into the room of a poor man who had no dowry to give his daughters. Perhaps because of this story St. Nicholas is thought of as one who leaves presents on Christmas Eve. Besides being the patron saint of children, St. Nicholas is also the patron saint of boatmen, fishermen, and sailors, and one of the patron saints of Greece and of Russia.

St. Stephen (died 33). Feast day, December 26. St. Stephen, the first martyr of the Catholic Church, had been made a deacon by the Apostles and was active in the new Church. The *Acts of the Apostles* relates: "Now Stephen, full of grace and power, was working great wonders and signs among the people." *Acts VI 8*. Stephen was falsely accused of speaking against Moses and against God. Brought before the council, he tried to show his accusers that Jesus, whom they had crucified, was the Messias announced by Moses. Stephen was cast out of the city of Jerusalem and stoned to death. "And while they were stoning Stephen he prayed and said, 'Lord Jesus, receive my spirit.' And falling on his knees he cried out with a loud voice saying, 'Lord, do not lay this sin against them.'" *Acts VII 59–60*. St. Stephen is one of the patron saints of stonemasons. His name is mentioned in the Canon of the Mass.

A LIST OF THE POPES
AND THEIR PONTIFICATES

NAME	BIRTHPLACE	REIGN
St. Peter	Galilee	29–67
St. Linus	Tuscia	67–76
St. Anacletus (Cletus)	Rome	76–88
St. Clement	Rome	88–97
St. Evaristus	Greece	97–105
St. Alexander I	Rome	105–115
St. Sixtus I	Rome	115–125
St. Telesphorus	Greece	125–136
St. Hyginus	Greece	136–140
St. Pius I	Aquileia	140–155
St. Anicetus	Syria	155–166
St. Soter	Campania	166–175
St. Eleutherius	Nicopoli in Epirus	175–189
St. Victor I	Africa	189–199
St. Zephyrinus	Rome	199–217
St. Callistus I	Rome	217–222
St. Urban I	Rome	222–230
St. Pontian	Rome	July 21, 230–Sept. 28, 235
St. Anterus	Greece	Nov. 21, 235–Jan. 3, 236
St. Fabian	Rome	Jan. 10, 236–Jan. 20, 250
St. Cornelius	Rome	Mar., 251–June, 253
St. Lucius I	Rome	June 25, 253–Mar. 5, 254
St. Stephen I	Rome	May 12, 254–Aug. 2, 257
St. Sixtus II	Greece	Aug. 30, 257–Aug. 6, 258
St. Dionysius	unknown	July 22, 259–Dec. 26, 268
St. Felix I	Rome	Jan. 5, 269–Dec. 30, 274
St. Eutychian	Luni	Jan. 4, 275–Dec. 7, 283
St. Caius	Dalmatia	Dec. 17, 283–Apr. 22, 296
St. Marcellinus	Rome	June 30, 296–Oct. 25, 304
St. Marcellus I	Rome	May 27, 308 or June 26, 308–Jan. 16, 309
St. Eusebius	Greece	Apr. 18, 309 or 310– Aug. 17, 309 or 310

NAME	BIRTHPLACE	REIGN
St. Milziades or Melchiades	Africa	July 2, 311–Jan. 11, 314
St. Sylvester I	Rome	Jan. 31, 314–Dec. 31, 335
St. Mark	Rome	Jan. 18, 336–Oct. 7, 336
St. Julius I	Rome	Feb. 6, 337–Apr. 12, 352
Liberius	Rome	May 17, 352–Sept. 24, 366
St. Damasus I	Spain	Oct. 1, 366–Dec. 11, 384
St. Siricius	Rome	Dec. 15/22/29, 384–Nov. 26, 399
St. Anastasius I	Rome	Nov. 27, 399–Dec. 19, 401
St. Innocent I	Albano	Dec. 22, 401–Mar. 12, 417
St. Zozimus	Greece	Mar. 18, 417–Dec. 26, 418
St. Boniface I	Rome	Dec. 28 or 29, 418–Sept. 4, 422
St. Celestine I	Campania	Sept. 10, 422–July 27, 432
St. Sixtus III	Rome	July 31, 432–Aug. 19, 440
St. Leo I (the Great)	Tuscany	Sept. 29, 440–Nov. 10, 461
St. Hilary	Sardinia	Nov. 19, 461–Feb. 29, 468
St. Simplicius	Tivoli	Mar. 3, 468–Mar. 10, 483
St. Felix III (II)	Rome	Mar. 13, 483–Mar. 1, 492
St. Gelasius I	Africa	Mar. 1, 492–Nov. 21, 496
Anastasius II	Rome	Nov. 24, 496–Nov. 19, 498
St. Symmachus	Sardo	Nov. 22, 498–July 19, 514
St. Hormisdas	Frosinone	July 20, 514–Aug. 6, 523
St. John I, Martyr	Tuscany	Aug. 13, 523–May 18, 526
St. Felix IV (III)	Sannio	July 12, 526–Sept. 22, 530
Boniface II	Rome	Sept. 22, 530–Oct. 17, 532
John II	Rome	Jan. 2, 533–May 8, 535
St. Agapitus I	Rome	May 13, 535–Apr. 22, 536
St. Silverius, Martyr	Campania	June 1 or 8, 536–Nov. 11, 537
Vigilius	Rome	Mar. 29, 537–June 7, 555
Pelagius I	Rome	Apr. 16, 556–Mar. 4, 561
John III	Rome	July 17, 561–July 13, 574
Benedict I	Rome	June 2, 575–July 30, 579
Pelagius II	Rome	Nov. 26, 579–Feb. 7, 590
St. Gregory I, the Great	Rome	Sept. 3, 590–Mar. 12, 604
Sabinianus	Blera in Tuscia	Sept. 13, 604–Feb. 22, 606

NAME	BIRTHPLACE	REIGN
Boniface III	Rome	Feb. 19, 607–Nov. 12, 607
St. Boniface IV	Marsi	Aug. 25, 608–May 8, 615
St. Deusdedit (Adeodatus I)	Rome	Oct. 19, 615–Nov. 8, 618
Boniface V	Naples	Dec. 23, 619–Oct. 25, 625
Honorius I	Campania	Oct. 27, 625–Oct. 12, 638
Severinus	Rome	May 28, 640–Aug. 2, 640
John IV	Dalmatia	Dec. 24, 640–Oct. 12, 642
Theodore I	Greece	Nov. 24, 642–May 14, 649
St. Martin I, Martyr	Todi	July, 649–Sept. 16, 655
St. Eugenius I	Rome	Aug. 10, 654–June 2, 657
St. Vitalian	Segni	July 30, 657–Jan. 27, 672
Adeodatus II	Rome	Apr. 11, 672–June 17, 676
Donus	Rome	Nov. 2, 676–Apr. 11, 678
St. Agatho	Sicily	June 27, 678–Jan. 10, 681
St. Leo II	Sicily	Aug. 17, 682–July 3, 683
St. Benedict II	Rome	June 26, 684–May 8, 685
John V	Syria	July 23, 685–Aug. 2, 686
Conon	unknown	Oct. 21, 686–Sept. 21, 687
St. Sergius I	Syria	Dec. 15, 687–Sept. 8, 701
John VI	Greece	Oct. 30, 701–Jan. 11, 705
John VII	Greece	Mar. 1, 705–Oct. 18, 707
Sisinnius	Syria	Jan. 15, 708–Feb. 4, 708
Constantine	Syria	Mar. 25, 708–Apr. 9, 715
St. Gregory II	Rome	May 19, 715–Feb. 11, 731
St. Gregory III	Syria	Mar. 18, 731–Nov., 741
St. Zachary	Greece	Dec. 10, 741–Mar. 22, 752
Stephen II	Rome	Mar. 23, 752–Mar. 25, 752
Stephen III	Rome	Mar. 26, 752–Apr. 26, 757
St. Paul I	Rome	May 29, 757–June 28, 767
Stephen IV	Sicily	Aug. 1 (7), 768–Jan. 24, 772
Adrian I	Rome	Feb. 1 (9), 772–Dec. 25, 795
St. Leo III	Rome	Dec. 26 (27), 795–June 12, 816
Stephen V	Rome	June 22, 816–Jan. 24, 817
St. Paschal I	Rome	Jan. 25, 817–Feb. 11, 824
Eugenius II	Rome	Feb. (May), 824–Aug., 827
Valentine	Rome	Aug., 827–Sept., 827

NAME	BIRTHPLACE	REIGN
Gregory IV	Rome	827–Jan., 844
Sergius II	Rome	Jan., 844–Jan. 27, 847
St. Leo IV	Rome	Apr. 1 (10), 847–July 17, 855
Benedict III	Rome	July (Sept. 29), 855–Apr. 17, 858
St. Nicholas I the Great	Rome	Apr. 24, 858–Nov. 13, 867
Adrian II	Rome	Dec. 14, 867–Dec. 14, 872
John VIII	Rome	Dec. 14, 872–Dec. 16, 882
Marinus I	Gallese	Dec. 16, 882–May 15, 884
St. Adrian III	Rome	May 17, 884–Sept., 885
Stephen VI	Rome	Sept., 885–Sept. 14, 891
Formosus	Portus	Oct. 6, 891–Apr. 4, 896
Boniface VI	Rome	Apr., 896–Apr., 896
Stephen VII	Rome	May, 896–Aug., 897
Romanus	Gallese	Aug., 897–Nov., 897
Theodore II	Rome	Dec., 897–Dec., 897
John IX	Tivoli	Jan., 898–Jan., 900
Benedict IV	Rome	Jan. (Feb.), 900–July, 903
Leo V	Ardea	July 903–Sept., 903
Sergius III	Rome	Jan. 29, 904–Apr. 14, 911
Anastasius III	Rome	Apr., 911–June, 913
Lando	Sabina	July, 913–Feb., 914
John X	Tossignano	Mar., 914–May, 928
Leo VI	Rome	May, 928–Dec., 928
Stephen VIII	Rome	Dec., 928–Feb., 931
John XI	Rome	Feb. (Mar.), 931–Dec., 935
Leo VII	Rome	Jan. 3, 936–July 13, 939
Stephen IX	Rome	July 14, 939–Oct., 942
Marinus II	Rome	Oct. 30, 942–May, 946
Agapitus II	Rome	May 10, 946–Dec., 955
John XII	Tusculum	Dec. 16, 955–May 14, 964
Leo VIII	Rome	Dec. 4 (6), 963–Mar. 1, 965
Benedict V	Rome	May 22, 964–July 4, 966
John XIII	Rome	Oct. 1, 965–Sept. 6, 972
Benedict VI	Rome	Jan. 19, 973–June, 974
Benedict VII	Rome	Oct., 974–July 10, 983
John XIV	Pavia	Dec., 983–Aug. 20, 984

NAME	BIRTHPLACE	REIGN
John XV	Rome	Aug., 985–Mar., 996
Gregory V	Saxony	May 3, 996–Feb. 18, 999
Sylvester II	Auvergne	Apr. 2, 999–May 12, 1003
John XVII	Rome	June, 1003–Dec., 1003
John XVIII	Rome	Jan., 1004–July, 1009
Sergius IV	Rome	July 31, 1009–May 12, 1012
Benedict VIII	Tusculum	May 18, 1012–Apr. 9, 1024
John XIX	Tusculum	Apr. (May), 1024–1032
Benedict IX	Tusculum	1032–1044
Sylvester III	Rome	Jan. 20, 1045–Feb. 10, 1045
Benedict IX, 2nd time		Apr. 10, 1045–May 1, 1045
Gregory VI	Rome	May 5, 1045–Dec. 20, 1046
Clement II	Saxony	Dec. 24 (25), 1046–Oct. 9, 1047
Benedict IX, 3rd time		Nov. 8, 1047–July 17, 1048
Damasus II	Bavaria	July 17, 1048–Aug. 9, 1048
St. Leo IX	Egisheim-Dagsburg	Feb. 12, 1049–Apr. 19, 1054
Victor II	Dollnstein-Hirschberg	Apr. 16, 1055–July 28, 1057
Stephen X	Lorraine	Aug. 3, 1057–Mar. 29, 1058
Nicholas II	Burgundy	Jan. 24, 1059–July 27, 1061
Alexander II	Baggio (Milan)	Oct. 1, 1061–Apr. 21, 1073
St. Gregory VII	Tuscany	Apr. 22 (June 30), 1073–May 25, 1085
Bl. Victor III	Benevento	May 24, 1086–Sept. 16, 1087
Bl. Urban II	France	Mar. 12, 1088–July 29, 1099
Paschal II	Ravenna	Aug. 13 (14), 1099–Jan. 21, 1118
Gelasius II	Gaeta	Jan. 24 (Mar. 10), 1118–Jan. 28, 1119
Callistus II	Burgundy	Feb. 2 (9), 1119–Dec. 13, 1124
Honorius II	Fiagnano	Dec. 15 (21), 1124–Feb. 13, 1130
Innocent II	Rome	Feb. 14 (23), 1130–Sept. 24, 1143
Celestine II	Citta di Castello	Sept. 26 (Oct. 3), 1143–Mar. 8, 1144
Lucius II	Bologna	Mar. 12, 1144–Feb. 15, 1145
Bl. Eugene III [1]	Pisa	Feb. 15 (18), 1145–July 8, 1153

[1] Cult approved October 3, 1872

NAME	BIRTHPLACE	REIGN
Anastasius IV	Rome	July 12, 1153–Dec. 3, 1154
Adrian IV	England	Dec. 4 (5), 1154–Sept. 1, 1159
Alexander III	Siena	Sept. 7 (20), 1159–Aug. 30, 1181
Lucius III	Lucca	Sept. 1 (6), 1181–Sept. 25, 1185
Urban III	Milan	Nov. 25 (Dec. 1), 1185– Oct. 20, 1187
Gregory VIII	Benevento	Oct. 21 (25), 1187–Dec. 17, 1187
Clement III	Rome	Dec. 19 (20), 1187–Mar., 1191
Celestine III	Rome	Mar. 30 (Apr. 14), 1191– Jan. 8, 1198
Innocent III	Anagni	Jan. 8 (Feb. 22), 1198–July 16, 1216
Honorius III	Rome	July 18 (24), 1216–Mar. 18, 1227
Gregory IX	Anagni	Mar. 19 (21), 1227–Aug. 22, 1241
Celestine IV	Milan	Oct. 25 (28), 1241–Nov. 10, 1241
Innocent IV	Genoa	June 25 (28), 1243–Dec. 7, 1254
Alexander IV	Anagni	Dec. 12 (20), 1254–May 25, 1261
Urban IV	Troyes	Aug. 29 (Sept. 4), 1261– Oct. 2, 1264
Clement IV	France	Feb. 5 (15), 1265–Nov. 29, 1268
Bl. Gregory X [2]	Piacenza	Sept. 1, 1271 (Mar. 27, 1272)–Jan. 10, 1276
Bl. Innocent V [3]	Savoy	Jan. 21 (Feb. 22), 1276– June 22, 1276
Adrian V	Genoa	July 11, 1276–Aug. 18, 1276
John XXI	Portugal	Sept. 8 (20), 1276–May 20, 1277
Nicholas III	Rome	Nov. 25 (Dec. 26), 1277– Aug. 22, 1280
Martin IV	France	Feb. 22 (Mar. 23), 1281– Mar. 28, 1285
Honorius IV	Rome	Apr. 2 (May 20), 1285–Apr. 3, 1287
Nicholas IV	Ascoli	Feb. 22, 1288–Apr. 4, 1292
St. Celestine V	Isernia	July 5 (Aug. 29), 1294– Dec. 13, 1294
Boniface VIII	Anagni	Dec. 24, 1294 (Jan. 23, 1295)–Oct. 11, 1303

[2] Cult approved September 12, 1713
[3] Cult approved March 3, 1898

NAME	BIRTHPLACE	REIGN
Bl. Benedict XI [4]	Treviso	Oct. 22 (27), 1303–July 7, 1304
Clement V	France	June 5 (Nov. 14), 1305– Apr. 20, 1314
John XXII	Cahors	Aug. 7 (Sept. 5), 1316– Dec. 4, 1334
Benedict XII	France	Dec. 20, 1334 (Jan. 8, 1335)–Apr. 25, 1342
Clement VI	France	May 7 (19), 1342–Dec. 6, 1352
Innocent VI	France	Dec. 18 (30), 1352–Sept. 12, 1362
Bl. Urban V [5]	France	Sept. 28 (Nov. 6), 1362– Dec. 19, 1370
Gregory XI	France	Dec. 30, 1370 (Jan. 5, 1371)–Mar. 26, 1378
Urban VI	Naples	Apr. 8 (18), 1378–Oct. 15, 1389
Boniface IX	Naples	Nov. 2 (9), 1389–Oct. 1, 1404
Innocent VII	Sulmona	Oct. 17 (Nov. 11), 1404– Nov. 6, 1406
Gregory XII	Venetia	Nov. 30 (Dec. 19), 1406– July 4, 1415
Martin V	Rome	Nov. 11 (21), 1417–Feb. 20, 1431
Eugene IV	Venetia	Mar. 3 (11), 1431–Feb. 23, 1447
Nicholas V	Sarzana	Mar. 6 (19), 1447–Mar. 24, 1455
Callistus III	Valencia	Apr. 8 (20), 1455–Aug. 6, 1458
Pius II	Siena	Aug. 19 (Sept. 3), 1458– Aug. 15, 1464
Paul II	Venetia	Aug. 30 (Sept. 16), 1464– July 26, 1471
Sixtus IV	Savona	Aug. 9 (25), 1471–Aug. 12, 1484
Innocent VIII	Genoa	Aug. 29 (Sept. 12), 1484– July 25, 1492
Alexander VI	Valencia	Aug. 11 (26), 1492–Aug. 18, 1503
Pius III	Siena	Sept. 22 (Oct. 1 (8)), 1503– Oct. 18, 1503
Julius II	Savona	Oct. 31 (Nov. 26), 1503– Feb. 21, 1513

[4] Cult approved April 24, 1736
[5] Cult approved March 10, 1870

NAME	BIRTHPLACE	REIGN
Leo X	Florence	Mar. 9 (19), 1513–Dec. 1, 1521
Adrian VI	Utrecht	Jan. 9 (Aug. 31), 1522– Sept. 14, 1523
Clement VII	Florence	Nov. 19 (26), 1523–Sept. 25, 1534
Paul III	Rome	Oct. 13 (Nov. 3), 1534– Nov. 10, 1549
Julius III	Rome	Feb. 7 (22), 1550–Mar. 23, 1555
Marcellus II	Montepulciano	Apr. 9 (10), 1555–May 1, 1555
Paul IV	Naples	May 23 (26), 1555–Aug. 18, 1559
Pius IV	Milan	Dec. 25, 1559 (Jan. 6, 1560)–Dec. 9, 1565
St. Pius V [6]	Bosco	Jan. 7 (17), 1566–May 1, 1572
Gregory XIII	Bologna	May 13 (25), 1572–Apr. 10, 1585
Sixtus V	Grottammare	Apr. 24 (May 1), 1585– Aug. 27, 1590
Urban VII	Rome	Sept. 15, 1590–Sept. 27, 1590
Gregory XIV	Cremona	Dec. 5 (8), 1590–Oct. 16, 1591
Innocent IX	Bologna	Oct. 29 (Nov. 3), 1591– Dec. 30, 1591
Clement VIII	Florence	Jan. 30 (Feb. 9), 1592 Mar. 3, 1605
Leo XI	Florence	Apr. 1 (10), 1605–Apr. 27, 1605
Paul V	Rome	May 16 (29), 1605–Jan. 28, 1621
Gregory XV	Bologna	Feb. 9 (14), 1621–July 8, 1623
Urban VIII	Florence	Aug. 6 (Sept. 29), 1623– July 29, 1644
Innocent X	Rome	Sept. 15 (Oct. 4), 1644– Jan. 7, 1655
Alexander VII	Siena	Apr. 7 (18), 1655–May 22, 1667
Clement IX	Pistoia	June 20 (26), 1667–Dec. 9, 1669
Clement X	Rome	Apr. 29 (May 11), 1670– July 22, 1676
Innocent XI [7]	Como	Sept. 21 (Oct. 4), 1676 Aug. 12, 1689
Alexander VIII	Venetia	Oct. 6 (16), 1689–Feb. 1, 1691

[6] Canonized May 22, 1712
[7] Beatified October 7, 1956

NAME	BIRTHPLACE	REIGN
Innocent XII	Naples	July 12 (15), 1691–Sept. 27, 1700
Clement XI	Urbino	Nov. 23, 30 (Dec. 8), 1700 Mar. 19, 1721
Innocent XIII	Rome	May 8 (18), 1721–Mar. 7, 1724
Benedict XIII	Rome	May 29 (June 4), 1724– Feb. 21, 1730
Clement XII	Florence	July 12 (16), 1730–Feb. 6, 1740
Benedict XIV	Bologna	Aug. 17 (22), 1740–May 3, 1758
Clement XIII	Venetia	July 6 (16), 1758–Feb. 2, 1769
Clement XIV	Rimini	May 19, 28 (June 4), 1769– Sept. 22, 1774
Pius VI	Cesena	Feb. 15 (22), 1775–Aug. 29, 1799
Pius VII	Cesena	Mar. 14 (21), 1800–Aug. 20, 1823
Leo XII	Fabriano	Sept. 28 (Oct. 5), 1823– Feb. 10, 1829
Pius VIII	Cingoli	Mar. 31 (Apr. 5), 1829– Nov. 30, 1830
Gregory XVI	Belluno	Feb. 2 (6), 1831–June 1, 1846
Pius IX	Senigallia	June 16 (21), 1846–Feb. 7, 1878
Leo XIII	Carpineto	Feb. 20 (Mar. 3), 1878– July 20, 1903
St. Pius X [8]	Riese (Treviso)	Aug. 4 (9), 1903–Aug. 20, 1914
Benedict XV	Genoa	Sept. 3 (6), 1914–Jan. 22, 1922
Pius XI	Desio (Milan)	Feb. 6 (12), 1922–Feb. 10, 1939
Pius XII	Rome	Mar. 2 (12), 1939–

[8] Canonized May 31, 1954

IMPORTANT MODERN
PAPAL ENCYCLICALS

Pope Pius IX (1846–1878)

TITLE	SUBJECT
Qui pluribus November 9, 1846	On faith and reason
Singulari quadam December 9, 1854	On rationalism
Gravissimas inter December 11, 1862	On a false liberty of doctrine
Quanto conficiamus moenere August 10, 1863	On indifferentism
Quanta cura December 8, 1864	On naturalism, communism, socialism
Syllabus * December 8, 1864	On modern errors

Pope Leo XIII (1878–1903)

Inscrutabili April 21, 1878	On the evils of modern society
Quod apostolici muneris December 28, 1878	On modern errors
Aeterni Patris August 4, 1879	On Christian philosophy

* Important document, but not an encyclical.

TITLE	SUBJECT
Arcanum divinae sapientiae February 10, 1880	On Christian marriage
Diuturnum June 29, 1881	On civil government
Humanum genus April 20, 1884	On Freemasonry
Immortale Dei November 1, 1885	On the Christian constitution of states
In plurimis May 5, 1888	On the abolition of slavery
Libertas praestantissimum June 20, 1888	On human liberty
Sapientiae christianae January 10, 1890	On Christian citizenship
Rerum novarum May 15, 1891	On capital and labor
Providentissimus Deus November 18, 1893	On the study of Holy Scripture
Longinqua January 6, 1895	On Catholicism in the United States
Graves de communi January 18, 1901	On Christian democracy

Pope St. Pius X (1903–1914)

TITLE	SUBJECT
E supremi October 4, 1903	On the restoration of all things to Christ
Lamentabili * July 3, 1907	Decree on the errors of the Modernists
Pascendi September 8, 1907	On the false teachings of the Modernists

Pope Benedict XV (1914–1922)

Ad beatissimi November 1, 1914	An appeal for peace
Pacem, Dei munus May 23, 1920	Christian peace and reconciliation

Pope Pius XI (1922–1939)

Ubi arcano Dei December 23, 1922	On the peace of Christ
Studiorum ducem June 29, 1923	On the sixth centenary of the canonization of St. Thomas Aquinas
Quas primas December 11, 1925	On the feast of Christ the King

* Important document, but not an encyclical.

TITLE	SUBJECT
Divini Illius Magistri December 31, 1929	On the Christian education of youth
Casti connubii December 31, 1930	On Christian marriage
Quadragessimo anno May 15, 1931	On social reconstruction
Non abbiamo bisogno June 29, 1931	On Catholic action
Nova impendet October 2, 1931	On the world crisis
Caritate Christi compulsi May 3, 1932	On world distress and the Sacred Heart
Ad Catholici Sacerdotii December 20, 1935	On the Catholic Priesthood
Vigilanti cura June 29, 1936	On motion pictures
Mit brennender Sorge March 14, 1937	On the Church in Germany
Divini Redemptoris March 19, 1937	On atheistic communism
Firmissimam constantiam March 28, 1937	The Church in Mexico

Pope Pius XII (1939–   )

TITLE	SUBJECT
Summi Pontificatus October 20, 1939	On the state of the modern world
Sertum laetitiae November 1, 1939	On the 150th anniversary of the establishment of the hierarchy in the United States
Mystici Corporis June 29, 1943	On the Mystical Body of Christ
Divino afflante spiritu September 30, 1943	On the promotion of Scriptural studies
Mediator Dei November 20, 1947	On the sacred liturgy
Humani generis August 12, 1950	On false opinions concerning philosophy
Fulgens corona September 8, 1953	On the observance of the Marian Year
Sacra virginitas March 25, 1954	On evangelical chastity
Musicae sacrae disciplina December 25, 1955	On sacred music
Haurietis aquas May 15, 1956	On the devotion to the Sacred Heart